A SAFE H
Evacuees in Keswick
1939-1945

The reminiscences of evacuees from elementary schools in the north-east of England, together with accounts of the evacuation to Keswick and district of scholars from the Central Newcastle High School, Hunmanby School (Filey), the Liverpool Orphanage, Roedean School (Brighton) and students of S. Katharine's College (Liverpool).

edited by
Brian Wilkinson

BOOKCASE

ELSIE HINDMOOR

© The copyright of the contributions remains with the writers
First edition 2010
Published by Bookcase
19 Castle Street, Carlisle, CA3 8SY
01228 544560 bookcasecarlisle@aol.com
Printed by CPI Antony Rowe

DEDICATION

This compilation of reminiscences of former evacuees in Keswick during the Second World War is dedicated to the Keswick and district people who welcomed children into their homes and gave them love and security.

In particular this dedication is to the late Elsie Hindmoor, at whose home the idea was born to collect the stories of evacuees.

The work of the teachers from the schools who accompanied the evacuees to Keswick is also acknowledged. As with the 'host families', their care and attention beyond the call of duty helped the children and young people to come to terms with separation from their homes, families and friends.

THANKS AND ACKNOWLEDGEMENTS

The thanks of the compiler for their help and encouragement in the bringing together of these reminiscences is due to Mrs Hilary French, Headmistress of the Central Newcastle High School and the School Librarian, Mrs Carol Elliott; Dr Janet Hollinshead of Liverpool Hope University and her colleagues; Mrs F King, Headmistress of Roedean School, Brighton, the School Archivist and the Old Roedeanian Association; Stephen Matthews, the publisher ('Bookcase' and 'Bookends'); Jeff Taylor, Keswick historian; Armathwaite Hall Country House Hotel and Bassenfell Manor Christian Centre for permission to use images and the contributors themselves.

Together we have been able to record for posterity an important period in Keswick's history that had far-reaching effects upon many of those who were involved.

The girls from Roedean in Keswick

CONTENTS

INTRODUCTION

REMINISCENCES OF EVACUEES IN KESWICK DURING THE SECOND WORLD WAR

The evacuation of children and adults at the beginning of the Second World War was the largest mass movement of people in British history. In the first few days of September 1939 nearly three million children and adults were taken from their homes in those parts of the British Isles likely to be the target of enemy bombing to safer, rural areas. Keswick was one of these.

In Keswick, Roedean School for Girls from Brighton leased the Keswick and Millfield Hotels together with Shu-le-Crow House and used other premises in the town for teaching and catering. S. Katharine's College, a teacher training college from Liverpool, leased the Queen's Hotel in Keswick and Derwent Hill at Portinscale and many other premises in the town for 'billets' and tuition. Girls from the Central Newcastle High School lived with 'host families' and also at Barrow House on Derwentwater. They shared classroom accommodation with Keswick School. The Junior and Middle Departments of Hunmanby Hall School, near Filey (a Methodist Foundation School for Girls) were evacuated to Armathwaite Hall and Bassenfell Manor near Bassenthwaite and The Liverpool Orphanage occupied Hause End House on Derwentwater.

One group from Newcastle came as an extended family, with ages ranging from a five-year-old to a grandmother of seventy-one years. Children of elementary school age (up to fourteen years at that time) came to Keswick in smaller groups from Newcastle-upon-Tyne, South Shields and Sunderland, arranged by their Local Education Authority or their parents.

Why Keswick? As a holiday resort, the town had ample

accommodation available in the hotels and guesthouses. Keswick was not a military target, apart perhaps from the Army Driving and Maintenance School based at Portinscale. Thirlmere Reservoir, supplying water to Manchester might have been of interest to enemy bombers, but it was perhaps beyond the reach of hostile aircraft and in mountainous country. In any event, it was protected by the Home Guard armed with several rifles, some wooden!

This 'invasion' of school children placed an almost intolerable burden on the local schools throughout the age range. Initially, in Keswick itself, some of the younger evacuee children shared school accommodation with Keswick children on a half-day basis. The organisational problems were not only confined to the education of the children. The evacuated teachers were also in *loco parentis* out of school hours and had to organise worthwhile activities on the half days when the children were not at school and tend to their emotional and social needs outside school hours.

The younger evacuees would have left their elementary schools with the obligatory gas mask in its cardboard box, a label giving the child's name, school and age, a small suitcase for clothing and perhaps a toy, and a packed meal for the journey. Some schools insisted that the children learn their Identity Card number by heart. A few of the youngest children were accompanied by their mothers. For most of the children every experience was a new one, as many had never left their homes before.

We can hardly image the thoughts of those children as they travelled into unfamiliar country, not knowing where they would be staying that night. On arrival at Keswick, the children from elementary schools were 'crocodiled' to a church hall, the Moot Hall, the Queen of the Lakes Pavilion or the Drill Hall where they were met by local volunteers and the residents who had come to choose a child or children to stay with them. A 'Local Billeting Officer' would have visited homes to ascertain if there was room for evacuees. Waiting for a 'host' to choose them must have been a traumatic experience. Roedean girls arrived by train at the Keswick Station and walked through the Hotel Conservatory into the Hotel. Girls from the Central Newcastle High School were accommodated in 'billets' arranged by the School and the Billeting Officer. Hunmanby Hall girls went directly to Bassenfell Manor and Armathwaite Hall, near

Bassenthwaite. Student teachers at S. Katharine's College found their own way to Keswick and their 'billets' – after all, they were aged at least eighteen years!

The 'phoney war' when no bombing took place during the first months of hostilities induced many parents to take their children away from their new homes, but the heavy bombing in 1940 saw many returned to the safety of Keswick. As time went on, some evacuees did return home, but many remained in Keswick until almost the end of the war and some beyond. But, for some parents the need to have a child at home and earning wages when they reached the school leaving age, fourteen years at the time, overcame the needs of the child to be in a safe environment. At least one evacuee stayed in Keswick for good, another came back to marry a local girl after National Service with the R.A.F. and apprenticeship to make his home here, and one other returned to Keswick on retirement.

The payment to 'host families' for having an evacuee stay with them was ten shillings and sixpence per week (fifty-two and a half pence), with the payment for a second or third child eight shillings and sixpence (forty-two and a half pence) each. This was hardly an amount that covered all eventualities in the home, but it was a welcome supplement to the income of a less well-off family. Payment was made at the Post Office in Keswick.

Many of the former evacuees who have written of their experiences have expressed their gratitude to their 'hosts' and said how happy they were to be with them and to live in such a beautiful part of the country. Indeed, some became so attached to their 'new families' that the eventual parting was such a wrench that all were in tears. Many of the evacuees kept in touch with Keswick and their 'adopted families', sometimes returning here for a social occasion such as a honeymoon or family get-together and taking delight in introducing their families and friends to the area on holidays.

It is somewhat difficult to imagine, more then seventy years on, what stress must have been experienced by the young evacuees, their accompanying parents and teachers and the local families who received 'guests' at the beginning of the War.

Concern for the younger children especially was felt by the wider community in Keswick. I have been privileged to see a letter from a Keswick father to his children, a son and a daughter, asking for their concern and thoughtfulness for two evacuees from Newcastle who were coming to stay at their house. I reproduce the letter here with thanks to David Hodgson, one of the children:

"To Anne Hodgson and David Usher Hodgson, You are both now old enough to know what good manners mean and now we are to have two children who are being sent away from their own homes, leaving their fathers and mothers and all their friends. So, both your mother and myself want you to do all you can , both in the house and outside, to make up for them what they are losing through having to leave their loved ones.

Also, you will both realise that it means extra work for your mother and you can both help in very many ways to make things easier for her. There are lots of little duties that you can do. Please don't wait to be told to do them, also remember that the two children are visitors to us and so you must both do what you can to make their stay with us both pleasant for them and us all."

The 'new homes' of evacuees to the Keswick area varied greatly. Some were accommodated on housing estates, others in larger houses on the outskirts of the town and in hotels and guest houses. Some, 'billeted' in farmhouses and rural cottages met with 'middens' (earth closets) for the first time – and oil lamps!

Evacuees met with experiences which they would remember for the rest of their lives. One evacuee was eye-witness to the crash of a De Havilland aircraft in Derwentwater and joined in an unavailing attempt to save the airmen involved whilst another was "pulling pints" at the King's Arms in Keswick at the age of eight years. Older scholars from Roedean School joined the bell ringers and the handbell ringers at Crosthwaite Church. A Central Newcastle High School girl played a church organ. Keswick also saw the game of lacrosse for the first time, played by the Roedean and Hunmanby girls. Needless to say, the game went with them when the girls departed! It is said that the local lads made an appreciative audience when games were played on Fitz Park by the Roedean girls!

Living in a small town surrounded by mountains gave many children the opportunity to explore the countryside for the first time, even climbing mountains - albeit in school shoes and overcoats. Many evacuees regarded their time in Keswick as the best time of their lives.

The situation concerning the impact of the evacuation of children and young people to Keswick upon the Keswick community appeared to be different for the differing status of the schools and the Teacher Training College involved. 'All-age school' children from state schools in the north east were assimilated quite easily in individual 'billets'. The children attended the existing schools, which at first experienced accommodation difficulties. These eased somewhat as the years progressed and evacuees left for home at the age of fourteen years to work. The girls from the Central Newcastle High School also came to live in individual 'billets' and some later went on to Barrow House. They retained their school 'ethos' and yet became part of the community.

The Roedean girls were more 'Roedean in Keswick' rather than integrated into the Keswick community. This is not to infer that the Roedean girls were quite separate from the town and its affairs, but their involvement was in a more controlled manner. The S. Katharine's College girls were older, eighteen years and more. Their time in Keswick was intended to equip them for teaching in state schools, and they were busy pursuing a concentrated two-year course of study for the teaching profession. The Liverpool Orphanage boys went to a local all-age school. Hunmanby Hall School, of which there are two contributors to this book, one a teacher and the other a pupil, was entirely self-contained at Bassenfell Manor and Armathwaite Hall. Their actual involvement with Keswick life was minimal – not much more than playing lacross with the Roedean girls on Lower Fitz Park.

There was no doubt that the Central Newcastle High School girls were welcomed in Keswick. An undated letter in the local press from a Mr George Little of Whitehaven sums up the local people's attitude (or at least his) to the evacuation of the secondary and further educational institutions based in the town in a humorous way. The letter, most likely written in 1990 or soon after, reads:

BOMBERS MADE AN IMPACT

Whatever happened to the Brown Bombers of Keswick – the Bonny Geordie lasses who suddenly descended on the town at the start of the last war and who became, by the end of hostilities, as much part of the natural scenery as the native beauties?

They were the girls of Central Newcastle High School for Girls – a rather toffee-nosed lot when they arrived but happily soon mellowed by the warmth of the Keswick welcome. And because they wore a brown uniform they were known simply as 'The Brown Bombers'.

Keswick schoolgirls, equally attractive in their green uniform, somehow never achieved a 'Brown Bomber' status.

Nor was that status ever achieved by the other imported evacuee beauties: Roedean School girls lived a cloistered nun-like existence in the palatial Keswick Hotel while S. Katharine's College girls were isolated in hotels in Keswick and Portinscale.

The 'Bombers', however, had to muck- in and shared people's homes and also shared Keswick School.

What a great lot of girls they were and what a pity no effort has been made by them to stage a reunion in the same way that the boys of Newcastle Royal Grammar School got together to commemorate their wartime years in Penrith.

Perhaps the girls, now sadly 60 years or more I suppose, were too shy to make the effort to turn back the clock.

Whatever the reason, it would be nice to know that some of them at least are still bombing along.

George Little.

How did this collection of reminiscences come about? In June 2006 I visited an elderly friend in Keswick, Elsie Hindmoor, who had another visitor whilst I was with her. The visitor was Ian Gumm who had been an evacuee in Keswick and lived with my friend. I had been an evacuee myself, from Derby to a small village in Derbyshire, and we exchanged memories of our wartime experiences.

I suggested that Ian might like to write about his evacuee days for the Keswick Museum, where, occasionally, visitors ask if there is any information concerning evacuees. He agreed to write an account, and gave me the addresses of several newspapers in the north-east. I had many responses as a result of letters I wrote to the newspapers, to 'The Keswick Reminder' and to newspapers in Liverpool asking other former evacuees to Keswick and district to write of their memories. Eventually two folders of reminiscences were placed in the Museum for visitors to see.

I am very grateful to the former evacuees who answered my request

Brian Wilkinson, Danny Robertson and Gerard Nuttney
in Keswick Museum

for their memories. The evacuated children and young people passed through very troubled times in the history of this country and their stories make absorbing reading.

Brian Wilkinson
Volunteer Steward at the Keswick Museum and Art Gallery

References:

An excellent account of evacuees during the Second World War can be found in:
'*Wartime Britain 1939 – 1945*' by Juliet Gardiner, published by Headline, 2004, from which some of the information above was obtained, with thanks.
"*Send Them to Safety*", by James Roffey, published by The Evacuees Reunion Association, 2009 gives the story of "*The Great British Evacuation of the Second World War*".

Ken and Derick Bell

14

EVACUEES FROM ELEMENTARY SCHOOLS IN THE NORTH-EAST

Cycling across frozen Derwentwater
KEN BELL, NEWCASTLE-UPON-TYNE
Chillingham Road School, Heaton, Newcastle

I was eleven years of age when I was evacuated with my younger brother Derick from our home at 35 Balmoral Terrace, Heaton in Newcastle. We were evacuated with my school, Chillingham Road School in Heaton, Newcastle-upon-Tyne.

Derick had not yet started school, being just turned five years of age, but he came with us. First we went to Bamburgh on the Northumberland coast. But, we were only there a few months. My brother got head lice and all his hair was shaved off. My mother was furious, and we were brought back home.

Then the Newcastle Railway Goods Station was bombed so we were sent to Keswick by bus. We ended up in the St John's Church Hall, waiting for a family to take us. A wealthy family, with a maid and chauffeur wanted to take me, but not my brother. I think their name was Spencer. I wanted to stay with Derick and that was when a Mrs Hayton said that she would take us both. It was the first time, apart from Bamburgh, we had been away from our family.

The first night in Keswick my brother and me went for a walk and got lost. We went to the Police Station and they took us home to Mrs Hayton in Windebrowe Avenue. I was with Mrs Hayton until I was fourteen and had left school. I had to return to Newcastle then but my younger brother Derick was seven years younger than I was and stayed on in Keswick until the war was over.

I went to Brigham School, but can't remember the teacher's name.

Keswick was a big difference to Newcastle. There was beautiful scenery and wonderful fresh air. I made friends easily and we played football and cricket. I got around Keswick and was a member of the Air Scouts. One very cold winter the lake was frozen and we cycled across it.

The Fisher brothers ran the Scouts and we played in Fitz Park. I can't remember getting into any trouble at School or at Mrs Hayton's, but Mavis may have a better memory than me. Mavis was one of Mrs Hayton's daughters and is now Mrs Mavis Clark. The other daughter was Eileen, now Mrs Atkinson and living at Portinscale. My wife Margaret and I still keep in touch with Mavis and Eileen.

I loved Keswick in the summer time and swimming in the lake. I can't remember if I was ever ill or not but I was very happy at Mrs. Hayton's.

I had a little job at Bargett's. They sold drapery etcetera and I went after school and on Saturday for pocket money.

I remember going to the pictures at The Alhambra and to the Pavilion for a show.

Yes, I think it was very worthwhile living in Keswick.

My grandchildren are very interested in my experiences as an evacuee, especially the younger ones. Sophie has helped with this story.

Later in life I did my National Service as a Royal Marine. I worked in Newcastle as a Co-operative Society butcher. I worked my way up to management and was there for forty-seven years. Before I was sixty years old I turned diabetic and other problems occurred, and now I am turning blind.

Oil lamps and earth middens
MARGARET BRAGG, KESWICK

Originally my sister and I were evacuated to Lupton, a small village between Kendal and Kirkby Lonsdale, in 1939. We stayed with an elderly couple named Cornthwaite, 'Aunty Alice and Uncle Tom' as we came to call them.

When we arrived at the village hall in Preston Patrick, after being taken there by buses from Oxenholme Station, we were lined up for people to 'choose' which child or children they would like to take to their homes. My mother had travelled with us and our three-year old brother as my father was dying (unbeknown to us) and he did not want us to be split up. It was almost like a cattle market. 'I'll have a girl', 'I only want a boy' etcetera. Eventually the Cornthwaites stepped forward and said they would take two girls, me and my sister. Imagine my mother's distress, what a dilemma for any parent to be in. Rather than have my brother go to someone away from us she decided to take him home with her and, as there were no trains home that night, the Cornthwaites said she could stay the night with them.

Uncle Tom had an old Jowett car outside, and piled us all in, letting down the 'dickey seat', which was like the boot of a car but pulled down to make another seat. Just as well it was a fine night as there was no roof over that part of the car.

We arrived at Cow Brow, Lupton in complete darkness and because of the 'black out' we had to go into the house in the dark and not until we were all inside were we able to put some lights on. First shock of the evening, oil lamps had to be lit and second shock, we were all desperately needing the bathroom and toilet, only to be told there was no such thing. There was a sort of cubby-hole on the stairs, in which there was a bucket. We found our way upstairs by my mother holding a lit candle. We did our 'ablutions' and I saw that our mother was crying. I think she thought that her precious children would probably be burnt to death in the 'safety' of the countryside rather than be bombed by the Germans.

When we got back downstairs there was a lovely smell of bacon and eggs cooking, and an enormous table spread with home-made bread and butter and a large jug of milk for us and a pot of tea for the grown-ups. We were all very shy and tired and after the meal my mother took us up to bed, once more carrying the candle. Inside the bedroom was an enormous feather bed and a small one. She tucked the three of us in the big bed, after using the chamber pot under the bed. She was to sleep in the smaller bed. She kissed us good night and told us she would take us all home the next day.

Mother must have told the Cornthwaites of my father's illness, and the circumstances in which they lived in South Shields. The kind couple that they were must have persuaded her to leave the girls with them, and they would look after them for the foreseeable future.

The next day we were shown where the outside 'toilet' was. It was down a flight of steps at the back of the house and along a path. There was a row of five, belonging to the five cottages on Cow Brow, which the Cornthwaites owned. The gloom inside took some getting used to, whilst the stench was overpowering. The old lady who lived at number three was allowed to live rent-free, on condition that she emptied the midden. This was at the end of the 'privies' where all the waste matter was put from the buckets in the 'toilets'. No 'Health and Hygiene' laws in those days!

There was another shock in store for me. When we got back in the house Uncle Tom asked me if I would like to go with him to get the milk. I thought that all I had to do was to get a bottle from the doorstep, which would have happened at home. But, he took me by the hand and we went across the road to where he had a barn type of building in which there was an enormous beast, which he explained was a cow. He sat on a stool with a pail between his legs and began to pull at the things which were dangling from the cow's stomach and squirts of milk started hitting the pail. I had no idea that milk came from cows. I thought it came from bottles, after all I was only six and three quarters years of age and a 'Townie' to boot.

We returned to the house to find my mother and brother getting their things together, for they were going home without us. I was absolutely shocked, as I thought we were going to go back with them. My mother explained that it was better for us to stay, and that she would write to us every day. I cried and begged her to take us home, but she asked me to be brave and look after my sister Betty, who was only five years old. However, she hugged us both, told us to be good girls and went outside where Uncle Tom had got the Jowett out of the garage. He put their luggage in and after one more grief-stricken hug and kisses we said our tearful farewells and waved and waved until they were out of sight.

With the resilience of children and the kindness of the Cornthwaites we soon settled into some sort of routine. We went to the village school and made friends with the local children (after a precarious start – our funny accents and different clothes were very much against us) and looked forward to the letters from home, not daily but certainly weekly. I wrote home but with orders from Aunty Alice not to say we were homesick or anything that might upset our parents.

Inevitably the word came to say that my father had died, in March 1940. In the following year my mother and brother came to Lupton. The Cornthwaites had had a new house built up the hill opposite the Plough Inn, for their retirement, and had arranged for my mother to rent the cottage which we lived in. The Cornthwaites moved into their new home with Betty and me. We stayed for a week – what bliss, there was an inside toilet and a bathroom. We had spent the previous eighteen months having a bath in front of the fire once a week.

My mother came with the removal van from South Shields and we moved back down the hill to number five Cow Brow again. We moved to Portinscale in 1942. A friend of my mother had been bombed out in London and had come to stay with us for refuge. She was a trained nurse, and when there was an advertisement in the Cumberland and Westmorland Herald for someone to look after an evacuee hostel at Portinscale, caring for about eight evacuees, so she applied and got the job.

I'll never forget sitting in the back of the removal van. We had taken it in turns to either sit in the back with the furniture or in the front with the drivers. I was in the front with the drivers for the last stage of the journey, crossing the river at Portinscale and thinking we would probably fall in and drown at some time.

I had become so responsible for looking after my younger siblings as so many grown-ups had impressed upon me to help my mother as much as I could because she was now widowed and I was the oldest. There were times, I must say, I resented the fact that I was.

We arrived at Derwent House which was opposite the Derwentwater Hotel. It had been commandeered by the Army as a base for the Officers of the D & M School (Driving and Maintenance). Down past the Harney Peak Hotel on the left hand side was the NCO's and men's quarters, rows of huts which included billets, Sergeants' Mess and NAFFI (Navy, Army and Air Force Institutes) where the men could buy various necessities, such as writing paper, shaving tackle and, whenever they had the coupons, soap, sweets and occasionally chocolates.

My mother was a very good pianist, and one day when she had been playing the piano there was a knock on the door and when she answered there was a Sergeant who asked if she would be willing to play for their band practices. They had started a band to play for dances for the soldiers and the A.T.S. (Women's Army). She said they would have to provide someone to look after us – I suppose they would have been classed as baby-sitters today. It was a marvellous time for her as she only ever conversed with children, since her friend had gone back to London.

Derwent House was a very big house with only three rooms on the ground floor, but the first floor had three bedrooms and a sort of washroom, but then the second floor had seven rooms which actually went over the three cottages adjoining the house.

Mr Just, who was a notable beekeeper, also kept hens, and we used to take buckets of left-over vegetable peel and old crusts to him to feed the hens and occasionally he would give us an egg.

Some of the evacuees returned home. One or two had turned 14 years and they were needed at home to help out financially, so my mother let some of the rooms to the Army personnel who came for a month's course in driving Bren-gun Carriers up the mountains in the area, to prepare them for embarkation to France etcetera. Their wives would come and stay for a couple of weeks before their husbands would be sent abroad. She also took in a couple of Land Army girls who were helping out on local farms where the usual farm labourers had been conscripted into the forces. The girls' love life was quite complicated as there were lots of single soldiers at a loose end in their free time and my mother always seemed to have one or the other with a broken heart confiding in her several times!

When I started at Crosthwaite School there were so many children because of the evacuation the class that I was in had to be held in the Tithebarn Street Methodist Church Hall. When I moved up, I went back to Crosthwaite School and we walked up to the Albion Hall for our school dinners. I passed my scholarship to go to Keswick School.

Due to the war there were hardly any new bicycles to be had. But, there were sales every month in the Drill Hall in Keswick and the list of things for sale was usually published in The Keswick Reminder the previous week. Well, there was a bike for sale, and because I'd done so well my mother asked me if I would like one. Of course. I was over the moon. She went to the sale and was there practically all day, and bid for and got the bike. Then she had to walk all the way back to Portinscale, pushing it as she didn't ride one herself. I was so disappointed as it was an old-fashioned 'sit up and beg' with a fixed wheel for a brake and a basket on the front. But how could I tell her after all the trouble she had gone to, I made all sorts of excuses as to why I wouldn't go out on it because I thought I would be a laughing stock. Anyway, one day when I had run out of excuses I got on it and rode past Braithwaite's Garage, where we used to take the accumulator batteries from the wireless to be charged in order to listen to 'The Man in Black' (Valentine Dyall) read some wonderful plays, when Mr Braithwaite came out and asked me where I'd got my bike from. I said that Mum had bought it at the Saleroom and he said would you ask her to come and see me.

Well, I was terrified, as I wondered if it had been stolen and Mum would get into trouble, but no, he just wanted to know if I would swap it for a brand new Hercules bike as he had just got his year's consignment of three brand new ones. But, he would rather have an older one for his wife, as she was more suited to the style. Mum said, well I'll have to ask Margaret, as it's her bike. When she asked me I daren't appear too pleased, but in the end I became the owner of ZL33, that was its serial number printed under the saddle. I've never forgotten it.

Bombed out and strafed in the street
JIM CHAPMAN, DARLINGTON

I was born in Newcastle-upon-Tyne, in Shieldfield and except for evacuation periods I lived there until I went into H.M. Forces in 1953.

In about 1941 I was evacuated from Newcastle to Ambleside and stayed with a lovely family, so I was told. The husband was a policeman. I do not know his name. After a few months I had to go back to Newcastle for eye treatment.

Sometime afterwards I came to Keswick and was placed with a family at 8 Borrowdale Road, with the Tyson family I believe. I was there for quite a while. I think that the Tyson daughter's name was May.

They were good times mostly, with a most loving family. I remember going down to the lake and other places.

I had to go back to Newcastle again for eye treatment. When I was there we were bombed out and strafed in the street. I was saved by a family friend, Mickey McGuire and taken to a shelter at Shieldfield Park and various other places until found by my mother who came on leave from the A.T.S. (the women's branch of the Army). I lived with my grandmother, my Nana, for most of the time. I then returned to Keswick, to 8 Borrowdale Road. I remember going to the 'movies' – payment being the newspapers, cans etc. that I collected for the War Effort.

In late 1943 – early 1944 I was sent to Dukes Wood School at Hexham and spent the rest of the war there before returning to Newcastle to my Nana.

Things being as they were, after the war I attended school etcetera and I saw my mother only three or four times as she had made another life.

My father was a soldier in the Royal Artillery and had served in Malta, then India. I did not see him until 1947 when he and my mother were divorced.

At the age of seventeen I joined the R.A.F. Regiment. Evacuee life gave me the foundations and what my Nana taught me has stood me in good stead for the rest of my life.

I moved away from Newcastle completely in 1962 after rejoining the Services and only went back for visits to my Nana before she died. After that I did not bother – though I still support Newcastle United Football Club as I have done for as long as I can remember.

My thoughts sometimes wander back to my life as an evacuee in Keswick.

In 2009 Jim wrote: After leaving Technical School in Newcastle I eventually became an apprentice tiler. Knowing that National Service would catch me up, I enlisted in H.M. Forces and eventually joined the R.A.F. Regiment. I am proud of my service of eighteen years with that outfit. I served in Germany, Kenya, Cyprus, Singapore, Aden, Northern Ireland, Cyprus again and Northern Ireland again. I was 'demobbed' in 1958 and had various jobs in 'security', and in 1998 went to London to be a caretaker for the St. John's Ambulance Brigade and then as caretaker for a block of flats in Hammersmith. Then came retirement in Cyprus, but I had to return to the U.K. in 2005.

My second wife, Barbara, comes from Darlington, so we decided to live there near her family.

I did not really know my father, and saw him only once, in 1948. He was a professional soldier, and I learned a lot about him from members of my family after his death. My mother had gone to the U.S.A /Canada until 1959/1960. My Nana was my inspiration in life. She taught me so much, seeing as I did not have parents as such.

I have never returned to Keswick, (except passing through about four or five years ago) though I would like to. Perhaps in 2010 Barbara and I will visit the town.

My brother was sure the teacher was a German spy !
IAN CRAWFORD, SUNDERLAND

My mother was born in Keswick and lived there until she married. Her parents were Mr and Mrs Bragg and the family home was The Beeches, Chestnut Hill, which I think is now a Bed and Breakfast Guest House.

My mother had two brothers, Sydney and Maurice. Uncle Syd's widow, Aunty Doris, died almost a year ago. Her daughter, my cousin Susan, still lives in Keswick and until recently owned and ran a ladies' dress shop in Bank Street – "Susan's". Susan was married to Les Reed who also died about a year ago. Les was well-known in Rugby circles, as was my other cousin, Tony Bragg. Sadly, Tony died a number of years ago aged just forty. Tony was also much involved with Keswick Rugby Club – I think he was Steward at the Club.

My parents married in 1925 with a wedding reception at the Keswick Hotel. My father worked for Lloyd's Bank in Keswick and was later transferred to East Boldon and then to Sunderland. I am the youngest of four children (two, sadly, are now dead). I was born in 1933.

Until my mid-teens my holidays were always spent at The Beeches with Grandma Bragg.

I was barely six years old when war broke out in 1939 so I did not have a comprehensive grasp of just what was going on. My parents, now living in Sunderland, quickly decided that we four children should be moved from the industrial north-east to the calm and safety of Keswick. So it was that my brother, then aged ten and I started at Brigham School. My two sisters, who were older, went to Keswick School, the school where my mother was educated.

We obviously missed our parents who, because of my father's work, stayed in Sunderland. However, in the care of Grandma and two great-aunts plus Auntie Doris, we were quite happy and well looked after.

My memories of Brigham School are really quite vague. The Infant

Department was a churchy-looking building across the playground from the main school. The main school was one big room with a partition down the middle – and all age groups were in together! My brother, George, used to regale me with stories about a teacher who he was sure was a German spy. We used to take a cup or mug to school each day – milk from a churn was ladled out at morning playtime. We played the usual children's games – tag, trains, chariot races and, of course in season it was conkers! Battles with conkers triggered many arguments and fights!

We had, I think, just one teacher in the infants' class – a lady who must have been pretty good because I seemed to master the basics of reading and maths quite easily. The Headmaster was called Mr Hartley and he lived in The Hawthorns – about two hundred yards up from The Beeches. He was very strict and had a bit of a temper but was very fair and well-respected.

Away from school life was wonderful – unfortunately it is only when one looks back that you realise how wonderful it was. It was like a "Swallows and Amazons" existence. Our rivals were the boys from the High Briary (the name Calperthwaite always makes me shudder!) They called us "townies" and yelled abuse at us at every opportunity. Strangely enough, it never came to physical combat – I guess we must have been good runners! Our most daring exploit was to search for and find their den, making sure they were nowhere about. It was a little hut in the woods near the Bobbin Mill. We didn't wreck it or anything like that but we left it to show that we had been there. They were furious! To walk home from school they had to pass The Beeches and they had a great fear of my great aunt Katie who, because of an illness as a child, had stopped growing when she was about seven years old and so was only about three and a half feet tall. The Briary boys would see her in the garden and were convinced that she was a witch!

At the back of the Beeches was a small wood, part of The Beeches' land. This was a fantastic playground for us. Hide and Seek, Cops and Robbers, English and Germans, etcetera. At the far side of this wood was a steep embankment down to the single-track railway line, the Cockermouth, Keswick and Penrith line. It was always exciting to watch the steam trains go by – especially exciting after dark when you could see the sparks shooting out of the engine's funnel and you could see people inside the carriages which were all lit up – shades of "The Railway Children"!

The Druid's Circle was less than a mile from The Beeches and we often walked up the narrow road past Mrs Walker's cottage (which was painted orange) then past "the cross old lady's farm" and on up to the Stone Circle. The field was a wonderful place to fly a kite!

If ever we had money to spend we would make for Dixon's toy shop. This shop was an Aladdin's Cave for me.

I also remember watching the salmon leap in the River Greta near the Pavilion. I think that was in the autumn. The Pavilion, by the way, served two purposes, cinema and dance hall - neither of which pursuits concerned me!

Climbing Latrigg, playing round the Bobbin Mill, getting stung by wasps, were all part of life for us – and not one air raid!

We actually returned to Sunderland before the end of the war – my mother hated being parted from her children. Consequently we did not have the excitement of air raids and bombs dropping nearby.

My wife and I visit Keswick regularly. We call on Cousin Susan of course and we go to The Theatre by the Lake for at least two of their summer season productions.

I refer to Keswick as "my spiritual home" and I always experience a tingle of excitement as soon as Blencathra, Skiddaw and Latrigg come into view. We leave the main road to come to Keswick on the old Penrith Road – past The Beeches, Townsfield, Calvert's Bridge and County Corner.

Keswick has changed a great deal since those childhood days but it retains its basic friendly atmosphere and is still a very special place for me.

Ian wrote in 2009: I attended Bede Grammar School until the age of eighteen. I was exempt from National Service because of eyesight deficiency so I went straight from school to Chester C.E. Training College.

My teaching career in Sunderland started in 1954 and following the usual promotion procedure I was ultimately appointed Head Teacher at Bishop Harland C.E. Primary School and held that position for twenty years until I retired in 1993.

I married Judith, who also became a Headteacher (two heads are better than one!) and we have two sons: Alastair has a high profile job with British Energy and Robin is in charge of the Arts History Library at the Victoria and Albert Museum in London.

In my younger days I played a lot of sport (despite deficient eyesight!) but my consuming passion has always been drama – musicals and straight plays, with a particular affection for the Gilbert and Sullivan operas. I took leading roles and/or directed many productions. I was recently thrilled to be awarded Honorary Life Membership of St. Andrew's Operatic Society – only the third person to be so honoured in the history of the Society.

My love for Keswick is as strong as ever. Judith and I visit at least three times a year – always taking in the current productions at Theatre by the Lake. We usually stay at the Keswick Hotel, where my parents had their wedding reception in 1925! We also keep in touch with my cousin, Sue Reid, who still lives in Keswick.

I always think of Keswick as my spiritual home!

I was one of Miss Siddle's fairies
LILIAN EDGAR, SEATON BURN
Heaton School, Newcastle

I was evacuated to Keswick when I was seven years old in 1941. Previous to this I had been evacuated to Horton Grange, on the estate near my home. Many years later, in 1949, I came to work on the Blagdon Estate and found the lady I had been evacuated with worked as a cook for Lord and Lady Ridley at Blagdon Hall. It is a small world.

After being at Horton Grange I went as an evacuee again to Ferryhill where my mother worked as a carer. I cannot remember much about these places but I can remember some things about Keswick.

I went to Keswick with children from my school in Heaton. We had been living near places that had been bombed, including Heaton Junction, Guildford Place and the railway goods station in Shieldfield.

I travelled to Keswick by bus along with the other boys and girls. Six of us went to stay with Miss Edith Siddle who lived on the veranda (Park

Lilian Edgar with Brownies in Keswick

28

Lilian Edgar and other evacuees
in the Veranda House with Miss Siddle

Villas I think) next to the Youth Hostel where we went to play. Miss Siddle is in the picture with four of us. I am on the right. This photograph was taken at the end of the veranda. It looked over to the River Greta and I remember there was a waterfall a few yards from the house and we used to watch the salmon jumping.

At the other side of the river was Fitz Park where we used to play very often. We also visited the lake sometimes and climbed the fells. This happened when we had visitors in the house as it was a boarding house, or when our families visited us. My brother was evacuated to Keswick with the vicar in the vicarage – but I cannot remember his name. We all went to Crosthwaite School, but I cannot remember the teachers there.

Keswick was a completely different place from where I lived in

Lilian Edgar with Miss Siddle's Dancing Girls

Newcastle. We all enjoyed being there, being six of us. We all helped in the house doing various jobs. We all slept in one bedroom with bunk beds and were all very happy. I cannot remember any time that we were unhappy there.

I am not sure when we came home but I went back to Keswick for holidays and we have had a few day trips there since.

I remember we went to the pictures and to shows. One of the places where we saw shows, I am not sure of its name, but it was at the top of the veranda [The Pavilion of the Lakes, now apartments].

Miss Siddle's sister was a dance teacher hence the picture with us all dressed up as fairies! I remember the girls from Roedean School who lived in the Keswick Hotel just up the road past the park.

Sadly, I did not keep in touch with the other evacuees. I wish I had done now. I did enjoy my time in Keswick, though I did miss my family.

In 2009 Lilian wrote: I still live in Blagdon, Seaton Burn and am now retired, of course. My husband died about five years ago. I worked as a secretary in various places, including working for Lord Ridley on the Blagdon Estate. I still think a lot about Keswick and when I was there once I went to see the veranda house where I was evacuated, but it has been altered a bit.

Pulling pints at the King's Arms – and I was only eight !
IAN GUMM, WHITLEY BAY

Thursday 12th September 1939 – that was the day I left my home in Jarrow on Tyne en route for Keswick. It was my eighth birthday!

That night I stayed at the King's Arms Hotel, in the Main Street. 'Tyson's King's Arms Hotel', as the sign proclaimed on the front, sandwiched in between Allinson's Grocery Shop and the Skiddaw Hotel. I was given a little room for myself – Room 6, and had meals with the staff in the hotel kitchen, where, for the first time, I saw a refrigerator!

The cook was called Alice, and one of the waitresses was Pat. There must have been other staff but my memory on this point fails. The lady who ran the Hotel was called Mary Forsyth.

My mother came with me for the journey, but left later that afternoon. I had never been away from home before.

I seemed to have been given the run of the Hotel pretty well, including (perhaps wrongly) the bar, and soon learned how to pull a pint and bring up bottles from the cellar. Remember, I was only eight! The beer, I remember, was mostly Jennings.

There was also a large ginger cat. I can't remember his name, but I do recall he came to a rather unhappy end one day, snoozing behind some crates. When the brewery men came – squashed cat!

My first taste of

Ian Gumm and Glenda at Castlerigg Stone Circle

schooling at Keswick was at Crosthwaite Junior and Infants, on the road out towards Portinscale. Miss Messenger was the Headteacher and lived in Stanger Street.

To come back to the Hotel for a moment, frequent visitors 'below stairs' were soldiers from the Driving and Maintenance School, which was based on the golf course behind the Station. One name which springs to mind was Freddie Frith, a well-known Isle of Man TT rider. I remember the D & M School gave demonstrations occasionally for the public at large (mostly I must say children) and gave rides around the golf course with half-track lorries and jeeps.

A real character who looked after pigs in the allotment behind the Hotel was Kebbie Speight, who was licensee of the 'Dog and Gun' further up the Main Street. He seemed to have his own particular language when dealing with the pigs – so even at eight I enriched my vocabulary!

Another small pleasure I well remember was a wind-up gramophone, kept in the tap room, plus a few old 78's – and one or two 'newer' ones. I was allowed to play these and it was, I suppose, my introduction to 'dance music'. Before this, in Jarrow, we had a gramophone, but the records were mainly semi-classical. There was one particular record I really enjoyed – *'Somewhere in France with You'* by Jack Hylton and his orchestra. I enjoyed it so much that I've still got it. It left, purely by chance, in my little case, and yes, sixty years on, it still plays!

I remember too the buses to Seatoller which used to leave from outside Storms Café in the Main Street. Some single deckers, very small, and looking very old! One green one, run by a man called Simpson and a white and cream one run by Weightman's. This was before Cumberland Motor Services took over.

King's Arms Hotel, Keswick

From the bus station you could get a bus for Carlisle, Penrith and Lancaster, and these were either Ribble Motor Services or Cumberland Motor Services. I remember going to Carlisle a couple of times and the single- deck buses were painted grey and had a door in the middle. Also, the vehicle driver didn't work right through. We used to meet the bus coming the other way at some point and the drivers changed over. Not the bus, just the drivers.

I cannot be sure what prompted my return to the north-east. Perhaps the hotel staff got sick of a small boy running around, or perhaps the fact that Hitler hadn't dropped any bombs on Jarrow up to that time could have had something to do with it, but sometime early in 1940 (I think it was March or April) I was sent for, and left by Wright's coach – back to Jarrow.

How was I to know that within a few short months I would be back in Keswick? Not to the King's Arms and not by myself – my Mum came with me this time – to a house in Southey Street, Carlton House, by the Methodist Church and we stayed with a lady I only knew as Mrs Mac. No electricity, no gas, lots of candles and oil lamps – and a lot of mice.

The reason why we came back to Keswick is well-documented. It was on the 2nd of July 1940 that a daylight raid on Jarrow left thirteen people killed and over a hundred injured when a lone German bomber, aiming for the shipyard, bombed a residential street nearby.

As fate would have it, I was playing in our local park when the bomber came over, very low. The pilot I remember wore sunglasses – yes, it was that low! The bomb doors actually opened as it passed overhead. And it wasn't too long afterwards that we realised that it would have been so easy for the crew to machine-gun the park. There were lots of children around. It was around 5pm on a summer's evening.

The very next morning my mum and I again set off, again by Wright's coach. Their coaches seemed to run all through the war, taking something like four hours for the trip, and as I said we ended up with Mrs Mac. We didn't stay too long there, but moved next to a house in Church Street and a lady called Winnie (I think Winnie McQuaker) who worked at the Alhambra Cinema, which in those days changed programmes three times a week plus matinees on Wednesdays and Saturdays.

There was also in those days the Pavilion on Station Road which also served as a hall for dancing, brass band concerts and suchlike, but also, on occasion, showed films.

About this time I was upgraded to Crosthwaite Old School, the bigger one by the church, and whose headteacher was Mr Slee. The other teachers I remember were Miss Rushfirth and a Mrs Douthwaite, whom I believe was also evacuated.

It was when I was at the school that I learned a valuable lesson. Sometimes it is better to tell a little lie. It was during the last lesson a Friday afternoon. We were all out in the school garden and like all small boys 'half-inched' one or two peas. Mr Slee spotted this, and asked around, "Were you eating?" Everybody said, "No, sir" except me, who told the truth, "Yes, sir, sorry, sir". "Ian, go in School at once and never come out to gardening again." And I never did. So, as a result of this …. I learned to tell the odd 'porkie'!

I suppose that having a lake in the area was a great attraction for small boys and I was no exception. I made friends with one of the launch boatmen called Bob Johnson. He ran a launch called "Doris" and must have taken me on free trips around the lake dozens of times, sometimes letting me steer. Wonderful. Oddly enough, all the times I've been back to Keswick I've never sailed around Derwentwater again!

Our next move was to number 15 Wordsworth Street, the home of Elsie and Billy Hindmoor and their little daughter Glenda – whom I once remember trying to teach her the words of *"You are my sunshine"* so that she could sing it for her Daddy when he came home on leave. Two things that happened at number 15 stick in the memory. One, the ceiling, or part of it, coming down in the living room. And secondly, me tripping on the stairs, landing on a slip mat at the bottom, sliding along the hall and ending up outside the front door on the pavement – none the worse for wear!

One of the things I used to do was to take the wireless accumulator to be charged on my way to school and pick it up on the way home. It used to cost 6d. I remember dropping it once and it cost 13/6d to replace.

Next door to the garage (Quirk's) was a bookshop run by the Chaplin brothers, Harold and Roy. Roy was in charge of the books and Harold was the stamp man, who kindled my interest in philately. I collected stamps, mainly Commonwealth countries, all through the war. That's where the pocket money went.

I remember the local Home Guard, going off most evenings to guard the reservoir at Thirlmere and the commotion one night when there had been a marvellous display of the Aurora Borealis, the Northern Lights. We all thought that the Germans had landed, even the Home Guard!

As well as my boatman friend, mentioned earlier, I also made friends with the Park Keepers in Fitz Park, who let me do small jobs. Mr Davidson was the Head Keeper. So, my exclusion by Mr Slee wasn't too bad after all. I even got the odd tip!

Sometimes I would venture to the Railway Station, to do a bit of train spotting – not that there was very much of that going on. The only locomotives I ever spotted, during the war, were old (even then) Webb designed 0-6-0 tender engines, known, for some strange reason, as 'cauliflowers'.

Just a few more thoughts. Gathering rose hips and getting, I think, 2d a pound for them …. queuing for torch batteries at Edmondson's Garage in the Main Street …. reading in bed by candlelight …. walking across Derwentwater to Portinscale, during the big freeze in 1940 …. an outbreak of diphtheria in Keswick, not sure of the year but having to be innoculated …. buying Ovaltine tablets, which weren't on the sweet ration

Digging for Victory

…. and Nippits! …and last but not least, spending some time being taught in a church hall of some kind in Tithebarn Street, opposite the bus station, can't be sure how long for, and I think it was only our class.

One last confession. In those far-off days there lived in the town a dachshund (a German sausage dog) which we, as children, loved to chase. Well, it was wartime!

So, after sixty odd years or so, a few memories of a small boy evacuated to Keswick from 1939 to 1944. I left the town in September 1944 for boarding school, and life was never the same again. But that is another story.

Perhaps the dachshund had the last laugh!

Ian wrote in 2009: I left Keswick in September 1944 to spend five very long unhappy years at St. Bees Public School in West Cumberland. Leaving in September 1949, with no qualifications (School Certificate failed) and got a job in the photographic department of A E Reyrolle, in Hebburn on Tyne – a dead-end job. National Service rejected me and in

1953 I went on to driving buses in Newcastle, which is where I met my wife to be. She was a conductress.

In 1955 we both left the buses and I joined Vickers Armstrong in Scotswood. We married in October 1955. Sadly, the department closed in 1960, and Vickers (a very good company to work for) found me a job in one of their other companies, this time X-Raying the welds in ships. This was rather dangerous, and after a narrow squeak in 1962 I left and joined the Photographic Department of the Newcastle Chronicle and Journal Ltd., moving on to their library in 1969 and remaining there until I took early retirement in 1987.

Ian Charlton

In 1969 I started doing Hospital Radio. Then, I was offered a job with BBC Local Radio in Middlesburgh (BBC Radio Cleveland), doing a programme of records of the thirties, forties and fifties. I had always collected records from an early age and had quite a large collection. My programme was called "Dad's Music" – a title I had no control over!

I retired from the BBC in 1994 and we moved back to Cumbria, to Grange-over-Sands. By 2003 my wife was getting a bit homesick for the North-East and we came back to live in Whitley Bay. Sadly, my wife passed away in 2008, but we had fifty-three years together, fifty three happy years.

I kept in touch with Elsie Hindmoor for a long time and while we lived in Grange-over-Sands often spent a day in Keswick, revisiting my old haunts.

Perhaps not a very exciting life, but I'm happy and can say with hand on heart – not bad for a drop-out!

The photograph is of me in my Radio Cleveland days – Ian Charlton was my Radio name!

Annie the maid gave us breakfast – cereals and fried bread with sugar

OWEN HUMBLE, NEWCASTLE-UPON-TYNE
Christ Church School, Newcastle

In 1940 my sister and I were evacuated from Christ Church School in Newcastle. I was five and a half and my sister was ten years old.

My mother requested that we went together. We gathered in, I think, a Methodist Church Hall in Borrowdale Road, almost looking down Lake Road. The Hall gradually emptied. Having to be kept together was understandably a difficult task. Finally, we were alone with despairing volunteers wondering what to do with us when an elderly lady came in.

She was forbidding-looking, with a porkpie hat, thick-lensed spectacles and black moles on her face. To our distress she agreed to take both of us.

A short walk up the road we came to a grand house (Castlehead House, now Castlehead Hotel). We were handed to a lovely maid called Annie. It was quite late in the evening so after a glass of warm milk and a biscuit we were tucked up in bed.

The following morning we were astounded to look out over a lovely garden and beautiful trees. Annie gave us breakfast – cereal and fried bread with sugar. This was a regular morning treat. After breakfast Miss Marshall, the lady of the house, walked us to Keswick and took us to the

clog shop where we were fitted out with leather clogs with large wooden soles and metal hoops. On the way back we called at two houses. One was the home of Judy Cartmell and the other Alistair Cartwright (?) who in later life

Owen Humble and his wife

38

became a local councillor.

They were asked to look after me and take me to Brigham School, which they did. I can't remember what arrangements were made for my sister.

Apart from Annie there was her husband Sid, gardener and handyman to the house. There was also Miss Moore, Miss Marshall's companion and an austere and rather frightening lady to two small children.

Miss Marshall was a Guider and Brownie Leader. My sister was quickly enrolled and I was enrolled in the Cubs.

I adored my evacuation very much and learned a love of Keswick and the Lakes in general which has lasted to this day.

Our time in Keswick came to an abrupt end after approximately fourteen to eighteen months. Sid was called up and Annie left. Understandably Miss Marshall couldn't cope.

My return to Keswick was for my honeymoon in 1954 at the Skiddaw Hotel. We returned every year until recently, introducing our children and many friends to a beautiful place.

Owen wrote in 2009: My principal hobby in retirement is being involved in an amateur operatic and dramatic society. My involvement in the community has been in Scouting and I am a District Commissioner for Scouts. (Owen was enrolled as a Cub-Scout as soon as he arrived in Keswick!)

[The Castlehead Hotel was destroyed by fire in 2009. The site has been cleared ready for another hotel].

"Come in, Thomas. Lemon curd for tea."
TOM JOYCE, NEWCASTLE-UPON-TYNE

My memories begin in my hometown of Newcastle-upon-Tyne. It was 1941 and the air raid sirens sounded their usual alarm, but this night was to be a turning point in my life.

I lived on City Road, opposite what was then Hedley's Soap factory (remember 'Oxydol" and 'Fairy Soap'?) On my way to the air raid shelter which was in the basement of Hedley's there was a blast which nearly burst my eardrums. This was a direct hit on the flats where I lived. Flames and debris everywhere, windows shattering in the heat. My mother grabbed me and we rushed across the street and made for the shelter.

Next morning in the light of day we emerged to a terrible scene. A high section of our Square (as we called our flats) had been obliterated and several families had lost their lives including childhood friends. This was when I realised that war was not a game.

Shortly afterwards with many other children I was at Newcastle Central Station, carrying a gas mask, cheese sandwiches – and what luxury – an apple! We were herded onto a train, no idea where we were going. My father was at war and my mother worked in the soap factory. I felt deserted, lost and very confused. I was eight years old.

I've little memory of the train journey. To say I was nervous was an understatement. I had never been out of the City before, not on a train.

Eventually we arrived at Keswick Station and can't remember much about the journey but I know we all finished up in the Moot Hall. Grown-ups with strange accents (to a Geordie!) were walking amongst us and gradually taking children away. We had been reading 'Oliver Twist' at school, so you can imagine what was going through our eight-year old minds!

Then suddenly I heard a voice. 'Hello Thomas! I'm Mrs Colbeck, would you like to come with me?' I know I didn't reply, my eyes were firmly fixed on the floor. She seemed very posh, but she smiled and took

Tom Joyce on Remembrance Day

my hand. I remember how gently she did it and somehow I knew she would be kind – and I was right. 'Come on, I'll take you to your new home and you shall have tea and cake – and don't worry, when this awful war is over, and maybe before, you will return home'.

Mrs Colbeck lived at 24 Manor Park, not too far from St John's Church. It was a far cry from the flats in Newcastle. I remember a grandfather clock just inside the front door, soft carpets and a lovely smell, not the carbolic smell of Hedley's Soap Factory.

True to her word, the table was laid with cakes and scones and what looked like a yellow jam – homemade lemon curd. I remember thinking, 'This must be like heaven'.

After tea and cakes I was shown my room – my own room! Never had one to myself before. A shelf full of wonderful books, 'Treasure Island', 'Wind in the Willows' to mention but two. I was to read them all. Everything seemed so grand, and from my window a view of the fells and outside a garden to the front and the back. You must realise that I'd never seen mountains and a garden was a rarity on City Road.

Mrs Colbeck's husband arrived home. He was called Arthur and she was called Maude. His arrival surprised me, all men were at war I thought, but Mrs Colbeck said he had an important position that helped the war effort, but couldn't talk about it.

So you see I was very lucky as Arthur and Maude were the warmest and kindest people you can imagine and very patient with me as I had quite a few rough edges as you would imagine.

Soon all my fears vanished and I settled in. To my delight there was a boy next door roughly my age, Ray Sewell. Now he loved rugby and I loved football so at first there was some friction. Ray was a giant of a boy and one day we scuffled over the merits of the games. I would like to say I defeated the giant, but after being picked up and deposited on the ground three or four times I rapidly decided that rugby was a great game and we became great pals. Ray decided I was OK and through him I was accepted by other local boys.

Many years later on a visit to Keswick, staying at a Bed & Breakfast Guest House in Stanger Street, I mentioned Ray and the owner of the Guest House said that he knew him and that he had connections with the Keswick Rugby Club. I was over the moon – I would look him up – then sadly she informed me that Ray had died. Even after all these years I felt a great sense of loss. He was a great pal of my childhood and I will not forget him.

Mrs Colbeck arranged for my schooling and I attended Brigham School, just opposite the River Greta and not far from Manor Park. The building is still there but not used as a school anymore. Every morning at playtime a large churn of fresh milk would arrive – we all lined up in the schoolyard and got our share. It was lovely and to this day I have never tasted milk like it.

After school in the summer I would join up with the local boys – and Ray of course – we knew a deep pool in the River Greta, up to an eight year old's neck – in the case of Ray up to his waist. We would swim and mess around as boys do, and every now and then the locals would duck under the water. I soon realised why. Have you ever been bitten by a clegg?

My job was collecting books and papers and any old scrap, all to be handed in, sorted and used again. Because Mrs Colbeck was related to the Maysons, now a bazaar on Lake Road, I had a great source of old books and paper. In those days the licence to photograph Tarn Hows was held by Maysons and it was an Aladdin's Cave of photographs and old books. I remember the old man – he seemed ancient to me and always had an air of mystery.

One day it was decided at school that we would put on a show at the old Pavilion Theatre. It was called 'TenLittle Black **Boys**'. The proceeds – to the war effort. To my humiliation, along with another nine evacuees I was cast as one of ten little black girls. The girls in the school were cast as the boys. It took a long time to live down. So that was my ultimate contribution to the war effort.

As time went by I explored more of Keswick and its surrounds – Friar's Crag, Walla Crag, Catbells and of course my favourite, Derwentwater.

Often I would stroll down the lane by the side of St John's, the lovely smell from the hedges and wild flowers was great. Now, of course, you have to cross a main road.

Skipping pebbles was one of my favourite pastimes. Each time I tried to beat the number of bounces. I became quite expert at it and only recently was teaching my grandson Conor the art. One winter it was so cold Derwentwater froze over. Mrs Colbeck took me skating on the lake. She lent me a pair of Victorian wooden skates – no metal runners. I never mastered them and spent most of the time on my backside. Still, lovely hot roasted chestnuts were ample compensation. The Bank Tavern used to have old black and white photographs of the event – they were displayed on the wall in the bar area.

Like most boys, my explorations led me into trouble. Three of us decided to climb Latrigg. Being foolhardy we climbed straight up, hanging on to the tree trunks to stop sliding backwards. We got separated so I persevered and eventually reached the top – I felt I'd climbed Everest. Then – big mistake – I lost my bearings, low cloud and mist had developed. I headed downhill, slipping and sliding, sadly down the opposite side to my climb, totally lost, hadn't a clue what to do – Ray wasn't there. I'm sure he could have got us back. I spent what seemed forever trying to find a way back, to no avail. I was so tired I just laid down and fell asleep, but jumped up with a start and found a dog, a collie I think, barking like mad. Its owner, I believe a farmer, realising my plight, took me home, gave me a good telling-off and guided me to the outskirts of Keswick, where I got another roasting from Mr Colbeck. No lemon curd that teatime.

I loved everything about Keswick, the mountains, the parks, the mini-golf course, my pals, the adventures but most of all Mrs Colbeck. She taught me so many things which have stood me in good stead throughout my life.

Sadly, all things must end. One day my mother arrived at No. 24. She wasn't expected and I had no warning. I was ten years old by now. Mrs Colbeck called me in. I knew she was upset. 'Thomas, your mother has called to take you home'.

I didn't know what to do or say. I knew I didn't want to go home, I burst into tears and my mother had to drag me to the railway station. I realised later how much that must have hurt Mam, but at that age you don't realise.

Over the years I visited Mrs Colbeck whenever I could but as I joined the Royal Navy (for twenty-two years) the chances were few and far between. I married and my wife Barbara and I took an opportunity to visit. At that time we had two children, boys. Arthur had died, but we enjoyed a wonderful day – tea and cucumber sandwiches.

That was the last time I saw Maude, Mrs Colbeck. She died when I was at sea. She was a genteel English lady and I will always remember her with affection.

When my wife and I visit Keswick, at least two or tree times a year, we often stroll past 24 Manor Park, but of course the occupants wouldn't know us. I've thought about knocking on the door – but then I like to remember Mrs Colbeck opening the door smiling. 'Come in, Thomas. Lemon curd for tea'.

Writing in 2009: I left school at fourteen years of age and started work as a paper ruler, part of the printing trade. I found the work mind - bogglingly boring, but stuck it for three years and them made the best decision of my working life. I joined the Royal Navy just before the death of King George VI. In 1953 I was 'loaned' with thirty-two others to the Royal Australian Navy for two and a half years. I mention this, because many years after returning to the Royal Navy and then leaving, after a service of twenty-two years, a couple of us traced the others. Sadly, some had 'crossed the bar' (died).

Our next reunion, already organised and booked, is in Keswick in May 2010 and twenty-eight will be attending. For my other sins I am the organiser. Some of those attending have never been to the Lakes.

I left the Navy in 1973 having risen to the rank of Chief Petty Officer Radio Mechanic 1st Class. During my service I circumnavigated the globe twice and have served in many areas, including Malaya, Singapore and Aden – in total over seventy different countries and islands.

I met my wife Barbara whilst shore-based in Paisley, near Glasgow. We had three sons, Paul, Stephen and Edward. Mrs Colbeck, who looked after me as an evacuee met Barbara and my two elder sons. I tried to keep in touch with her. She was so kind to me.

On leaving the Navy I worked as a TV Engineer. Later on, returning to my home town, I became a section leader responsible for all electrical equipment and maintenance at Parsons, later Rolls-Royce.

In retirement I help out with the Alzheimer's Society. Now 76, I am well and truly retired but still fit and active. On April 24th last my wife and I celebrated our Golden Wedding. We went on a Mediterranean cruise, so it was full circle and back to sea. My wife calls my memories 'nautical nightmares'!

On the farm, it was all a boy could wish for ….
JACK LAMB, BORROWDALE
Cruddas Park School, Newcastle

How do you start writing after all this time? I went to a school in Newcastle called Cruddas Park on the famous Scotswood Road (Blaydon Races), a tough and run-down area but the people had hearts of gold.

We had a big school – three storeys with playgrounds on the roof for hundreds of girls and boys.

Just before war was declared we had to say if we would like to be evacuated or not – so I was on my way leaving mother, father, big brother and two sisters behind, setting off from the Central Station and arriving at Keswick in the afternoon. Seven of us from the same school were put on the bus to Grange School. After a lovely tea we were all sent to different homes.

Some children from the school stayed in Keswick and others went to West Cumberland. Those staying in Borrowdale were Nevison

Above:Horse drawn sledge in Borrowdale

Jack Lamb (second left) with fellow workers at the Pencil Mill

Lorraine, sister Rosie, George Dunwoody and Emily, Irene and Billy Gordon, but after six months we were down to Nevison and myself and also a teacher called Miss Barris who had to help out Mr Watson Boustead, the Headteacher and a Miss Davidson.

A week later from South Shields came twenty or more boys and girls but too many to join us at Stonethwaite so they had to go in the village hall at Rosthwaite.

For the first few weeks I was with a family called Mr and Mrs Baker and their son Teddy. They were very kind to me but they had to move out of the valley down to the Kendal area. After all these years we still keep in touch with Christmas cards and visits.

I spent most of the time out of school at Hollows Farm, which had a family of five, Bob, Mary, Peter, Billy and Ted, so when they heard the Bakers were leaving took me in and it was all a boy could ask for, learning to milk, going round with the milk float (horses) and a big churn with pint measures – no bottles in those days. Hay-timing was mostly hard work but many hands made light work of it.

After a few weeks my mother turned up at school to see how I was settling down. She came up the valley on Weightman's bus driven by John Atkinson who said, "Don't worry about him, he's alright and by the way I'll wait at the road end for you and make sure you catch Wright's bus back to Newcastle".

In the 1939 – 1940 winter there was so much snow and ice I remember helping to make a snow plough. With Mr Jenkins on and with two horses we set off from Grange to his brother at Brandelhow. It seemed to take all day. When the ice was thick enough we skated under Grange Bridge for weeks. Alan Mounsey, who lived at Grange, found skates for most of us. The war hadn't got to Grange!

I had two wonderful years in Borrowdale before I left school. Mother wanted me to go home and start my apprenticeship as an engineer working at the Vickers Armstrong Works.

Nevison, who left school at the same time, went into farm work at Manesty Farm, then on to Martin Raven at High Hill Farm. We lost each other after that, but a strange thing happened about forty years later. My sister and her husband were on holiday on the south coast and in the hotel her husband was talking to a lady and as usual, "Where do you come from?" etcetera and it turned out she started school on the same day as my sister, sitting together until leaving at fourteen and not seeing each other in forty years. Also, her half sister had married Nevis Lorraine and was living in Gateshead.

I still managed to get back to Grange whenever I could, long weekends when I was moving from day work to night shift. We had air raids most nights and had the work's sirens which went on long after the city sirens, also some of the big machines couldn't be turned off.

After the war in 1945 I was called up in the Royal Air Force, spending most of my leaves at Grange and doing a bit of courting, a Dinah Pattinson, whose father farmed at Longthwaite in Borrowdale. After three years service I had to go back to finish my apprenticeship, which I did and got married in December 1948.

I got a job in Keswick at the Cumberland Pencil Mill lasting forty-

Jack and Dinah Lamb

two years, enjoying every minute.

We had one daughter, Elizabeth, who later married a farmer, David Bland, and had two sons, Gavin and Peter, and one daughter Liza.

Liza also went to College in Newcastle and it turned out she was in the Halls of Residence at Cruddas Park, a stone's throw away from where I was born and went to school but with the slum clearance it looked different.

Not a bad life for a boy in short trousers, cardboard box with gas mask, a paper carrier bag with my clothes in leaving for Borrowdale all those years ago. All the Jenkinson family keep in touch, thanks to them all.

Jack wrote in 2009: Since the 1950's and my National Service married life has been good for my wife and I. Last December we celebrated our Diamond Wedding – and received a card from the Queen. We had a small party with family and friends at the Borrowdale Hotel.

After forty-two years at the Cumberland Pencil Mill I was invited to see the new factory in Workington. I wish the firm well and to get plenty of orders in these troubled times.

Since my retirement I can't see how I had the time to go to work! We have two grandsons in farming, one in Grasmere and the other in Thirlmere and one grand-daughter living away in Cheltenham. We have five great-grandchildren and they help me fill my days.

My interests are in hunting, hound-trailing, horse racing and last but not least fell running, which has taken us to most of the Cumbrian fells, Scotland and Wales – but as a spectator. Our great grandchildren are into most sports so we have so much to look forward to in the coming years.

It's a funny thing, but the war has done me a favour and given me a wonderful life here in Borrowdale with my wife and family.

I remember the smell of cedar wood in Keswick

MARION LOWNDES, MIDDLESBROUGH
Kirby Secondary School, Middlesbrough

During the invasion scare of 1940 I remember my mother (Marion Jane Weaver, nee Zealand) coming into my bedroom one morning and telling me to go to school (Kirby Secondary School, Middlesbrough) and tell Miss McCombie, the Headmistress, that I would not be coming any more, as Mother and I were going to Keswick. I was in the middle of examinations, but I never did finish them!

My late sister, Eileen, was married to Hubert A Lowe. He worked in Martin's Bank, Middlesbrough, which was a "reserved occupation", that is, he would not be called up. He was also in the Auxiliary Fire Service, and on call every night. Eileen and her first son, Martin, were already in Keswick, staying with the manager of Martin's Bank who lived between Bank Street and Fitz Park, and what is now Mill Row off Otley Road. I remember going round to the house, which had an awful lot of steps, and helping Eileen with the pram.

Mother and I went by train, as there was no petrol for 'pleasure trips'. We changed trains at Darlington and Penrith, arriving at Keswick in the evening. A man with a pony and cart took the luggage to the County Hotel on the Penrith Road near the junction with Station Street. Mother and I walked to the Hotel, which was not far and there was no extra petrol for taxis. It was rationed, and in short supply, having to be brought by ship to Britain. My father had booked a room for us, and we stayed there while we looked for accommodation, as we did not know how long we would be staying in Keswick. Rooms were hard to find, as there were so many people there, all looking for somewhere to rent.

There were a lot of Middlesbrough people at the hotel, and mother knew most of them, as Middlesbrough was a much smaller place then. Three ladies, who lived nearby in Linden Grove (we lived in Cambridge Road, Linthorpe) were Jewesses, and like others of their faith, were very kind. One afternoon they went out as usual, looking for somewhere to

Marion Lowndes (centre) with friends

rent, but came back looking very dejected. They asked if they could have a word with Mother, 'in private'. It appeared that they had been to see some rooms in a bungalow, but the lady who lived there would not let them have the accommodation. They knew that it was because they were Jewesses and had come back to tell Mother and said, 'If you hurry, you will get the rooms'. We did get the rooms, at 20 Heads Road, at the corner of Heads Mount, and our hostess was a Mrs Dent, who was the Manageress of Judge's Post Card shop in Station Road. Her late husband had been Manager of the garage (I think Quirk's Garage), in Tithebarn Street, near a car park. I always thought how kind it was of these three ladies to come and tell Mother about the rooms.

We knew a lot of Jews and Jewesses in Middlesbrough who lived quite near to us in Cambridge Road. Many of them were refugees from Austria and Germany and they were all very kind. I never knew why people didn't like them.

Our life at Heads Road was very pleasant in spite of food rationing, although we were worried about our loved ones at home and my brother Harry who was in the Army, in the Royal Corps of Signals. After a while

51

Mother decided to leave me in the capable hands of Mrs Dent and return home.

Mrs Dent was a very strict chaperone, but she was great fun to be with. She used to tell me all about the local climbing club, of which she was a Founder-Member, and take me to dances at the local Dance Hall, next to the River Greta. It also doubled as a Cinema, called, I think, The Pavilion. When the river was flooded the dance floor was inundated and took some time to dry out! The Youth Hostel is next door, near the old pencil mills on the River Greta. (My memory was never very good!) The Pavilion was demolished in 1988 to make way for flats,

I got to know several of the local girls of my own age. There was one, whose name I cannot recall, but her uncle had a jeweller's shop opposite the Royal Oak Hotel, which had a lovely barometer in a glass case on the wall outside his shop. It was there for years (no vandals in those days!) I remember all the little ginnels we used to walk through between the Market Square and Tithebarn Street and on into Heads Road. They have nearly all been blocked off now. My friends and I walked miles around Keswick. One time we were walking up to Ashness Bridge, and met 'The Borrowdale Hermit'. He was quite frightening with his long hair and long beard! We were quite young then.

I remember the peace and quiet of Keswick, and the smell of the cedarwood for making pencils, and the friendliness of the local people, who were wonderful. It all seemed a world away from the War.

After about six weeks Mother decided I should return home, but I shall never forget my time as an evacuee.

My parents used to take me to Keswick every Easter before the War, ever since I was born, and I used to go back with friends on the train, taking our bicycles with us. I have been to Keswick every year for eighty-four years, and I still love it!

Marion (Paddy) wrote in 2009: I kept in touch with Mrs Dent, my Keswick hostess, until her death. After school I began work as a clerk at the Midland Bank in 1941. We hated 'Balance Night' on New Year's Eve. We could not leave until the books balanced, though the girls could go home at 10 pm in time for the last buses. Sometimes the men stayed all night! My next job was in a solicitor's office, leaving to get married to William Lithgo, who was a Captain in the Merchant Navy.

He died in 2005.

Now I am 83 and I have my nephew Martin drive me to visit Keswick. He too was an evacuee in Keswick, aged three months, in 1940. Like me, he loves the town, a truly wonderful place.

The two ladies, our hosts, had been debutantes at Court
NORMAN MIDGLEY, SUNDERLAND

My special place would be in the Newlands Valley, just after the start of the 1939 – 1945 War. It was 1940, and my father, unfit for war service, took me and my sister aged six and a half years and nine years respectively with mother on a short holiday in Keswick.

One day as we walked on Catbells, the sole of my shoe became separated from the uppers. My father called at the house at Gutherscale to see if we could have some string to hold my shoe together until we got back into Keswick. There we met two ladies – a Miss Fisher and Miss Layton. It transpired that the latter would have to do war service if she was not doing a job of national importance.

Our parents, there and then, decided the north-east coast was no place for children due to the prospect of excessive bombing and suddenly we were EVACUEES. After lots of tears from us and our parents, we were on our own with two ladies we hardly knew.

Life seemed hard for two small children, particularly when we were fitted with clogs and yellow sou'westers and sent to Newlands School. It was an age 5 to 14 years school in one small classroom. I remember well the teacher, who was an elderly lady who worked and tried so hard to keep us in order.

Later we were joined at Gutherscale by two more girls from South Shields, Moira Parker and Margaret Collins. We all shared one bedroom and it was hard for me, the only boy with three girls!

At school we were friends with the sons of Mr Graves' Farm, Skelghyll. I remember some of the activities – which included Maypole Dancing (the pole is still stored in the church I am told) and knitting was taught (plain) because at six and a half years old I was too young to do woodwork. I remember we were knitting scarves for the White Russian troops. Mine just got bigger and bigger, becoming a shawl for my granny.

Saturdays we played on Catbells and wrote letters home. Sunday

Gutherscales

morning was a walk along the Manesty road to Sir High Walpole's house to post our censored letters home. Occasionally we were invited to the Rev. J Steel-Smith's (Vicar of Newlands) house for tea, and were presented with prayer books.

The ladies we stayed with were both presented at Court as debutantes and many parties were held at Gutherscale. I remember that we were all packed off to bed early on these occasions, however we didn't go to sleep and spied on the visitors – mostly local gentry, including Lord and Lady Lonsdale.

Times changed and we were transferred to Crosthwaite School – the girls to the junior section by the church and me to the infant section. We walked each way through the Great Wood, leaving Gutherscale about 7.30 am with torches and gas masks in the dark in winter (double summertime) and returned when we arrived! We were known throughout the area as the 'four yellow bellies' because of our sou'westers. We were not allowed to accept lifts, because we were told German spies operated in the area!

In 1942 we were brought home to the north – east to see out the end of the war. However, nearly sixty years later I look back at Newlands with affection. I know where the best hazelnut trees are – the short cuts across the fields, and remember how things were. And – if you happened to drop into Newlands Church some Saturday – you may hear me playing the organ and my wife singing a few hymns!

Norman wrote in 2009: I have many happy memories of my evacuation, when along with my sister and two other girls from the north east of England, we stayed at 'Gutherscale' with Miss Fisher and Miss Layton. We went to the local school at Newlands which was one mixed class of ages ranging from 5 to 14, and taught by one teacher, namely Miss Pooley. Many of the pupils in the class were local children whose names I cannot recall, however I do remember John and Norman Graves from the neighbouring farm.

In 1942, which was the worst part of the war, my parents missed us very much and decided to bring us home. My mother had been ill after a serious operation and my father had survived a bombing at his railway office. They both felt that if they were to be bombed it would be better if they went as a family.

My education was continued at the local school and at the age of eleven I passed the 11+ examination and went to the Bede Grammar School in Sunderland. When I left school I took up an apprenticeship in marine engineering which resulted in me joining the merchant navy in 1956. My fiancé Valerie was then training to be a nurse so we thought it was better that we both followed our careers before settling down to marriage.

In 1959 we were married and I continued to travel with the Merchant Navy, doing such trips as taking the £10 immigrants to Australia. When I left the Merchant Navy I took a job at Barrow-in-Furness working on nuclear submarines. Our first child was born in Barrow-in-Furness in 1963, a son named Peter. We returned to live in Sunderland and I took up work in the shipyards as a draughtsman.

The shipbuilding depression began in 1964, and then I went to work as a draughtsman for the Pyrex glassworks in Sunderland. Our second child, a girl named Linda was born in 1965. Valerie and I then began to think about the future and how we could further our careers for the good of the family. I began to train as a teacher of mathematics in 1968 and when I qualified Valerie attended college to train as a primary school teacher.

My love for the Lake District never left me, and when the children were young we spent most of our school holidays camping and caravanning. We also enjoyed walking and brought up the family to go along, hence they too developed a fondness for walking the lakes and hills.

Sadly, in 1990 my wife Valerie died after a long illness battling for many years with cancer. In 1993 I married Elizabeth, my second wife, and we have now spent sixteen happy years together sharing many interests. Now that we are both retired we pursue our interest in music together and sing in two choral societies as did my first wife. In fact she introduced Elizabeth to me a few years before she died. We enjoy walking and travelling and share a fondness for the Lake District and places such as Switzerland.

We have two grandchildren who have never known any other grandmother but Elizabeth, and she gets along with them and my family very well.

"Come and Join Us." Well, I did just that!
PAT MUCKIAN, OVINGTON, NORTHUMBERLAND
St. Theresa's R C School, Newcastle

My name is Pat Muckian and I was five years old when World War Two began. Together with my sister Eileen, who was then 12 years old and with other pupils from St Theresa's R C School at Newcastle upon Tyne we were evacuated, heading first for Keswick. Eileen and I did not have our parents with us, but some children did, and our Headmaster, his wife and three children accompanied us.

We had a bag on our backs with clothes, but not a toy between us. Eileen was scared, but I was too young to understand. I loved the journey, but Eileen didn't. Keswick was just a name to us. We walked from the train station down to the bus station where we were 'selected'. Eileen and I were separated, I went to Scott's Court and Eileen went to Myrtyl Villas, which was quite near.

My first night was great. I was allowed to take Fluffy the cat to bed with me and we became great friends. I stayed with Emily and Jimmy at Scott's Court for the duration of the war and one year longer.

There was no Catholic School in Keswick so we went for lessons to the Congregational Hall in Lake Road and Mr Cain the Headmaster taught us, but he took his wife and family home not long after as they were homesick. My education was badly neglected. My sister Eileen went home after two years. In those days you left school at fourteen years of age. I missed Eileen, but soon got over it.

I had a lot of friends and played in Fitz Park. When the lake froze over we walked on Derwentwater. One child fell through the ice and sadly died. We climbed the fells and went bleaberry picking. Happy days.

Jimmy was an agricultural worker and exempt from being in the forces. He hired himself and tractors out to farmers and took Emily and myself with him to various farms – an ideal life for me. I must have slipped through the system, but do remember going to Brigham School and walking through a wood to get there. I have no idea how long I attended Brigham School and don't remember the teachers' names.

We went to Mandell's Farm and there was a boy and his mother from London staying there. They were escaping from the bombs. His name was Charles Button. His father was a doctor but he stayed in London.

I remember the farmer sitting me on his knee and teaching me to read the clock. It was a great big grandfather clock and this went on each night after we had churned butter, milked cows and fed cattle. Rationing meant nothing to me as I lived on the fat of the land.

How I loved the Lakes and still do. Delightful. I think that the thing I liked best about Keswick was the people and the surrounding hills. I still come back now at the age of seventy-one years and when I come through Penrith I always say, "I'm home now". I visited Emily and Jimmy often and my husband was fond of them. Emily died and six months later we attended Jimmy's funeral.

When I was seven I had diptheria and was put in isolation in a Hospital in Penrith (I don't know if it still exists) and Emily and Jimmy could only look at me through a window on the ward. When I was discharged my first words were, "Where is Fluffy " and was told the cat had died of diphtheria. I never did find out what happened to it.

To recap on my school days, we had to attend Mass. On a Sunday I was sent to Church and went past the Salvation Army Hall and they were singing, "Come and Join Us." Well, I did just that. It was fun. After all, the Mass was in Latin, a language unheard of!

Come Monday morning the Priest called at School and asked. "Stand up if you missed Church." So, I was at Church, but the wrong one. The priest came to the house and I was told that I would be taken away from Emily and Jimmy if I didn't attend. I never told anyone what I did, but I was found out somehow. Emily was crying, so I agreed to go back. Ugh!!

There was one character I remember that we called Charlie Norris, the Skiddaw Hermit. He had a shop on Lake Road and in the window was a full set of dentures. I was fascinated and used to go back often to see if they had been sold. He had no teeth and I drew the conclusion that they were his own. Rumour had it that he lived in the white cottage half way up Skiddaw and came down for the summer. The cottage has gone now so he must have departed.

One of my friends had family who were Romanies and each year they came to Keswick with Gypsy caravans pulled by horses. We used to visit them in the evening and sit round the campfire, eating pancakes, which were lovely. They parked in the field across the road from the Pencil Mill. Happy, happy times. I don't remember having money but there didn't seem any need for it.

We went to the pictures at the Alhambra and to the Pavilion with the School about three times, but I wasn't very impressed. Later I went to dancing classes and we went on stage in the Pavilion. I loved that, the dancing and the bright lights and I was always in the front, being little. At the end of the show we made a Union Jack with strips of sheeting dyed red and blue and, of course, white. That has always stayed in my mind. The Pavilion has gone now, but I did attend Saturday night dances there when I was between sixteen and eighteen years old.

The Keswick Hotel put on a party for us at Christmas and I remember what a beautiful place it was and still is. We had lovely food and a Christmas tree and were given a present each. Fond memories indeed.

At Christmas I would wake up, run downstairs to see what was in the sock (one of Jimmy's socks) and was delighted to find hazel nuts, a very shiny red apple and an orange. I may have had other things, but don't remember one single thing, but I was very happy. What more can I say? 1946 came and I had to return to Newcastle. I was heart-broken as were Emily and Jimmy. My mother, whom I could not remember, made arrangements for Emily and Jimmy, who hadn't any children, to adopt me. My father came out of the Royal Air Force and came to take me home. That was when World War Two began for me. The name 'mother' to me is meaningless. I was born of this woman, so be it. My father was a lovely, loving dad. I consider myself very lucky as the war did me a favour. I wonder what kind of life I would have had if I had stayed in Newcastle. Nobody, but nobody wins in a war.

I do not believe in God, but believe in fate. When I was nineteen I met my Terry and we were married at the age of twenty-three. Alas, we have no children but have been very happy, and still are. We both worked and saw a lot of the world and will celebrate our Golden Wedding in 2007.

All's well that ends well.

Pat Muckian wrote in 2009: I returned to Newcastle after evacuation

Pat and Terry Muckian

in 1946. I had not seen my parents in six years. I was twelve years old and I was sent back to the school I was evacuated with. It was the time of the scholarship and because of my lack of education I wasn't able to sit the examination. I wasn't happy with my mother, nor her with me, but we made the best of it.

When I left school I started in the wages department of C A Parsons, but found it hard. After seventeen and a half years I left the firm to work for a coachworks and was taught book-keeping and accounts. I later worked in the Civic Centre at Newcastle in Education Accounts and stayed with them until I was fifty-six.

My interests now are walking, swimming and gardening. My husband and I meet up with friends and we walk every week-end.

Every year for thirty years we went to the High Lodore Farm in Borrowdale. They stopped catering for visitors a few years ago, so now we go to the Keswick Country House Hotel, which brings back lovely memories of the Xmas parties they used to put on for the evacuees.

The only achievements I can boast of, having reached the age of seventy-five years -I have a free television licence. Nothing to boast about – I don't even care for television – but life's like that. Ha! Ha!

Whenever I go to Keswick, I still feel that I am going home
GERARD NUTTNEY, NEWCASTLE-UPON-TYNE
St Theresa's R.C. School, Newcastle

During the early part of 1940, my elder brother Thomas and I were evacuated to Keswick. Our ages at that time were nine and six respectively.

We were with a school group of children from a school in Heaton in the East End of Newcastle, St.Theresa's R C. We were from St. Dominic's School nearer to the city centre.

Travelling with the group was the Headmaster Mr Cane and his wife and two children, Michael and Hilary. I can only remember the name of one teacher, Miss Boucher.

On arrival, there were a lot of voluntary helpers assembled in a room above the town centre market hall, along with a number of people who had said they would look after one, or possibly two of the evacuees. My brother and I were taken to No.10, Windebrowe Avenue to stay with Mrs. Turner until a more permanent accommodation could be found for us.

My feelings, in hindsight, are that the voluntary helpers thought that

all children from a war-ravaged city must be very dirty, because the first thing that happened to us was that we were immersed in a bath full of hot water and thoroughly scrubbed. The estate was fairly new, and we used to play on a piece of waste ground covered with bricks and various other builders' rubble, having a great time as young kids do.

After a week or two we were transferred to a more permanent billet to No. 3, High Hill. This was the house of Mr.

Thomas and Gerard Nuttney

and Mrs. Raven. He was the son of Mr Raven, senior who owned Raven's farm. Mr. and Mrs. Raven had a daughter Margaret, two years old. We thoroughly enjoyed our stay there, seeing the circus arrive and set up in a field between the farmhouse and the river; being allowed to toast bread on a large toasting fork at the living room fire; and generally wandering around the farm to look at all the animals being fed and watered. However, all good things come to an end, and when Mrs Raven became pregnant, and could no longer cope with us, we were transferred to another house in Wordsworth Street.

This was the home of Mrs. Campbell, known to us affectionately as 'Granny Campbell'. Her stepdaughter Betty lived there and she did virtually all the looking-after of us. I well remember the long Sunday afternoon walks, while Granny had her nap for about four hours; we were taken to places like Friar's Crag, the great Bowder Stone, the Druid's Circle, Portinscale, and at times up Skiddaw, as far as the lemonade shack. We stayed with Granny Campbell until early 1944.

Our schooling took place in the Congregational Hall. The Town Council had very kindly given this over to the school for the term of our stay. On my last visit to Keswick, I checked it out, and it is still there. Approaching from the lake uphill, turn left at the T junction and look to the right, and there it is.

I well remember on at least one occasion, during a very cold spell, we all wrapped up in scarves and gloves and were walked OVER the frozen lake to a place called, I think, Brandlehow. We did our lessons there and had our lunch before walking back. Quite an adventure for a seven year old city boy. On the way back across the lake we were amazed to see not only people ice-skating, but also a horse and trap, equipped with runners instead of wheels.

Our normal outdoor school activity was to be taken to the lower slopes of Latrigg, to go wool gathering; this, we were told, was to help the war effort.

Another great activity to help the war effort was collecting waste paper. The man next door to Granny Campbell let me store my collection in an outbuilding in his yard. The local butcher's boy very kindly offered to help me get my paper to the local cinema to be weighed. They were giving a ticket to everyone who had collected two hundred weight of paper. The film on show was in Technicolor called 'NORTH-WEST MOUNTED POLICE AND INDIANS'. Wow! I had never seen anything like it in my life.

One day at school during morning assembly, one of my classmates, a young lad from the Channel Islands, told me that his mother was visiting, and he was allowed to have the day off after he had his mark, and would I like to go with them. Yes, I said and in due course left with him and his mother. We had a great time, playing crazy golf, having lemonade and ice cream, then off to see a matinee performance at the cinema. Great! Unfortunately for me, on returning to Granny Campbell's house at about four thirty, I was in deep trouble: no one at school knew where I was, or who I was with. I had gone missing without telling anyone and without permission from the headmaster.

One activity we thoroughly enjoyed was with the local Boy Scout and Cubs Group. We regularly played a game at Castlerigg where the troop would be split into two groups. Group A would have three spent matches tucked in the garter of their sock near the green uniform flash.

They would then go up the hill and wait till the appointed time, before making their descent. Group B would set off at the same appointed time to climb the hill. The object of the game was that for Group A to avoid being caught by Group B. If they were caught, they had to submit a match. The wining group was the one with the most matches at the end of the exercise. I think there was quite a lot of cheating went on.

Our parents were able to visit once a year. The first time was to show us our new baby brother. I never realised just how well I would get to know him; I had to look after him after my days as an evacuee were done. Now I visit him regularly in Australia.

Happy days, long gone; I don't think I suffered in any way through being an evacuee. In fact I think I really enjoyed the experience.

Whenever I go to Keswick, I still feel that I am going home.

In 2009 Gerard wrote: In 1944 I arrived back in Newcastle and was adjusting to city life, renewing friendships with the boys in my street, etcetera. In 1947 the family moved three miles away to an estate that provided us with a new council house. Two years later, I started an apprenticeship in the plumbing trade, and then I was uprooted from home to do my two year National Service in the RAF. This was a completely

new experience however, because I was stationed on Anglesey, North Wales. I was able to enjoy cycling all over Snowdonia, an absolutely wonderful eighteen months of miles and youth hostelling.

After National Service, I enrolled in a dance class. I met a young woman and danced with her through bronze, silver, gold and gold cross medal ballroom dancing classes before treading the boards in the manner of 'Strictly Come Dancing'. (She still insists that I have led her a merry dance ever since).

We have recently celebrated our 46th wedding anniversary and have a son, daughter and two adorable grandsons.

Evacuation and Keswick obviously did me no harm mentally or physically. I still visit Mrs Raven, my 99 year-old Lakeland mother.

An Aladdin's Cave of Sports Equipment!
DANNY ROBERTSON, NEWCASTLE-UPON-TYNE

My brother Raymond and I were evacuated to Braithwaite at about the beginning of the war (1939). We were fortunate to be staying with the Barnes family, Gladys and Matt, at Seldom Seen, Thornthwaite.

Eventually Raymond and I went to Braithwaite School.

I remember playing football for the school. Unfortunately, I did not have any football boots, but I remember my headmaster, Mr Caleb Barnes, allowed me to go up to the roof space of the school where I was delighted to witness an Aladdin's cave of sports equipment. There I found some football boots.

I was also very friendly with my next - door neighbour, Vic Gardner. Being the same age as me, he would take me fell running which started at his house, across the road, into the trees, and up to the top which led us towards the mountain Barf. I remember Barf was a very steep climb. Apparently, so steep they had horse riding events, which started at the bottom of Barf.

I believe there is a whitewashed crag where a bishop managed to get to. Unfortunately, he fell back down the hill and was killed.

I have happy memories of school, mainly because of the football team. I recall two sisters who used to go to the same school. One was called Freda. At that time, her parents managed the pub "The Royal Oak". Their name was Litt.

Whilst still at school, in the month of September, we would go blackberrying and sell our produce to friends in Keswick.

On leaving school, I had my first job with the Forestry Commission. I must have stayed there for about nine months before returning home to Newcastle.

Over the years since leaving Seldom Seen, I kept in touch with Vic Gardner who had a taxi business.

To end this little note, in the past, I have taken friends to Seldom Seen and they have all been amazed how beautiful a place I lived in.

I am now 80 years of age and I am looking forward to seeing Vic once more.

After a little thought, I remember the Green between the White Swan and the foot of the Barf was used for "Hoying the Wellie" competitions.

Sadly, Danny died in 2008. He is remembered with affection in Braithwaite and by his friend, Gerard Nuttney.

Mrs Telford taught us proper knitting – with four needles

HILDA SNOWBALL, NEWCASTLE-UPON-TYNE
St Theresa's R.C. School, Newcastle

I was a nine-year old pupil at St Theresa's School on Heaton Road, Newcastle. We were evacuated to Amble on the Northumberland coast on September 1st, 1939. After spending nearly a year there, enjoying half-day schooling, enjoying the sea and sand dunes and all the delights of rock pooling, we had to come home to Newcastle.

After the air raids became more frequent over Newcastle it was decided that those parents who wished could evacuate their children to Keswick.

I was eleven at the end of November 1940 and I enjoyed every day in Keswick. I lived in Porch Cottage on High Hill with Mr and Mrs Telford. I remember a real spinning wheel in the tiny room off my bedroom above the porch. The view from the bedroom window was of Skiddaw straight in front of me with the white mountain shelter hut visible halfway up. The River Greta was just a step across the road. A farmyard was at the back door and an orchard with fields down to the river where it flowed after passing under Greta Bridge.

The elderly couple I lived with were lovely. Mr Telford worked for the pencil works just across the road. He worked with the huge horses leading the felled trees down from Latrigg. On our walks he explained about felling timber and making the Cumberland pencils. He had a trail hound called 'Latrigg'. I was allowed to go with him on trail evenings and watched the man dragging the aniseed sack across the lower slopes of Skiddaw. I can still hear the shouting and whistling and tins of food rattling as the hounds returned to their masters.

Mrs Telford taught me 'proper' knitting. I made a blue cardigan for myself while she knitted dozens of socks for the forces. I was shown how to use four needles, how to 'turn' the heels and shape the toes on a pair of grey socks I made for my brother, a soldier.

What with lovely rabbit pies and warm gingerbread and blazing log fires I was well-fed and warm.

Hilda Snowball (right) with friend at the Boat Landings
Hilda and friend climbing Helvellyn (bottom left)
and on the summit

Hilda Snowball

The greatest joy again was half-day schooling, alternating every week. We split into groups after meeting our teachers at the Catholic Church on High Hill. Naturally, sometimes we played in the park but if the weather looked promising we climbed Latrigg and on many days walked around the Applethwaite roads. On longer holidays we climbed Skiddaw, walked along the Borrowdale road to Grange then back home the other side of Derwentwater via Portinscale. I don't remember anyone grumbling about being tired.

Some of us learned to row on Derwentwater. A boatman always had our favourite boat called 'Dorothy' ready for us. Mr Irvine, our teacher, taught me all I know about rowing, controlling the rudder and landing a boat gently. We did geography lessons and map-making by going to and from the islands and following the shoreline. We were taught how to watch the sky and any change in the wind.

One day a friend and I with Mr Irvine rowed to the end of the lake and up the River Derwent. Rain began to fall and we all helped to shelter under the boat. We ate our picnic as the swollen river swirled past us. That was when we had a very important lesson – how the rain collects on the hilltops and finds outlets to the waterfall (Lodore) and thence to the lake.

On holidays we had time to climb Great Gable, Helvellyn and Scafell. I remember going to Honister Pass and learning about screes and talking to the slate miners who told us where the slates went to. They made us 'knackers' for playing tunes. We saw an eagle gliding overhead. We waked across the frozen Derwentwater in 1941 to play on a small island. We watched the snow lying thicker and thicker on the mountain tops. We remembered all the names of the mountains around Derwentwater.

We shared Brigham School and thoroughly enjoyed passing the hotel where the Roedean girls were having their lunch. They wore gowns with bright embroidered panels down their backs. They sat at snow white covered tables with shining cutlery and sparkling glassware!

But all the good things had to come to an end. I sat the 11+ examination in Keswick. I passed and I knew I was on my way to Kendal where the Convent Grammar School from Fenham was evacuated. We returned from there after a year.

Mr Irvine was a keen photographer. I have a few printed memories of my happy days rowing and mountain climbing in school shoes and ordinary coats!

Always, when I have been asked about being evacuated some people are inclined to remark 'Oh, you poor child – all those years away from your family!' – I have my answers ready.

Those three years I have never forgotten, nor will I ever forget.

So, thank you Keswick for the best years of all.

Roedean girls threw notes from their bedroom windows
A KESWICK LAD - NORMAN TEASDALE, BRAITHWAITE
Brigham School, Keswick

I'm 76 years of age and attended Brigham School, so I was there during the time when the evacuees came to Keswick.

I first became aware of them when one day, passing the Pavilion, I saw a large group of people, adults and children, outside and inside the entrance to the Pavilion. They had just come from the railway station. I learned later that they had come from Newcastle.

At the time I lived in Wordsworth Street and the next thing I knew about the evacuees was when a young lad about my age came to live with us. His name was Peter Gray and was from South Shields. He called it 'Shields'. He went to Brigham School but he seemed to go at different times to me. At that time locals went to school in the mornings and others in the afternoon.

Peter was always singing '*Little Sir Echo*'. Before he came to Keswick he had been in the Gracie Fields Orphanage at Peacehaven in Sussex. His father was in the Green Howards serving in India. He died whilst in India and it was after this that Peter's mother came to collect him and presumably took him back to South Shields. That was the last we heard of him.

Another lad living in Wordsworth Street at the time was Dennis Quayle who was from Sunderland. He lived with Mr and Mrs Boyd at the top of Wordsworth Street. I seem to remember he once said he lived in Byron Street, Sunderland.

Another lad was George Crawford from Sunderland. He lived in

Greta Street with Mr and Mrs Cullen. He stayed on with them long after most other evacuees had left Keswick. It seems that George became an Army reservist and was called up at the outbreak of the Suez invasion in 1956. He was a parachutist.

In 1954 I was at the Police Training Centre at Warrington when I got talking to a policeman from Liverpool. He told me that when he was a lad he had been evacuated with his school to Hawes End, Keswick. He would most probably be one of the evacuees from the Liverpool Orphanage, who were at Hause End until 1952 when they returned to Liverpool.

When I was at Brigham School we used to go down to the 'Albion' in Keswick for school diners. On the way back we passed the Millfield Hotel which is where the younger girls from Roedean School at Brighton were living. They used to lean out of the windows above the front door and talk to us peasants (even then we thought they were 'posh'). They sometimes threw notes down to us as well.

It's hard to think that people I refer to were schoolboys at the time but if they are still around they will be in the 75 to 80 years of age group.

In 2009 Norman wrote: I was born in Bassenthwaite but moved into Keswick when I was a year old. My father worked at Weightman's Garage in Keswick, and I attended St John's Infant School and then Brigham School until I was fourteen, the leaving age in those days. Like my dad, I worked as a motor engineer.

National Service with the R.A.S.C. came and after that I left to work with the Keswick Motor Company. The great change in my life came in 1954 when I joined the Cumberland and Westmorland Constabulary, now the Cumbria Constabulary. I retired from the police in 1984 after thirty years' service.

I have a wife Valerie, son Kevin and daughter Karen, with a grand-daughter Laura. I now live not far from Keswick, in Braithwaite.

CENTRAL NEWCASTLE HIGH SCHOOL (CDST)

The Central Newcastle High School (Girls' Day School Trust) was opened in 1895 and moved to its present location in Jesmond, Newcastle-upon-Tyne in 1900.

The CNHS is an independent all-girls' school, with pupils aged three years to eighteen years in two separate buildings (Senior School and Junior School). At the time of writing (late 2009) there are some 940 girls on roll with a teaching staff of about 120.

The CNHS is one of twenty-nine schools in England and Wales who form part of the Girls' Day School Trust. The aim of the schools within the Trust is *'to provide affordable day school education for girls'*.

A Schools Enquiry Commission set up in 1864 concluded that there was a general deficiency in the provision of secondary education for girls. As a result of this the sisters Maria Grey and Emily Shirreff launched the *'National Union for Improvement of the Education of Women of all Classes'*. The Union was supported by major figures of the time, including Mary Gurney and HRH Princess Louise, daughter of Queen Victoria. The Princess later became President of the Union.

The Union aimed to provide *'good and cheap day schools for all classes of girls above the level of elementary* education'. Towards this end the 'Girls Public Day School Trust' was founded in 1872, and opened

Central Newcastle High School girls prepare for evacuation to Keswick, September 1939

its first school in 1873.

The school uniform of brown during *'The Keswick Years'* gave rise to the name in Keswick for the girls of *'The Brown Bombers'* - the nickname of a famous boxer of the time, Joe Louis, who was world heavyweight champion from 1937 to 1949.

The School's song is *'The Keel Row'* and the Latin motto *'Ante Deum Asto'* translates into English as *'I stand before God'*.

EVACUATION TO KESWICK

Adapted from 'A History of Gateshead High School and Central Newcastle High School' by Olive Carter, circa 1956 and other sources with acknowledgements and thanks.

The Headmistress of CNHS in 1939, Miss W A Odell, had realised that evacuation from Newcastle-upon-Tyne would be necessary if a state of hostilities was declared. It was thought unlikely that the CNHS would be included in the evacuation arrangements organised by the Local Education Authority, so Miss Odell began to organise an evacuation herself. But, the L.E.A. offered to include the School in its arrangements. Towards the end of August 1939 the schools were warned by the

Government that evacuation could occur any day. The code words for the evacuation were *"Operation Pied Piper"*.

Before the school left Newcastle it became known that it was to share the buildings of Keswick School under the headship of Mr W H Howe. At the time additions to the Keswick School buildings were under way, including the construction of an assembly hall with classrooms above which was to be known as the Rawnsley Hall. The arrival of the CNHS girls made it necessary for the new building works at Keswick to be continued.

Whilst the building operations were underway, arrangements were made to share the existing accommodation. Mr Howe agreed that the CNHS should use the school for the morning sessions and Keswick School children for the afternoon sessions – except on Saturdays, when the arrangement was reversed. Fortunately, the very good weather of the 1939 autumn enabled the CNHS girls to take walks and play games when not in the school buildings. It was noticeable how the Kindergarten children from Newcastle, unaccustomed to much walking or climbing, quickly became capable of increased distances and speeds. *'.... It was only necessary to take them to the bottom of Latrigg for them to disappear upwards at an astonishing pace, and it became something of a task to collect them together again'*.

Three-hundred and nineteen girls travelled to Keswick by train in early September 1939 – seventy two per cent of the roll in the previous term. Numbers dropped by a further 87 during the first year, as parents decided to have their children return home. The *'flat uneventfulness'* of the first eight months of the war, when no bombing occurred, did not make the transition from homes in Newcastle to 'billets' in Keswick any easier for parents to accept.

The most serious difficulty was finding sufficient and suitable homes for the children. Some girls spent the whole of their time in Keswick with one 'hostess', but there were invariably some miss-fits and new 'billets' to be found. Classroom space was another problem – there was never enough space at Keswick School and a great variety of other teaching spaces, scattered over the town, had to be sought. But by ingenuity, patience and good humour the difficulties were overcome.

The Headmistress herself and her secretarial staff had difficulty in arranging accommodation. The school office had four moves in the first year. Its final home was at the premises of an undertaker in Main Street!

Some 'hostesses' could not provide a mid-day meal. So, school meals had to be introduced for most of the girls. The after-school supervision of girls was undertaken by staff who undertook 'evening patrols' to check that girls were actually in their 'billets'. For the teachers this, in a strange town in the blackout, was difficult to say the least. By the end of the first year a regular pattern had emerged, but other staff duties were needed for girls who stayed in their 'billets' over the weekends (some girls travelled home by train at weekends and others had to stay in Keswick for part of the holidays).

On Sundays groups of girls were organised into Church parties – and a register was taken! For many girls church-going was obviously enjoyable. Some became actively involved in the church activities, some were confirmed and some joined the church choirs. One played a church organ.

'House meetings' became regular functions for the girls and staff. The main activity there appeared to be knitting for the forces. The generosity of the staff in giving up their own time in the evenings and holidays impressed the girls and engendered a much closer relationship. In addition, the mothers who had accompanied the girls to Keswick proved an invaluable source of help, as did many Keswick people, a few of whom had been pupils at the CNHS.

Miss Odell was aware that, as the summer holidays approached, Keswick landladies would wish to take holidaymakers into their homes, rather than CNHS girls. With some difficulty, she arranged to rent Barrow House on the eastern shore of Derwentwater. Barrow House was built in the 1790's by the famous 'King Pocky', a local eccentric and now owned by Lord Rochdale, who lived at Lingholm on the other side of Derwentwater. The house had its drawbacks, one of which was that electricity was generated by a stream-fed turbine. This gave a fluctuating electricity supply.

The house at that time had a private shore onto the lake, which was to prove invaluable for the outdoor activities fostered by the Teacher / Warden, Miss Walkinshaw. This teacher became very much a legend amongst the schoolgirls for the innovative way in which they were introduced to out-door activities, including Girl Guiding and the climbing of trees! Barrow House was converted into several dormitories and partly furnished by Lord Rochdale, the Newcastle-upon-Tyne Local Education Authority and the school itself. According to one girl, *'The only memory of the move-in that remains is the sight of a small horse and cart bringing along a load of children's luggage from Keswick, the whole surmounted by a teddy bear with a label round its neck!'*

The girls at Barrow House were organised into 'patrols', and were responsible for some washing-up and cleaning duties. They were also responsible for putting up the blackouts to the windows. It appears that on one occasion this duty was forgotten, resulting in a visit by an infuriated Air Raid Warden from the other side of the lake complaining of a light shining from Barrow House. In due course an appearance in Court took place and a £2 fine was levied.

Miss Odell left the CHNS shortly before the girls moved to Barrow House to take up an appointment in London, but her initiative in obtaining the use of Barrow House was of great advantage to the school during the following seven terms.

Many of the girls who stayed at Barrow House enjoyed the experience enormously – the boarding school stories of Angela Brazil come true. Story-telling after 'lights out', melting chocolate in tins by the living room fire, chopping wood, experimenting with small garden plots (radishes appeared to be the only real success!) and in the summer, bathing in the lake after homework and sometimes, *'to show off'*, before breakfast in the pool under the waterfall.

There were disadvantages. The girls who spent all their Sixth Form years in Keswick had limited use of the school library out-of-school hours. Jurisdiction over out-of-school activities was no longer under the supervision of parents and now undertaken by the teachers. According to one girl, this seemed to increase the possibilities of getting into trouble immeasurably. These included illegal visits to the cinema, the superseding of the R.G.S. (Newcastle Royal Grammar School) boys by the Keswick Schoolboys in masculinity appeal and the mass production of homework. But, she thought that it would have been worth expulsion for the memories of the forbidden moonlit skating on frozen Derwentwater.

Miss Leale became the Headmistress in September 1940. She wrote that she thought the best in the School was brought about by the difficulties of evacuation and that the children showed unselfishness and understanding of difficulties in their 'billets'. She welcomed the staff involvement in activities that they had never thought would be met in the evacuated school and that of parents who gave their help ungrudgingly. She valued the co-operation of the Headmaster of Keswick School who saw his school invaded by hordes of girls in brown uniforms - and who proved to be a constant and kindly ally.

The CNHS and Keswick School shared the same building but remained essentially distinct. But, there was a certain amount of academic co-operation, a joint choir was formed and Keswick School boys invited CNHS girls to Saturday evening dances.

As far as numbers of girls in school were concerned, during the second year these remained steady, but after that they began to drop again. Recruiting from the Newcastle district declined and the reduction in bombing encouraged parents to have their girls return home. Some parents in Newcastle asked for a 'nursery class' to cater for the younger returnees and new entrants until the return of the School proper to Newcastle. This problem was solved when an offer was made to sell the premises of St. Margaret's School in Gosforth to the CNHS.

The Trust agreed to buy the school and the school building was opened as the Gosforth branch in April 1942.

For the next two terms the school worked in two sections, one in Keswick and one in Gosforth. Eventually, there were very few junior children left in Keswick. By the end of 1942 preparations were made for the return of the remainder of the girls to Newcastle.

The doctor extolled the virtues of Kendal mint cake.

STELLA ALDER, NEWCASTLE-UPON-TYNE
CNHS

I was evacuated with other girls from the Central Newcastle High School (nicknamed 'the Brown Bombers' because of their uniform colour!)

I was 'billeted' with a succession of others in a house on the Headlands, and looking back at the number of people who shared that house I cannot believe how we all fitted in!

We had swimming lessons in the lake and tried ice skating in the winter and sledged down the miniature golf course. We enjoyed milk shakes at the Dairy on the Main Street and queued for cough sweets called 'Hacks' as they were available without coupons at a small shop somewhere near the Post Office.

There was a doctor who extolled the virtues of Kendal Mint Cake and I believe he had been on an early expedition to Everest.

I didn't consider this as a happy time in my life – I felt we were shut in by the mountains – and said I would never go back. Needless to say that sentiment didn't last long and with my husband and children on more than one occasion have appreciated the real beauty of the area.

Stella wrote in 2009: After gaining a B.A. in Social Studies at Durham University I worked for a time with various charitable organisations and the Citizens' Advice Bureau with the then Newcastle Council of Social Services prior to my marriage. I have two children. My son, a Cambridge graduate, lives and works in the south whilst my daughter is a primary school teacher in Newcastle.

My husband was a Technical College lecturer but died before retirement and I have been a widow for twenty-four years. Before my retirement I was employed as a research assistant by Oxford University. Not a very exciting life compared with some!

Mr Adamson was a huge man.
He let us wear his ARP helmet
JOAN CRESSWELL, NEWCASTLE-UPON-TYNE
CNHS

It was on 1 September 1939 that we were told we were to be *evacuated*. I remember wondering what *'evacuated'* meant, and also for the *"duration'* – a new word.

I was five years old and I think the youngest girl from Newcastle Central High School. We first had to meet at the Junior School (I suppose the seniors went to the Senior School). We were fitted and given gas masks, which we thought were very funny and we went round grunting

Above: Joan Cresswell, sister Honor and Miss Odell

81

Joan and her new bicycle

like pigs. We had to keep them in square cardboard boxes with string straps to go over our shoulders. I was lucky as my sister Honor (aged 8) and my mother came too, so I wasn't alone.

I suppose we went to the station but I can't remember that but I do recollect the train which I think the whole school took over. It didn't have a corridor and I was worried in case I had an accident in front of the 'big girls' - after all I was only five.

When we got to Keswick (I don't remember the journey) all the girls had to go to the Pavilion cinema and we sat in the audience seats. The 'hostesses' sat at the back of the platform (the cinema screen must have been removed) and a man read out the name of a hostess who came forward and then I think probably one of the school staff read out the name of as many girls as there were places in the hostess home. When our turn came my sister was called first and then my mother and me and another girl called Betty Emerson, and we joined our hostess. No one could have been as fortunate as we were as we were billeted with Mr. and Mrs. Adamson. They were a wonderful couple. Mr. Adamson had the butcher's shop on the corner of Station Street and St. John's Street (subsequently absorbed by Dixon's stationers).

It was dark when we left the Pavilion and it seemed a long way to St. John's Street (24 I think), although I realise now that it wasn't far at all, but Mrs. Adamson took my hand and helped me along. The house was a big three-storey building and we slept in the attic, my mother, my sister and I in one room and Betty in another. However Betty was homesick and she changed places with my mother after a night or two.

Very soon we were joined by Elizabeth and Richard Havery who had been bombed out in London. The Adamson's son George and daughter Mary joined us at weekends and then their other son Joe's wife Pru (he was away in the army) came from London with her year-old son Nicky. So there were six adults and six children, quite a houseful so we all had to help. My job was to set the table in the kitchen for meals and I remember it was so big I used to crawl across it.

Friday night was bath-night and as I was the youngest (apart from Nicky) I went first and had the clean water. The bath was magnificent with a very wide mahogany edge which I found quite difficult to negotiate! The plumbing was amazing with brass taps and jets all over the place – I was VERY impressed.

On Sundays we went into the parlour after dinner and could play quietly while Mrs. Adamson read to us from a 'good' book. She read very softly as was her wont, she was a calm, good person with a serene expression and we always behaved for her as I think we realised what a wonderful person she was.

Mr. Adamson was a huge man with a big voice and a grip like a vice. He was great fun and let us wear his ARP hat if we were good. I remember one afternoon he was left in charge of us as Mrs. Adamson, who was a devout churchwoman, and my mother had gone to St. John's Church and he initiated us in sliding down the banisters. He had grown up in the house so he knew the joys. You could begin at attic level and come right down to the hall as there were no newel posts at any level. At the bottom there was no post but the banisters ended in a swirl. Mr. Adamson showed us how to put a pile of cushions on the hall floor to land on and if you were going fast enough you could slide along the brown lino to the front door! Heady stuff for a five year old! (What would 'Health and Safety' say about it now?) All too soon Mrs. Adamson returned and her look of horror and her expostulation of "FATHER!" left us in no doubt as to the error of our ways (especially as the cushions were the best ones from the parlour). I remember feeling so sorry for Mr. Adamson as he looked so contrite and he had given us a marvellous time.

There was a large garage with a loft at the bottom of the yard and it was there that the hens had their necks wrung and they were plucked. I didn't like this or when the hens flopped and twitched afterwards.

Next door to the yard was the bakery for the Co-op. Deliveries were made by wagons pulled by shire horses. They had to back down the side alley between the Adamson's and the bakery with the wagons being pushed backwards by them. The noise of the horses' feet was very audible in the house and I used to worry that the horses would slip and fall. Once they were in the Co-op yard we could go and stroke them – they were huge!

At first we juniors shared Keswick School classrooms with their children but I think that must have been difficult for the staff as we soon had school on the second floor of the Conservative Club in Borrowdale Road. We were there for a year or two and it seemed to work very well and we could go into the yard at playtime. The only thing that was sacrosanct was the billiard table and we knew we must never touch it or run round it! The senior school remained in Keswick School but I wasn't involved in that although my sister must have been.

For games and exercise we used to go into Cockshot Wood where one of our very enlightened teachers, Miss Walkinshaw, taught us how to climb trees and to swim in the lake. She was exceptional and organised hikes, climbs and taught us the names of flowers and birds. During the severe winter of 1940/41 when Derwentwater froze for six months and they drove cars on to it, Miss Walkinshaw organized us to borrow tin trays and we sledged down the hill on the far side of the lake and we had to see how far out over the lake we could go. Many bruises but great fun – 'Health and Safety' would have hated half the things we did! She also took us up Skiddaw when we were about seven years old.

In a year or two the CNHS rented Barrow House which became a boarding house for quite a number of girls as a number of the billets weren't satisfactory. Later for a term or two the junior school stopped going to the Conservative Club and we had lessons at Barrow House which we loved. There must have been about twenty children – boys and girls – in the junior school and several children from abroad and from London. Lucy Brach was Austrian/Jewish and her mother taught German at the senior school. We never heard anything about her father. We also had Noosia Mogadam (spelling?) who was the Persian Ambassador in London's daughter. She was very naughty and great fun and lived with her mother at the Royal Oak Hotel. In the afternoons she used to be sleepy and giggly and my mother told me years later that she used to have at least two glasses of wine at lunchtime and her mother could not understand why she shouldn't!

84

Going back in time. After about six months my father (in Newcastle) developed TB and had to go to a sanatorium near Aberdeen and we didn't see him for two years. My mother then moved from the Adamson's to a rented house which she shared with the headmistress of CNHS, Miss Odell. This was No. 3 Limepots Road – opposite the Roman Catholic Church. My sister and I hated it as she was formidable and couldn't relate to young children. I think I was naughty and disobedient as I was sent to eat with the maid in the kitchen when my mother was away visiting my father. I liked this but it was very hard on my sister.

Fairly soon Miss Odell moved to another school so we had the house to ourselves and were very happy and I made lots of friends with the children round about and we used to go and play in Fitz Park, going in "the back way". One time I got up early and rode right round the lake on my tricycle! I remember the bridges at Grange and the hairpin bend at Swinside being very exciting going down with my feet up off the pedals. I got into big trouble over that and my trike was taken away for a week.

My mother busied herself with helping with evacuees when they arrived from the south. I remember her telling us that she had to take children in her car (a Morris 8) and go round to addresses she was given and the owners would come out and look at the children and select the one they thought was the least bad. She said it was awful and once no one would have one little boy as he had a squint, wore specs, was dirty and had wet himself (he got a good billet in the end). She also helped with school milk at break-time. She had her piano brought over from Newcastle and the music teacher Dr. Hutchinson used to come to our house once a fortnight to give the girls piano lessons. My mother had to make sure he got away in time to catch the Carlisle bus as he was giving a singing lesson to someone who he told my mother would be famous one day – that was Kathleen Ferrier.

Sometimes when my mother went to see my father we went to stay at North Bridge House, opposite Keswick School. I hated this and was very unhappy about it so my mother used to get Mary Elliott (who helped her in the house) and her husband George to come and stay, which was a good arrangement.

Eventually CNHS returned to Newcastle, I think around 1943/44. My mother wasn't happy about this so we went to Keswick School for a few terms. I was very happy there under the tuition of Miss Gilchrist. I really felt that I belonged.

When my father came out of the sanatorium and came home to Newcastle, we had to return too. It was very sad and I can remember crying in the train to Penrith. I returned to CNHS but all my old friends had gone and I was like a new girl and never really settled. I was frightened of my father who was a kind and gentle man and would have been devastated if he had known my feelings and it took years before I could relate to him, but that is another story.

We kept in touch with the Adamsons until they died. They moved up to Castlerigg Cottage above Manor Brow and we used to visit them there. We used to go and stay at Barrow House when it became a hotel owned by Mrs. Lambert and her brother who was a well-known local climber called Bob (I can't remember his surname). We had climbed all the mountains near Keswick during our visits.

When my father retired (he was a Chartered Accountant) they bought a house in Millbeck – Rowling End, near Applethwaite. Unfortunately my father died before they actually moved but my mother went on her own and for eight years became very involved in Keswick life and we visited her frequently, especially my elder son, Nicholas who was at school at Seascale.

Now we tend to frequent the South Lakes as my younger son Guy has a house at Levens. However, whenever we are there I like to go to Keswick as it is still home to me.

Joan wrote in 2009: After I returned to Newcastle I went to the Junior School in Gosforth. When I was eleven I passed to the Senior School and remained there for two years until I was sent to boarding school, St. Leonard's in St. Andrews and spent probably my most unhappy years. I finally left to study physiotherapy in Newcastle although I wanted to be a vet (not suitable for girls!)

I married David Paton, a Civil Engineer, soon afterwards and never practised physio. I had two sons and a daughter and domestic life occupied me. My marriage ended and I worked as a general administrator for a charity for ten years. In the meantime I married Bryan Cresswell, a civil servant and a classical musician.

Music played a big part in my life and I was in several choirs, performing in the north and very occasionally on radio. I also had a life-long interest in dogs and bred Norwich Terriers and then Labradors in a small way. I competed in obedience shows and working trials and for many years was a trainer in several obedience clubs. Increasing age and arthritis eventually curtailed this but now I interest myself in family history research and I still have two Labradors and sing in Newcastle Bach Choir.

When the school returned to Newcastle Miss Odell left, to be replaced by Miss Leale, and went, I think, to Putney High School. Miss Walkinshaw also did not return to Newcastle. I missed her very much. I don't know where she went but I did hear about twenty years ago that she spent the spring / summer at Bridge of Garten in Scotland working at the Osprey Watch as cook to the watchers. I can just imagine her there – it would be right up her street! I did hear that she later suffered from Alzheimer's but I don't know how true that is – I hope not.

My main worry was – would I be chosen? Would I be left?

MARY DRISCOLL, CROOK, CO. DURHAM
CNHS

I was just twelve years old when I was evacuated. We hadn't experienced any bombing where I lived, since I was evacuated on Friday 1st September 1939.

It was my parents' decision to send me with the Central Newcastle High School for Girls to Keswick. I had often stayed with relatives, so I was used to being away from home. We stayed in Keswick for three and a half years, returning home at Christmas 1942. I remember travelling by train to Keswick – more especially as my parents and younger brother were being evacuated to Carlisle. My father taught at Rutherford College so for a few days there was no point of contact.

My main worry about going to Keswick was concerned with the 'choosing by hosts'. Would we have to line up and would I be left? I had never been to Keswick before.

I was chosen, but actually stayed at a neighbour's house since my 'host family' had visitors. I remember panicking during the night because I could hear a baby crying.

During the first year I was in two separate 'billets' with kind families who looked after me very well. After that I moved, with about fifty others, to Barrow House, which now, I believe, is a Youth Hostel, about two miles along the shores of Lake Derwentwater, just below Ashness Bridge.

From Barrow House we were conveyed daily into Keswick for schooling. We shared premises with Keswick School and also had the use of various halls – the Parish Room being one. Even at this distance in time I remember many of the teachers and their subjects. At lunchtime a 'crocodile' meandered through the streets to the Masonic Hall in St John's Street for lunch. The most wonderful bread pudding I have ever tasted springs to mind! After lunch we returned to School via Fitz Park.

Keswick was a very small town compared to the City of Newcastle. The only friends I remember were the children of neighbours before

Mary Driscoll and friends at a Barrow House reunion

I went to Barrow House. I do remember we played a game called 'racing demon' at Barrow House. Our teachers took us for walks around Keswick. Latrigg was an evening walk from my first 'billet'. We often visited the lake, more especially from Barrow House.

One of the main delights I experienced was the arrival, by train, of my bike. This enlarged my horizons considerably. I did, on occasion, ride to stay with my parents outside Carlisle – a journey of more that thirty miles each way. Sometimes, with a friend whose father taught with my father, I travelled to Penrith to meet up with my father.

One local 'character' I remember was an old man who lived in a caravan who used to give out 'perpetual calendars', slightly larger than a half-crown.

I caught chicken pox whilst at Barrow House. One of the teachers, Miss Walkinshaw, took me to Brampton near Carlisle on the way to Newcastle and my father picked me up there. It was Christmas.

Eventually our home was in Carlisle but we did occasionally stay with an auntie in Newcastle.

I kept in close touch with the lady at my second 'billet' until she died in November 1966.

I remember visiting the Alhambra Cinema on St John's Street and the Pavilion of the Lakes on Station Road.

A Guide Company was started up at Barrow House, run by Miss Walkinshaw. I remember camping along the Applethwaite Road at, I think, Millbeck. I, along with other Guides, made my only ascent of Skiddaw 'up the back way'. I regarded my days at Keswick as an evacuee very worthwhile – but I may have got better examination results under my father's eye!

I have often spoken to my children and grandchildren about my wartime experiences and I have helped my granddaughter with her school project for which I wrote a long account of my days as an evacuee. Probably the best thing I experienced at Keswick was the companionship of my school friends.

My days in Keswick bring back many happy memories but I don't think I realised how lucky we were to live in such wonderful countryside until I was older. I still have friends from schooldays and about twenty-five years ago a group of us, about ten people, got together and began meeting for regular gatherings – even having a return visit to Barrow House, where we were provided with lunch - celebrating the words of the song sung at every end-of-term assembly – 'Forty Years On'. Sadly, our meetings, through age, distance and depleted numbers aren't as frequent, but we still keep in contact.

I have spent several holidays in Keswick since those days and always spend a lot of time 'remembering when .... '.

Mary wrote in 2009: In 1944 I was again 'evacuated' – to Berwick-on-Tweed to study domestic science and subsequently taught for six years in Newcastle, marrying after four. We moved to Co. Durham, living first at Wilton-le-Wear, then Crook and had two daughters who now live in Oxford and Colwyn Bay.

In 1966 I returned to part-time teaching of general subjects and remedial work.

My husband died in 1978.

I attend church and my interests include W.I., Meals-on-Wheels, Friends of Guiding, needlework of all kinds and gardening. I have a grand-daughter and a grand-son who are a source of great pleasure.

I have happy memories of my evacuation in Keswick

MARGARET FAIRCLOUGH, WENDOVER
CNHS

I was evacuated with the Central Newcastle High School for Girls in September 1939. At that time I was living in a neutral area north of Newcastle and for a week or so there were great debates by my parents as to whether I should go to Keswick with the other High School girls or transfer to a school near home. I was not wanting to leave my friends to start in a new environment.

It was finally decided that I should go to Keswick. I went about a week after the rest of the School had gone.

It was a move I never regretted as it gave me a love of Lakeland which has lasted until the present day.

I was billeted in a house on Manor Brow with Mr and Mrs Pollock and their daughter Marjorie. The house had the most beautiful view right down the lake and the surrounding fells.

Mr Pollock was a retired chemist, Cumbrian born but came to Keswick from Scarborough. He worked part-time in a chemist's in Keswick. Mrs Pollock came from an old Keswick family, the Lowthers, so she knew the town in and out. The family were Quakers and their beliefs teach them anti-warfare. But, over the war years they certainly did their bit in taking quite a number of evacuees into their home. It certainly was a home from home and I kept in touch with Marjorie until about three years ago.

School was shared with Keswick School; we were at School in the morning and Keswick School in the afternoon. It cannot have been easy for the teaching staffs but our lessons didn't seem to suffer. The new hall at Keswick School was in the process of being built. I was reminded of this the other day when I saw a programme of 'Bargain Hunt' filmed in Keswick School's Hall! Another memory I have of the Hall is a performance of '*The Messiah*' that was performed when the Hall was in use.

Mr Pollock was a keen hill walker and over the time I lived there we were taken on walks that covered the whole area; Watendlath, Buttermere, Grasmere, nearly all the fells. It was a total change from the coast and moorlands of Northumberland! Living in Buckinghamshire now I often wish for the open spaces and views. Especially the sea during the past few weeks!

We shopped in Keswick, played tennis in the park and sat in the cheap seats of the two cinemas.

While I was in Keswick we had a very severe winter. The lake was frozen for weeks, and the Pollocks fitted us up with skates and we ventured out, far out from the shore. I often think that we didn't realise what the depth of the lake was under the ice.

We attended church and I was confirmed whilst in Keswick.

In all, despite the reason for being in Keswick and the home-sickness, I have the happiest memories of my time there. It gave me a love of the countryside which has, I am sure, been to my advantage for the rest of my life.

I was so miserable, I was physically sick
MARGARET FURNESS, RIDING MILL
CNHS

I was eleven years old when war broke out, and living with my father, mother, an older brother and a much younger brother. Also within walking distance lived my grandfather, three sets of aunts and uncles and sundry cousins. We were a close-knit extended family living in Newcastle-upon-Tyne.

I went to the Central Newcastle High School and my brother went to the Royal Grammar School.

Arrangements had been made since Munich that the Central High would go to Keswick if war should be declared. We all knew about this but I think we had romantic notions of a boarding-school type of existence – shades of Angela Brazil! The reality was very different.

I did not go with the School that first week. My parents could not decide whether to send me to boarding school or join my School and friends. After much debate I went to Keswick.

So my parents took me by car to my allotted 'billet', 1 Springs Road, and yes, it was the first time I had been away from home with strangers. So there I was, left on my own in a strange house with this person. She was a maiden lady, unused to children and really didn't want to know; of indeterminate age - probably 55-ish who had tried always to avoid having an evacuee, but with three bedrooms she had no excuse. But, I was deeply resented.

I remember the first week I was so miserable that I was physically sick, but after that I must have accepted the inevitable and settled down.

Mum and Dad came through to Keswick about once a fortnight during that first term. They would pick my brother up from Penrith and then stay over one or maybe two nights at Fletcher's Hotel, opposite St John's Church. Obviously during the winter the weather made the journey impracticable and petrol rationing became tighter, but they came if and when they could. We corresponded every week.

We shared Keswick School premises but otherwise we remained

completely separate. One year they had the use of the classrooms in the mornings and we had the afternoons. The following year we had the mornings so in effect we had half-day schooling for three and a half years – and I still managed to pass a Durham School Certificate at the end of it.

The Mistresses were fantastic and would keep us occupied during the other part of the day with games of hockey, tennis, rounders and nature rambles in summer. I can still name all the wild flowers in the district.

We had knitting sessions in the Crosthwaite Parish Room in winter and it was freezing. I was allowed to knit for the R.A.F. because even then I was a good knitter. The R.A.F. wool was lovely and soft and pleasing to handle. The Army wool was harsh and the Navy wool thick and oily!

Of course I walked to School, winter – knee deep in snow - and summer. We had to be there for 9am regardless of whether we had the classrooms. We had Assembly in the gymnasium and then we would be told the arrangements for the day. We had our lunch in St John's Parish Hall then back to School and back to our billets.

The winters were spectacular with snow on the hills and drifts of ten - twenty feet deep and the lake froze over completely each year we were there. In 1942 it was frozen solid for six weeks. Skating was possible from Borrowdale to Portinscale so we revelled in it. The sledging was great too.

I spent as much time as possible out of the house. Of course I was not allowed a key but little did she know I could get in through the kitchen window if she was out!

We would walk around the lake at weekends. We climbed Castlehead, Walla Crag, Catbells, Swinside and Latrigg. I never went up Skiddaw but many did.

In the summer we would sit for hours on the bank of the Greta with a trimmed branch, length of string, bent pin and a worm, hopefully fishing. We never caught anything obviously, but we talked, watched the wildlife go by and enjoyed it.

Once we had bicycles we went further afield to Cockermouth, Grasmere, Borrowdale and Seatoller. There was no traffic and we would ride four abreast, singing at the top of our voices.

We used to go swimming in the summer. There was a bathing pool at the head of the lake with diving boards and changing rooms. I can picture the diving boards and the steps. I can't visualise the changing rooms. I just assumed that there must have been changing rooms, which one should never do! I know we put our costumes on underneath our dresses but have no recollection of how we got dry afterwards. I don't know if it still there but I suppose it was where the caravan park is now.

One day a friend and I swam over to Derwent Island and back. That was grand. That was the longest swim I did, we usually stayed around the bathing area.

We did have a tragedy. Two of the mistresses were out in a boat which somehow or other they must have capsized for one hit her head on a stone and died in hospital a week later. She was greatly missed.

We spent a lot of time in Fitz Park, walking, talking and playing tennis. There used to be a very good fish and chip shop along from the Post Office in Bank Street. We didn't have fish but bought three pennorth of chips, in newspaper of course, which were eaten out of sight of any mistresses – no eating in the street! They were delicious. Milk shakes were another favourite but we couldn't indulge too often. They were expensive – about one shilling and six pence. Sweets, of course, were rationed by weight, so we had to decide whether to have smaller unwrapped or slightly larger wrapped sweets. The unwrapped always won even though you often ended up with a sticky mess in a paper bag!

Yes, we did do jobs. I remember three of us went on our bikes to Whinlatter Pass and spent the whole of the afternoon in the hot sun picking bilberries for my hostess. I brought them back proudly, it having been hot, tedious, backbreaking, fly-biting work. All she said was, "Is that all you've got?" About one and a half pounds. Never again! Every time I went near a wood I was supposed to bring wood back for the fire.

We also collected everything possible for the School. Acorns, to feed the pigs; rose hips, for the syrup. I tried eating one. Quite disgusting, it was hairy and full of pips! Brambles, for jam or jelly at my billet; sheep's wool from the hedgerows for blankets, sphagnum moss for the hospital and conkers for our own amusement.

I never did housework – she was too house-proud to let me loose on dusting or hoovering so that was fine by me! Nor was I allowed to help with baking or cooking – food was rationed and too precious to waste.

I got into trouble regularly at my billet, so regularly that, although at first I used to argue and state my case, I soon gave that up and just switched off. It was always at teatime so I would first carry on eating my tea until she ran out of breath and then ask very politely for more bread - or whatever. It seemed to work because after a while she gave up!

We were never paid for any jobs done. We would do something because we were asked or because it was expected. Money never entered into it. Not then.

I got pocket money, I think about two shillings per week. There were increments of sixpence per year and it had to last. We used to go to the Alhambra Cinema on wet Saturday afternoons – six old pence downstairs and nine pence upstairs if feeling very flush. We did go to the Pavilion – I remember seeing Walt Disney's *'Fantasia'* there, but not often. I think perhaps it was more expensive.

The School had its own Guide Company of which I was a member and worked for a number of badges. The School took over Barrow House in, I think, the late 1940's and I pleaded with my parents to be allowed to go there, but they said, "No". But we used to hold the Guide meetings on the lakeshore across the road from Barrow House with a campfire, songs and cooking. I remember being entered for the cookery badge and asked to make drop scones and serve tea for two people. I had never made a drop scone in my life but found out before what was the general idea. The result was predictably awful, more suited to mending shoes! But the tea was good and nicely served so I got my badge.

We were able to go home for half-term - half day Friday, back Monday – and our holidays. Although, if I remember rightly, the 1940 May half-term coincided with the German invasion of the Low Countries. We got as far as Carlisle by train (Keswick had a bustling station in those days) but were turned back. It was deemed unsafe for us to go further.

I remember going into Fitz Park on our return from Carlisle and borrowing a friend's bicycle and practising until I could stay on!

In the summer of 1940 Keswick held a fete in aid of the Royal Air Force, which was opened by Hugh Walpole. He, of course, lived on the other side of the lake at Manesty. We must have been in uniform because he came over and had a word with us. Sadly, he died shortly after that event.

96

Crosthwaite Parish Room

It would be about ten years later when I was working in Carlisle when I went back to Keswick to spend the day with my hostess. I was glad that I did for we spent a very pleasant day together but then the circumstances were totally different.

The best thing about Keswick was the road home. It was an unhappy time, cut off from the family, shut in by the hills, knowing we were resented. But I learned self-confidence and independence. No use grumbling - don't you know there's a war on? – just get on with whatever it might be.

We returned home in time for Christmas 1942 and back to School in Newcastle in January 1943.

In 2009 Margaret wrote: After training at Newcastle General Hospital (Gold Medallist for the year!) I worked in nursing at Newcastle and Carlisle. Whilst in Carlisle I visited my wartime "hostess" in Keswick for the one and only time. After qualifying in midwifery I returned to Newcastle. In 1955 I became a theatre sister and stayed in theatres until my retirement.

My personal interests are in local history, music, literature – and cruising, the only way to travel!

A hockey stick, a tennis racquet, oh yes – and brown knickers!
PAT LOWTHER, SEATON, DEVON
CNHS

It was 61 years ago that I sat my eleven-plus exam. Oddly enough, it was over forty years later that I found I had actually passed. I always thought that my father had to pay for me to go to High School although I don't suppose it was free, and I never thought to ask. I suppose that within our rather fractured family, each one thought someone else had told me, and with the upheaval of the war years I expect that, manlike, my father just forgot.

In any event, Auntie Ethel, his sister, took me to Keswick to which the school was evacuated, to have my interview. I don't remember much of it, but the next event was the buying of my school uniform at Raymond Barnes, the school outfitters. The uniform consisted of a brown gym tunic with a cream coloured square necked blouse, brown blazer with school badge; brown knee socks and shoes completing the winter outfit. In summer we wore brown and cream checked cotton dresses and panama hats. Winter hats were felt ones with the school band above the brim. To this day I can't abide wearing a hat, and yet oddly, I still like the colour brown. Added to this was a hockey stick, a tennis racquet and a swimsuit. Oh yes....and brown knickers. Suitably equipped I was packed off to Keswick.

The school was called the Central Newcastle High School, or C.N.H.S. for short and we were made aware that it was part of The Girls Public Day School Trust, whatever that meant. I never did find out, which just goes to show that grand titles are rarely self-explanatory. At Keswick, we shared premises with the Keswick High School and were known locally and quite naturally as the 'Brown Bombers' (Joe Louis fans will appreciate the reference). Next door to the school was the pencil factory with its pervading smell of cedar.

I don't remember first arriving there or what my mode of transport was, but the first house at which I stayed was situated up the hill away from the lakeside and was owned by Mrs. Pettitt, an elderly widow, and her middle aged daughter Miss Pettitt. Miss Pettitt also owned and ran a large and well - stocked gift shop in the town. I really can't imagine why they thought it would be a good idea to take in an evacuee, as you couldn't have found two women less well equipped to care for an eleven year old girl. While I was there they also bought a spaniel puppy, an appealing little dog. The poor thing disgraced itself on the hall carpet and had its nose rubbed in the resultant mess which no doubt turned it into a nervous wreck. Once, feeling hungry, I helped myself to a couple of biscuits in the pantry and was duly scolded when I was found out. It made me wonder what they might want to rub my nose in.

I hadn't immediately made any friends at school, so at weekends I would roam the woods as I had been used to doing in Morpeth. Thus I came across one of the most delightful experiences of my childhood. Beyond the row of houses where I lived there was a lane and then rough meadows, which led up to a wood, set against a sloping hill. I spent a lot of time in this wood with its autumn smells; at school we were making miniature gardens with a piece of mirror in the centre to simulate a pond, and mosses and toadstools around about. In my search for the most colourful toadstools, I roamed higher and higher up the hill, until one day I came to a jumble of rocks at the top. Working my way around them I clambered on to a sheltered ledge where, spread out before me, was the whole of Derwentwater, with its islands, its beaches and woods sweeping down to the water's edge. It was south facing, and often I climbed up there to enjoy the peaceful scene.

I sometimes wonder how many other people have discovered that spot in the intervening years. I expect the meadow is full of housing now, and if it has been found, perhaps it is featured on the tourist trail complete with tearoom, gift shop and eager Japanese tourists with the latest technology in camcorders. And if so, why not, for why should I deny anyone else the everlasting pleasure of that memory, (and here of course, Wordsworth springs to mind) which is the bliss of solitude.

I didn't stay long at the Pettitts. I doubt if there was much sorrow at our parting on either side, we were not suited to one another. I do remember my arrival at the railway station at the beginning of the next term - we had been home for Christmas - and once more I found myself staggering down the road from the station, this time with a large suitcase. A very kind gentleman offered to carry it for me and so I arrived at Mrs.Thwaite's. She lived in a council house on an estate which lay on a rise between the town and the Lake. It was a small semi-detached house but it held an alarming number of people. Apart from myself, there was also Stella and Jean who were in my form at school and Joan who was a couple of years older than us. We had the sole use of the front room for our meals and doing our homework, except occasionally during the better weather when the odd visitor was taken in for bed and breakfast. Fortunately for us, visitors were few and far between during the war years, but I remember one famous occasion when six girls shared a double bed lying head to tail like sardines. There was a Mr.Thwaites, a slip of a man, and the two daughters of the house. Outside in the garden was a variety of sheds, which probably catered for the rest of the inhabitants, but this was out of bounds to us. There was a sister and her rather feeble - minded son Freddie who drooled and didn't say very much; there was Frankie, her nephew who had been evacuated to her from Birkenhead and of course her two daughters, Elsie and Audrey. If I had felt lonely before, this was now an overabundance of company, but I have to say that as an only child I revelled in it.

When I was six or seven years old I used to pray at night that God would give me a baby brother or sister and I would lie right on the edge of my little blue bed to show God that there would be plenty of room for another one, not realising that with my mother gone, this was not going to happen and it was a great disappointment to me and strained my faith in God. Now it was like all my Christmases come at once and I revelled in this swarming mass of people crammed into the little house. Sixty years on I have lost touch with all the others apart from Stella with whom I keep up an intermittent correspondence. As she says, at our age it is largely a question of an exchange of symptoms.

Stella was and is very clever with beautifully formed hand - writing. She was the only daughter and the middle child of her parents with an elder brother Donald and a younger called Stanley. Jean was the eldest daughter of a Methodist minister and had two younger sisters. Joan, being older, did not figure so highly in our lives and I knew nothing of her family.

Our school was not the only one to be based in Keswick, Roedean School for Girls had taken over a very large and plush hotel on the edge of town and were occasionally to be seen walking in strictly regulated crocodiles around the town.

School was enjoyable, our French teacher was called Miss Sorrel and we were initiated into that language with the memorable phrases of 'la plume de ma tante' and 'ouvre la porte' or alternatively 'la fenestre'. I never really got to grips with the masculine and feminine gender of words, much less the grammar with its past imperfect, but on my first visit to France some forty years later I found I had retained enough phrases and vocabulary to be of use. Miss Sorrel, who later unaccountably exchanged her name to Mrs Sidebottom, must have done a good job.

Our geography teacher was called Miss Horne and her grandfather had been the master of a sailing ship who used to regale her with stories of sailing around The Horn of South America. She also introduced us to the world of the National Geographic magazine which brought the things she taught us blazingly to life. It was one of my favourite subjects and gave me a lifelong interest in the rest of the world and the placing of various countries within it. Miss Horne also filled in as needlework teacher and in those days of rationing, whatever we made had to be of some use. Consequently we were set to making a pair of summer knickers in brown and white checked cotton. There were two sewing machines, hand operated, but one could not gravitate to them until one's hand sewing had passed muster. Alas, I never reached those pinnacles, my hand sewing was terrible and on one never-to-be-forgotten occasion, Miss Horne looked at my work in disgust and tore the whole seam from end to end. Having sweated blood and tears over that work, I had no wish to have it repeated, so when it came to stitching the hems, I enlisted the help of Audrey who was able to place endless neat little stitches exactly where she wanted them to go. When I produced this wonderful piece of work, Miss Horne must have been well aware that it did not spring from my own efforts, but perhaps she took pity on me, because after a very long look, she made no comment.

Our English teacher was Miss Forrest and English lessons were a joy. I had learnt to read and write at a very early age-before I started school, actually, and our early classes had always included spelling and vocabulary on a regular basis. Thus I was well - grounded, and, always an avid reader, I enjoyed the literature we studied. I think at that time we did not go on to the science subjects in the upper third class. It may have been that the facilities being shared with Keswick High school were not sufficient for us all. I don't really know, but I expect that allowances had to be made.

Our teachers were all referred to as 'mistresses' of course, and our Headmistress was Miss Leale, a quiet lady with an underlying strength of character who never raised her voice.

That winter we had very heavy snow falls and we went sledging on the small golf course between the town and the lake. There was also a small kiosk just inside the park gates where there was a roulette wheel on the wall. It would take pennies and the balls were released and then sent off with the aid of a pull back spring. If you were lucky, they might drop into the right hole and you would get your penny back, but after losing a large proportion of my pocket money, I decided that although it was quite a thrilling pastime, I had no wish to lose my money, and so I never became an inveterate gambler. Another slot machine was on the high street, and for a few coppers you could get a small packet of Woodbine cigarettes and some matches. We would take these into the outside toilets and puff away in an amateurish fashion, feeling very grown-up and daring.

School lunches had to be taken at another venue further up the High Street where we had to wait in a room without any windows until the meal was ready. We would douse the lights and play 'murders' where after a terrible shriek the lights would be put back on and we had to guess who had 'done for' the body on the floor. The meals were generally of a poor standard, the so-called meat being mainly bones and gravy with very little in it of substance, but had we ever complained, which we didn't, I dare say we would have been told briskly that there was a war on. (Not that that had escaped our notice, or else why were we in Keswick?)

The River Greta swept around the back of the town and my friends and I spent a lot of time watching the salmon attempting to jump up and over the weir. The grey stone houses and the greenish coloured local slates blended well with the surrounding mountains and always gave a clear cut and ordered feel to the town.

In the summer we were taken down to the lake to swim away from where the tourist rowing boats were drawn up on the way to Friar's Crag. Further along towards the Bassenthwaite end of the lake was a jetty into the deeper water and here we could splash and swim. I remember going there on one occasion when a thunderstorm was in the offing. The water in the lake was warm, and rose and fell in oily swells, the air became oppressive and still and eventually the rain came down in torrents and there was such a feeling of exhilaration in being so much a creature of the water, both in it and under it.

We could choose which church we wished to attend, and although I used to accompany my grandfather to the Baptist church on Heaton Road as a small child, I revelled in the choice and took to trying them all. My favourite, for its beauty rather than its services was Crosthwaite Church, the C of E church at the head of the lake. The large Presbyterian Church was imposing if rather cold and the Methodist Church felt welcoming.

One half term when we had a few days off, I decided to go and visit my aunt by marriage on the farm above the lake at Bassenthwaite. Aunt Ada and Aunt Belle were the sisters of the young man who had gone to Australia and sent for my Aunt Gladys as his bride. My cousin Marian was staying with them at the time and attending the village school, so, unannounced, I caught the bus from Keswick and got off at the end of the long lane that led uphill to the farm. It was a delight to walk up as it went through a small scented tree - lined valley at one point, where wild strawberries could be had for the taking. So tiny, and yet such a luscious taste. The farm at the top was windswept with a wide selection of barns and outhouses adjoining and surrounding it. The dairy was always spotless and cool and the stone shelves would hold wide earthenware dishes of milk from which the thick cream was skimmed. Next to them was the butter churn, which I loved to take a hand at turning and see the miracle of the butter eventually thumping around the barrel when it was taken out and shaped and patted with the butter paddles. The remaining buttermilk would be fed to the calves and I loved the task of weaning the young animals by bringing the bucket of butter milk to them, putting my hand into their mouths where they sucked with babyish enthusiasm, then guiding their heads down into the liquid so that they drew the milk up for themselves. It never ceased to amaze me how quickly they got the hang of it, and even now I remember the feel of their warm mouths and their rough tongues.

Upstairs in the house, in one of the unused bedrooms, the floors would be spread with newspapers and the season's apple harvest would be laid out to dry off before being wrapped and stored for winter. The huge kitchen was warm and comfortable and I envied Marian living there. On this occasion, Auntie Ada was surprised to see me and explained that she had to go to Cockermouth market to sell her butter and eggs while Marian had to go to school. I could choose to go with her or with Marian, so I chose to go to the school. It was quite a long walk and the teacher must have been surprised to have another pupil, but she made room for me and I had a very enjoyable day. The highlight for me was the singing class when we sang the Skye Boat Song. I must have had quite a strong voice even then as I remember the teacher walking up and down past me as I sang, probably wondering where all the noise was coming from.

And then it transpired that my father had put my name down for Barrow House, and at the start of the next school year, there was a place for me. Barrow House was a private hotel which the school was leasing. It lay on the north shore of the lake just before Lodore House and Falls. It also had a waterfall at the back of the house where the electricity generator lived, and which occasioned ominous flickering of the lights when the water ran low. About fifty girls could be housed here and we had dormitories with bunk beds, a large dining room and a library and studies for doing homework.

My friend Jean was also there and we used to beg some flour and buy a tin of golden syrup and some matches. Thus equipped we would climb up the hill at the back of the house above the waterfall and up onto the moors. Here there was a bridge and a ruined barn beside it; we would get water from the stream, light a fire and mix our 'dampers' in a purloined pan from the kitchen. Any stick would do to wrap the dough around and we would sit over our smoking fire and eventually, when patience ran out, eat our half-cooked dampers smeared with golden syrup. The beauty of it was that all the stickiness and the washing-up could be done in the cold racing stream. And then we could relax and gaze across the beautiful view of the bridge and the lake. It was only in later years that I discovered we were enjoying a famous beauty spot, the Ashness Bridge.

Hallowe'en saw us draping blankets down the sides of our bunks

Pat Lowther, author

and having midnight feasts with candles in hollowed - out turnips. Fortunately nothing caught fire. In the hard winter, the lake froze over and we skated and slid on its surface. To begin with, we used to walk back to Barrow House from Keswick in a 'crocodile' but later on we had a bus and we used to sing *'The woman stood at the churchyard door....'* with great gusto as we drove back along the lakeside.

They were very happy times, one that any schoolgirl who has read Angela Brazil would have recognised and I would happily have stayed there to the end of my school days, but it was not to be. The bombing of the North of England had declined somewhat, and the school in Newcastle, which had originally been requisitioned for some war purpose, was now available, and so we were to be brought back to Newcastle. It seemed it wasn't all over completely however, because as our train returned to Newcastle in the dark, we had to stop some way outside the city for some time as there was an air-raid in progress. The windows were all blacked out and we were forbidden to fiddle with the blinds, but we could hear the explosions and we knew that if the furnace in the engine could be seen by the enemy, we could become a target. But one thing I learned at that time, and that was that young people have very little fear. We shuddered among ourselves and worked ourselves up into a mild hysteria, but really we had no concept of what the consequences of an attack might be.

And so we settled into our school, a new experience for most of us, and also had to make a space for ourselves in our old homes. For me this was not easy. I had left the home which I shared with my father and our maid Florence three years before, I returned to my grandparents' house next door, the house now owned by my Auntie Ethel and which was shared with her sister, Auntie Marian and my father. And I was homesick for Keswick.

My one consolation was my dog Ross who, having belonged to my aunt, now became my own and faithful companion.

In 2009 Pat wrote: To have the experience of living in safety in the beautiful Lake District during the Second World War is an experience which shaped my life in many ways, principally by giving me a life-long love of the English countryside in all its seasons, but mostly by the inculcation of a sense of adventure and an awareness of fresh horizons and new experiences.

Perhaps because of that, as an adult, I never settled down to live in one place for very long. We returned to school in Newcastle and I later went to the Newcastle General Hospital to train as a nurse. But fate intervened when I lost my father in an accident shortly before I was to marry and with my husband we moved first to Lancashire and then to South Africa. After his death, I returned to England with my four children, joined the Civil Service and spent the last four years of my career at the Fees Office at the House of Commons helping M.P.'s *"to be good employers"* according to my job description.

I remarried and when I retired, I returned to live in South Africa for another five years. Now living on my own in Devon, I have written two books of autobiography *'Vintage 1930'* and *'Picking up the Pieces'*.

The children of Keswick would shout "Brown Bombers" at us.
DENISE RAMSAY, KESWICK
CNHS

I read with interest a letter in the 'Keswick Reminder' - June 23rd - written by Ian Gumm about his experience as an evacuee in Keswick as I too was an evacuee there from the beginning of September 1939 when war was declared. I lived in Newcastle-on-Tyne, where the armaments factory Vickers Armstrong was a sure target to be bombed, and all the schools in the city had to organise the children to be evacuated. I was at the Central Newcastle High School, but my sister was still at the local Council School - so she was to go to Kendal. I was nine and she was seven - a young age to be separated from each other and our parents and to go and live with strangers!

I was taken to school in the morning with suitcase, identity card and gasmask, which was issued in a cardboard box with string to go round our necks. Needless to say some manufacturer caught on to make cases for the boxes and of course we girls pestered our parents to buy us one.

Buses came to collect us from school to take us to the railway station to board a train for Keswick, which arrived there in the afternoon. I remember a lot of officials lined up on the platform to welcome us; one looked very important, wearing a gold chain - he would probably be the mayor. We were then sorted into groups by teachers, and some parents who came along volunteered to be helpers. My little group (five of us) were taken to High Hill Farm where we met Mr and Mrs Raven and their two grown up daughters - Sadie and Maisie, who showed us to our bedroom which we were to share. I ended up sleeping in a double bed with Florence; she had impetigo on her legs and no-one wanted to sleep with her so I just had to avoid touching her somehow. We were all so homesick that there was a lot of crying the first few nights. Three of the others including Florence managed to persuade their parents to let them go home - but not mine - I had to stay. At least it meant I had a bed to myself.

One of my first impressions on arrival was the feeling that I was trapped in the bottom of a basin - the huge surrounding mountains gave me that feeling. I had always lived in the city so living in the country was new to me. Now I just love them in their different moods and appreciate gazing at them through my window here in Keswick.

I realize I was lucky living on a farm, seeing how the farmers lived - at the crack of dawn one was aware of the movement from their bedrooms nearby (the floor coverings were lino - no soft carpets to absorb the noise!). When we went down for breakfast they were finishing theirs after having already done a good session of hard work - bringing in the cows, milking them and returning them to the fields.

When they took the bulls out, leading them with a rope or rod attached to the ring on their nose, I was fascinated and imagined them getting loose and chasing us. Sometimes I played a game of dare, going up to them as they were being led out to the fields. The farmer had a couple of farmhands - young lads who used to tease us. They all wore clogs which they kept on when they came into the kitchen, which made quite a clatter on the quarry tiled floor and gave off an odour of cow manure which disappeared at the end of the day when it was swilled out - just as well, as we lived in the kitchen except on Sunday for dinner, teatime and the evening, when we went into the front sitting room. I don't ever remember seeing the men folk dressed in a suit or anything other than their work clothes, which were breeches, a waistcoat with a watch and chain and a striped shirt with no collar and the sleeves rolled up. Theirs was a long day - from dawn to dusk; if it wasn't time for haymaking it was lambing time, and in between there were always plenty of other jobs to do.

When it became dark blackout curtains had to be drawn - no chink of light had to be seen. The enemy had a completely black country to fly over - so no towns or habitation were obvious to bomb. When we went to bed we carried a candle, and I remember hoping it wouldn't go out - as it once did making it very frightening along the long dark corridor - and then having to feel my way along by the walls and doors.

The orchards were exciting for us - we played hide and seek, climbed the trees, and pinched an apple or two. However we got found out, so were banned from going there! We loved to climb up the ladder and play in the hay loft – hiding, jumping and rolling. What a mess we made of our clothes as the hay clung to us.

My Gran left Newcastle too and my uncle paid the rent for a lovely little bungalow in Coldstream - on the Scottish borders - and there we spent all our summer holidays each year of the war. The garden had fruit trees and bushes and in the autumn she would send us a cardboard box of apples, pears and plums from time to time, plus a few bars of Duncan's chocolate sent to her by the factory where my uncle had worked before being called up, but the apples tasted of cardboard and the chocolate of mothballs!

School was just over Greta Bridge so it only took us a few minutes to get there. Keswick School let us share it with them - one term we went in the mornings and the next in the afternoons. When we weren't at school we went to other buildings and did knitting for the forces - gloves, mittens, socks, hats and scarves. I remember I had to go to the Parish Hall (just off the Main Street) and in winter it was freezing - no central heating then - only a little black primus stove with holes in and lit by paraffin to provide some heat, so we all huddled round, knitting endlessly away. Sometimes the teacher would read us a story. Hymns at school were always repeatedly about "those in peril on the sea".

Not long after we arrived in Keswick - only about a couple of weeks, a terrible event happened on Derwentwater. Our Art teacher Miss Hanson and History teacher Miss Ransom went out on a canoe. The boat capsized and they both went into the water. Miss Ransom struck her head on rocks at the bottom - became unconscious and tragically drowned. Miss Hanson managed to swim to the shore, leaving her wig to float on the water - her secret was out! Naturally it was a traumatic shock for the whole school so soon after arriving.

We were soon to have a nickname. The children of Keswick would shout out *"Brown Bombers, Brown Bombers"* as we walked through the streets. This was because our uniforms were brown with yellow trimmings. The Roedean School from Brighton came to Keswick and they occupied the Keswick Hotel, keeping themselves to themselves and were not seen wandering about town on their own like us. Their uniforms were navy blue with a bit of red. S. Katharine's Teacher Training College came over from Liverpool and took over the Queen's Hotel. Their uniform was purple with silver trimmings.

On Sunday mornings we went to the church, according to our

religion (I went to Southey Street Methodist Chapel). In the afternoon Sadie or Maisie would take us out on a walk even if it was raining! I remember going to Walla Crag, Calf's Foot Bay and Friar's Crag, Portinscale, Castle Head - in fact all the walks that were possible to do on foot from the house!

Every Monday evening we looked forward to sitting round the kitchen fire - all the family together - to listen to "Monday Night at Eight" - an hour's programme on the radio. I specially liked the detective story where you had to work out "who did it" and they told you later in the programme. As we listened, I would hold Mrs. Raven's wool and was intrigued to watch her winding it in the shape of an egg with a hole in the top and bottom where she held her finger and thumb. She showed me how to do it but unfortunately I've forgotten.

It was coming up to the Christmas holidays and strangely enough we were allowed to go home - but it was still a risk going back to Newcastle. I'd saved up to buy Mum and Dad a Christmas present. I felt really proud of myself as I thought I'd chosen some useful presents that looked quite expensive - one was a glass fruit dish for trifles, stewed fruit etc. and to me it looked like crystal. It cost me a shilling .The next Christmas I bought her a little blue jam pot with flowers round the top border. It had a lid with a hole for the spoon and stood on a saucer (it cost 1/6d). They have come back to me now since my mother died and they remind me of the war days at Keswick. I bought both of them at Dixon's, which has just been sold - adding yet another clothes shop in the town. My father smoked a pipe so I bought him his favourite 'Three Nuns Tobacco' each time.

After we came back from our Christmas holiday we saw the mountains transformed from their sprinkling of white before we left to a thick covering of snow coating every mountain. The air was so dry and cold. The lake at that time froze every winter - it was a lovely sight to see all the ice skaters gliding gracefully on the ice. Our games lessons always took place on the lake and the lucky ones who had ice skates were well away enjoying the freedom of movement on ice, racing each other, doing figure of eights and turning, while we others had to make do making slides on the ice; we still enjoyed it, making up our own games - and pulling each other to see who could make the longest slide etc.

One of my friends, Irene, was billeted in Greta Street. Often we met

110

each other and explored the different areas of the town, being careful not to go too far along Borrowdale Road, as someone told us that a Chinese lady had been murdered along there and it made us a bit frightened. I don't think the parents of today would be happy to see their daughters let loose on their own! We played a lot in the park and I remember the thrill I had when I eventually could turn and swing upside down on the iron bar! We enjoyed tennis too. When Irene's mother and aunt came to see us for the day in their old "banger" they would include me in their outing. Her Aunt Peggy had a sweet shop and she always brought us a lot of sweets! Actually I had more sweets when they were rationed than I had before, as I only got a Saturday's penny to spend then, and it only bought one tiny 1 oz bar of chocolate, whereas the ration gave me double that amount and my parents did not deprive me of my due! Nevertheless I discovered we could buy a certain lozenge – 'Victory V' - from a little tobacconist and grocer on a corner near the bus station called Hoppers which is no longer there. The lozenge had an ether-like taste which was very addictive (it was for sore throats really) and you could buy as many as you liked, but about three or four of them made your mouth very rough and uncomfortable. I'm sure they can't have been good for us but we carried on buying them when we had a few pennies to spend from our allowance.

I loved to go to the library which was in or beside the Parish Hall near Keswick School just on Main Street. I remember avidly reading all the fairy books (The Red Fairy, The Green Fairy, The Yellow Fairy etc.) as well as many others.

As petrol was rationed I can only remember two occasions when my parents came to see me in the car. One visit was for the day and the other was to pick me up and take me to Kendal to see my sister and we had a lovely weekend staying with her and her host and hostess. They were fairly young but had no children so they really enjoyed having my sister. She was very happy with them - calling them Uncle Hubert and Auntie Olive - and kept in close touch, writing and visiting over the years till they both died. I must say I felt a little jealous of how much they loved her and she took to them right away. They were certainly a real uncle and aunt.

It must have been a year later that we had to leave the farm - the sisters were leaving home to get married - Sadie to a widower who lived in a house under Skiddaw. Once or twice she took us there to visit. The old parents couldn't manage to look after us on their own so sadly we had to leave to go and live with the Wilson family (49, The Headlands, by the red phone box, which was handy for phoning my parents). They had a very barky dog of which I was frightened but I did eventually get used to it. Mr. Wilson worked at the Pencil Mill. They too had a grown - up family of which four were called up to fight in the war: Tom, who was killed (we went to visit his grave every week), Willie, Roland (both were married), and Leonard. There were three daughters: Hettie (married - surname Wells, with a daughter Joyce aged about fourteen who went to Keswick High School), Annie, who worked in a grocer's shop and Mary, the youngest, who joined the Land Army working in forestry. I went back about ten years later with my husband-to-be, to give them a surprise and hoped they would remember me - which they did; we had lost touch over those years. There was only Annie and Mary living there - they never married. Mary, however was working in Young's the furniture shop, which closed over a year ago.

There was one big bonus when I moved to another family - my friend Irene was able to change her digs and move in with me, so I wasn't lonely on my own with a new family.

There was a council house on The Headlands near the town end where the bus station was and the family who rented it were so poor, that during one very cold spell in winter they took the wooden banister rail down to make a fire!

A memory of a winter's morning comes to mind. We set off for school with our school bags. I had a satchel and Irene a briefcase. There had been an extremely heavy snowfall through the night and there were big drifts down the pathway through the houses. Irene was ahead of me and suddenly I couldn't see her - all I could see was her case lying on top of the snow - she had disappeared into the snowdrift! I thought it very funny, but at the time she didn't. The snow was so soft we had a struggle to get her out.

Another friend Sheila Bell (now Aitkin) played the piano beautifully, running off Chopin's Revolution, the Warsaw Concerto and many other impressive pieces at the age of ten! This inspired me to want to learn so I started piano lessons which we had in the Masonic Hall nearly opposite the Alhambra Cinema. The Music Teacher, Dr. Hutchinson, travelled all the way from Newcastle to give piano lessons to the pupils of our school (he used to teach singing to Kathleen Ferrier!). To be of this standard Sheila practiced for an hour before coming to school and an hour after coming back home. She didn't come out to play with us much as she was always at the piano. Of course learning to play the piano meant boring piano practice for me - especially with starting from the beginning and we had to find a house where the owner was willing to put up with the noisy practicing every day. I persevered, but it was very difficult playing in the winter in an icy cold room with numb fingers. Later Hettie Wells (Mr. and Mrs. Wilson's daughter) let me go to their house - it was better as it was only a few doors away along The Headlands).

We enjoyed going to the cinema. On Saturday mornings there was a children's cinema club at the Alhambra and we'd sometimes go there if there was something we wanted to see. It was extremely noisy however, and it was difficult to keep everyone quiet enough for us to hear. My favourite stars were children - Shirley Temple, Mickey Rooney and Judy Garland, among others, so I always tried to go and see them. The Pavilion in Station Road provided entertainment - dancing as well as a cinema. I remember we used to stand outside asking adults to take us in, as children were not allowed in on their own; some agreed and we gave them our money and they got our tickets along with theirs and then once inside they gave us our tickets and we left them to sit on our own! Sometimes we had to wait a long time as many just ignored us so we weren't always sure we'd get in to see the film. Along with the film there was always a newsreel (Pathe News) for about ten minutes, showing news of the war - fighting, bombing, news of the troops etc.

Everyone was encouraged to "Dig for Victory" so the small back garden of the Wilson's council house was taken over to provide us with vegetables and also eggs from a hen run they put there. I remember loving to dig the hard earth and seeing all the worms crawl out. The hens would come rushing to my spade to gobble them up.

Some of the changes for good that I have noticed since I was there in the wartime are the now traffic free area in the market square, the building of a theatre, the lovely light cheerful library and the approach down Lake Road with the by-pass over the top. I'm glad to see many of the features I liked are still there - the little kiosk where I used to get a drink and ice-cream and sit to enjoy them in Hope Park after a game of crazy golf. The big bus station has gone but the new stands seem adequate and it has made room for a very good supermarket. It is nice to see a few of the old shops and buildings left - the Keswick Reminder office with shop, Friar's, Fisher's, the Pencil Mill, Moot Hall and even some of the old pubs, e.g., The King's Arms, The George and the Four in Hand - all helping to retain some of the old character of the town. I can't remember whether the market was still going on during the war, but it certainly is now, giving a lively atmosphere to the town on Thursdays and Saturdays.

While I've lived here during the last few years it is sad to see Firn's (the only ironmonger in the town), Young's (the furniture shop) and the Health Food shop all disappear, many to make way for more clothing shops and charity shops - we never had the latter in my day!

When I first arrived in Keswick - as a city girl - it took time for me to appreciate the lovely scenery, as I felt a bit homesick, but it grew on me and I kept returning for holidays, to enjoy all the lovely walks and to climb the mountains, and to show my children a bit of the life I had here. Now having bought a bungalow a few years ago we are loving every minute being here thanks to my school choosing Keswick for our evacuation town.

Denise wrote in 2009: Before the end of the war I was back at Newcastle and, later, training to be a teacher specialising in Advanced Needlework at the Northern Counties College of Cookery and Domestic Science. The war was over by then but there was still food rationing and clothing coupons were required to buy fabric, which was limited in colour, design and type, so uninteresting compared to nowadays.

I met my future husband whilst at College and we spent holidays cycling and Youth Hostelling, including a trip to Keswick to look up those I had stayed with. Sadly, they had died though their daughters still lived at the same address.

My first teaching experience was in the Scotswood area of Newcastle-upon-Tyne (strangely, my last school post some thirty years later was in Newcastle-under-Lyme).

After marriage, we moved to Kent, firstly into two rooms in Gillingham until we found a house in Maidstone. There our two sons were born. After a few years we moved to Saltburn by the Sea in Yorkshire

Denise Ramsay, husband and grandson

where our daughter was born. More moves were to follow, first to Cambridge for a couple of years then a relatively long stay of seventeen years in Leek, North Staffordshire, on the fringe of the Peak District.

Over that time we spent a lot of our spare time hiking and acted as host and hostess on holidays of the Countrywide Holidays Association, leading walks and organizing the social events. As the family became older I was able to start my teaching career again doing part-time teaching – Cake Decoration at the Art College, then a year teaching in a primary school, before full-time teaching needlework at a secondary school in Macclesfield. There I started a Ramblers Group and at weekends I booked a coach to take the girls out hiking in the lovely Peak District. We made all the anoraks in the lunch hour and I was given a grant to buy hiking boots and rucksacks. After three years there I took a post as Head of Needlework in Newcastle-under-Lyme – very congenial compared to the challenging early years in the other Newcastle! I held this post until, reluctantly, we moved to Bolton following my husband's redundancy. I then obtained a job as Lecturer in Needlework at the North Cheshire College in Warrington and stayed there for thirteen years until my retirement. I joined the Warrington Craftworkers' Guild and am still an active member.

I have five grandchildren, three of whom live with my daughter in France, where I recently celebrated my 80th birthday.

After my retirement we bought a small bungalow in Keswick where we have enjoyed many walks among the mountains; it just had to be Keswick which held memories of my evacuation years.

THE 1987 KESWICK REUNION 45 YEARS ON

Phyllis Robson
CNHS

Phyllis Robson was a pupil at C.N.H.S., evacuated to Keswick and eventually became the Headmistress of the Junior School of the C.N.H.S. In 1987 a group of 'Old Girls' visited Barrow House on Derwentwater. This is the account of the reunion visit written by Phyllis who has since died.

We left Keswick in 1942. Miss Leale, the Headmistress, wrote in the School Magazine, 'At last the long-hoped for day of our return is at hand. Though the prospect of being once more at home fills us with joy, our feelings are tempered with very real regret at leaving Keswick and all the good friends we have made. Those ties of friendship will never be forgotten and we shall always look back on them with gratitude and we shall look forward to happier days when we can renew them all once more. We cannot tell what lies before us, but in this we may be certain that, richer by reason of our opportunities and experience during three happy years of evacuation, we shall be better equipped to face the future'.

Comment from the Sixth Form: 'We realise we have had many thrilling and amusing experiences; we have learned afresh the value of self-reliance and co-operation. The time we spent here will always be memorable in the history of the School'.

It is no wonder that many of us who had lived through the Keswick experience wanted to return together for a rather special reunion. After forty-five years we have reached the age of retirement or near-retirement, careers successfully completed, families reared – time to reflect.

The first mention of a reunion was greeted with enthusiasm. A certain amount of detective work followed, trying to trace the whereabouts of colleagues last seen forty years ago! It all came together on 30th April, 1987.

The day dawned, bright and fresh. As friends gathered outside School in Eskdale Terrace the years rolled away. 'I feel I should be wearing my hat and brown gloves' said one. 'Are we really allowed to enter by the front door?' said another. The library was the meeting point because, after all, libraries don't change very much do they? It was reassuring to see again the curved wooden seat, its well-worn polished surface looked friendly and reminded us of the day we sat there waiting to go into the Hall to take the School Certificate examination. But the window looking out over the playground was no longer there, and a large modern extension stretched far beyond the original cosy panelled walls. Girls were bustling about preparing for the day's work. As nine o'clock approached we were called to the Hall. Not the galleried Hall that we had known, where the staff sat in a row looking down on us and latecomers had to enter noisily down the creaking wooden staircase! This beautiful new Hall was opened by the Duchess of Gloucester in 1977. It has a fine stage at one end and room for everyone to sit comfortably in chairs. The girls looked smart in the familiar brown uniform, though they were all wearing ties that were once for the privileged few in the sixth form!

After Assembly, the coach was waiting and we left promptly on our pilgrimage. Some who had thought apprehensively, 'Will I know anyone after so many years?' quickly realised that no-one had changed so much. Yes, there were grey hairs, rather more lines on the faces, but everyone was instantly recognisable and basically just the same. The volume of conversation rose as the miles passed by and we all relaxed.

Turning into the drive of Barrow House was an experience it is difficult to describe. It was as if we were children again. There were the sheep peacefully grazing in the grounds as if nothing ever happens, just as they have always been. The house, standing majestically, well-preserved and exactly as we remember it. We strolled on the gravelled terrace and looked out across Derwentwater. This was the view that greeted us each morning as we dressed for school, yet we hardly noticed it then. Weren't we lucky to be surrounded by such beauty? The Lake seemed to cast a spell on us as we stood there remembering – yes, it really could be 1940 all over again. It was no easy task to break the spell and persuade everyone to assemble for a photo session – this was an opportunity not to be missed.

Entering by the conservatory (as we always did) the memories flooded back – the boot cupboard is still there! We toured the dormitories upstairs which looked remarkably as we remembered them as they are still furnished with bunk beds for Youth Hostellers. We were amazed and delighted to see our huge mirror and the beautiful marble fireplace intact in what had been an elegant drawing room before it was quickly converted to sleeping accommodation in wartime. I put my hand on the very bunk in which I had slept all those years ago, and could so vividly hear again the owls hooting through the night in the darkness of blackout and the comforting ever-present sound of the waterfall. One could almost feel the presence of Miss Walkinshaw, our teacher, friend and stand-in mother. There was her bedroom in the centre of the house – a door at either side left open during the night lest we should call. We crept through there one night when she was sleeping, but she never knew! Finally we reached the 'Singing Hills' dormitory, so called because the eight of us who slept there sang a hymn together last thing at night. How small it looks now – it seemed such a large room at the time.

Downstairs had changed considerably to meet the needs of a thriving Youth Hostel. It was difficult to locate the staff sitting room where we queued every Saturday morning to receive our pocket money from Miss Randall. The tuck cupboard was only faintly discernible as an oblong shape on the plaster wall where it had been filled in. Only in the dining room did we feel the comfort of a place well-remembered. Was it not here that we returned each evening from school, ravenously hungry? One jar of jam a month and two ounces of butter per week were put out in individual pots to be picked up from the trolley on entering. Today there were no such restrictions. The Warden and his staff had prepared a delicious three-course meal, and the voices grew louder as the memories returned. We used to do our homework in here – quite often the lights failed and poor Miss Randall had to brave the elements to go to a hut, strictly out of bounds, near the waterfall, to tend to the generator. Being a science teacher she was expected to know about these things I suppose. We almost enjoyed the periods of oil lamps, especially cosy when huddled together singing *'The Day Thou Gavest Lord Is Ended'* at evening prayers, whilst thinking longingly of home and parents.

There was the history of Barrow House on the Y.H.A. board but strangely no mention of its wartime use – we were affronted! How could such an important episode be omitted? - perhaps it never happened!

Reunion, 1987: CNHS at Barrow House

As we left, the Warden was preparing for his daily influx of campers. He was out of stock of the postcards of Barrow House. The coach returned to Keswick by the lakeside. We used to walk in the middle of that road, there was so little traffic. How different it all is.

Once in Keswick, we walked to Friar's Crag to enjoy the beauty of the lake as the sun broke through on this glorious Spring day. Others retraced their steps to Keswick School. Hardly any visible change at all. There was the playing field where we had to assemble on our very first morning, mountains close by (very few had actually ever seen a mountain before). How did the two schools fit into one? – what a headache that must have been for those in charge. In the event, we attended half-day only at first and then became familiar with every church hall, library, Masonic Hall and hut in the town, moving from place to place down an open covered way at Keswick School which is still there!

The journey home passed all too quickly. We were warmly welcomed back by Mrs Chapman who offered us some refreshment. A final look at the School which has played such an important part in our lives, then we dispersed, tired, emotional, happy.

What a day to remember!

There were many tears – would they see their parents again?
IDA TAYLOR, NEWCASTLE-UPON-TYNE
CNHS

In August 1939, aged eleven years, I was on a week's holiday with a friend in Keswick. Her grandmother owned the Hazeldene Hotel on the Heads and her mother ran the annex called Lane Rigg.

One day we were swimming in the lake when we noticed a group of girls in brown uniforms watching us. To my surprise I discovered that they were friends from the Newcastle Central High School who had been evacuated to Keswick. Instead of my parents coming to take me home that Saturday, they brought my uniform and told me I was staying.

My friends had been gathered at School in Newcastle to be taken by train to Keswick. There were many tears because they didn't know when they would see their parents again – if ever. Taken to the Youth Hostel in Keswick, they were then shared out to willing hosts and taken to their new homes. Some parents did manage to visit the following week.

We soon settled in, sharing Keswick School and using other premises like the Masonic Hall and Parish Hall. I think we had dinners where Bryson's shop is now. To begin with we had school on Saturday afternoons and always had to wear our school blazers. Hence our nickname *'The Brown Bombers'*. We had to attend church on Sunday mornings and often walked to Friar's Crag in the afternoon. We soon climbed Latrigg and Skiddaw, swam in the lake and played tennis in Fitz Park.

I'm not sure what happened to Lane Rigg, but I was soon sent next door to Miss Blackburn at West View which I loved. At various times there were families from Newcastle, Gravesend, London and Whitley Bay, so I always had company. I was given a party for my twelfth birthday that December. At one time three of my teachers stayed there – and much to my surprise they were really nice ladies. One taught me to knit and darn, and the others took me to the Alhambra Cinema as a Christmas treat. When six soldiers were billeted on us we had great fun and they taught me

Ida Taylor and her family

to play poker. I spent a lot of time in the park across the road where I fed the pets and played novelty golf. They gave me a rabbit 'Mickey' to look after but when 'he' had thirteen babies 'Minnie' had to go back to Pets' Corner. I had kept her in the greenhouse at Hazeldene where I was always made welcome by my friend's aunts who ran the hotel. It was during my week's holiday that her uncles took us up Scafell and Helvellyn.

When Miss Blackburn gave up West View I moved to Lake Road where I was miserable, it was such a contrast from before. I then got moved to the Atkinson's in Wordsworth Street who were very kind to me. The School had taken Barrow House as a hostel and Mr Atkinson drove the bus which brought the girls in to school. I often heard they had been noisy and up to mischief on the bus. I walked to school every day through Fitz Park and loved to watch the fish jumping the weir. Bystanders watching would applaud when one made it.

Meanwhile, my brother who is three years older than me was sent to Penrith and could not settle, so my parents bought a small house there. My mother moved in and my father and I joined them every weekend. Two other friends were doing the same thing. We had our bicycles there and went with the boys to Pooley Bridge or to swim in the river at Langwathby.

One winter it was so cold that we were able to skate on Eden Hall pond. I remember skating on Derwentwater too, and the bangs as the ice began to thaw and crack. We got stuck at Penrith for three weeks because the road and railway were blocked at Troutbeck. When we got the first train the snow was higher than the carriages.

When my brother left school Mother returned home and I stayed in Keswick full-time. Previously all the holidays had been spent in Penrith, but after that I came home to Newcastle each holiday until it was declared safe for us to finally return.

Being evacuated to Keswick was an experience I have never regretted. It was generally a happy time with freedom to enjoy everything about the countryside. I have had so many wonderful holidays with friends since then, and meet my family there every year. They have heard all about my time there and think it odd that we were 'billetted' out with 'hosts and hostesses', but they were the terms used then. They were also concerned that parents agreed to their young daughters being sent to live with complete strangers – it probably would not happen today. We were the lucky ones!

Ida wrote in 2009: After leaving school I worked for my father, a builder. I married Rowland in 1952 and had four children, a son, a daughter and then twin daughters. I am immensely proud of them. They all have degrees, and two doctorates. When the twins were ten years old Rowland had a stroke but made a good recovery and we opened a restaurant in Corbridge. After Rowland died in 1975 I began a Bed & Breakfast business, working part-time at Robbs of Hexham.

I met up with some school friends who were also single ladies and we spent holidays together in the Lakes. My family also love the Lakes and we have spent many reunions there.

In 1987 I returned to Newcastle to care for my parents. Father died two months later and my mother in 1989. About this time I returned to the church where I had attended Sunday School in the 1930's. I met old friends and made new ones who I now holiday with. They accept that I need to return to the Lakes and put up with my stories.

I have had two knee replacements this year and can now walk freely again, my health is good, and I still drive. In my busy life I have much to be thankful for.

HUNMANBY SCHOOL, FILEY, NORTH YORKSHIRE

Hunmanby Hall School was opened in 1928 as a Methodist boarding school for girls. The School was evacuated in 1940 to the Lake District and Ilkley. The Middle and Junior School pupils were accommodated in Armathwaite Hall and Bassenfell Manor, near Bassenthwaite and the Senior School girls went to Ben Rhydding, near Ilkley in North Yorkshire. The School closed in 1991. The building has since been converted to luxury flats and a nine-hole golf course has been constructed in the parkland.

Armathwaite Hall

I remember being a fairy in
"A Midsummer Night's Dream"

PATRICIA PEARSON, ADELAIDE, SOUTH AUSTRALIA
Hunmanby School

Patricia Pearson wrote of her memories of life at the School in the Lake District for the magazine of the Old Girls' Association and these are reproduced here with her kind permission.

It is Sunday morning in May 1942, two and a half years into World War Two. A corn coloured 'caterpillar' moves slowly down the Bassen Fell to the Armathwaite Hall road. Two by two, fifty junior girls in uniform, maize dresses, white wide-brimmed panama school hats and white gloves proceed to morning service at the 'Middle School'. I am one of them, a new girl, and this is to my first visit to Armathwaite Hall.

As I sit now, a world away, in my home in Adelaide, South Australia, it is all so clear in my memory. The 'halfway house' reached so quickly on the downward trek, later to be left behind so much more slowly as we plodded uphill towards our cold beef, mashed potatoes and beetroot (almost work-free on Sunday) luncheon.

Then the massive iron gates of the Hall are looming up before us. These gates were taken away in 1943 – metals of all sorts were commandeered to help the war-effort; old cutlery, pans, tools, railings, even rings were given to be melted down and used for armaments.

To the right, the little road where, in 1944 and 1945, we picked wild rosehips growing in the hedges beyond the gamekeeper's cottage. Rosehips were high in vitamin C, which was extracted commercially and returned as a syrup supplement to our meagre and citrus-free rations. Along this road too were many unusual wild flowers – all food for my flora, for I was already interested in botany and soon would compile a list of the species to be found around Armathwaite.

Past the lodge and into the curving drive lined with rhododendrons (now putting me in mind of '*Manderley*' and '*Rebecca*') and overshadowed by huge beech trees. The beeches, pale green and lovely in spring, golden red in autumn, shedding their glory in deep litter. We schoolgirls,

124

Bassenfell Manor

standing in for the gardeners away on Active Service, raked this into high piles to be burnt by the one remaining groundsman. Drifts of acrid smoke would fill the air in November – *'air polluting and biologically unsound, should have been composted'* we would say now!

Round the last curve of the drive and nearing the wide forecourt and formal entrance to the Hall, which we were not allowed to use, the tennis courts lay to our right. Used also for netball, I remember the early morning practices for the 'Manor' competitions; the half dark, crisp air, beat and bounce of the ball, heaving chests and steaming breath as we organised ourselves to achieve for the sake of our 'Manors'. Again in the games period every afternoon, we would practise to win against our arch-rival Roedean Ladies' College – evacuated to the Station Hotel, Keswick.

Adjacent lay the wonderful parkland where we played lacrosse in winter, cricket and rounders in summer. How I loved being bowler at rounders – I could throw hard, fast and straight over short distances, yet could never throw-in long passes from the outfield in cricket! I also loved being 'keeper' at rounders or cricket (in spite of my spectacles – wartime issue, round and owlish, tortoiseshell!) In those days, too, the parkland carried a picturesque herd of red deer and, possibly because of them, the railings skirting the driveway were not removed with the Hall gates.

We turned left to enter the Hall by the back entrance, passing first into the courtyard. Cobbled, it grew weeds which we, at times, were required to remove! On our right we had passed the wing of the Hall devoted almost entirely to the domestic staff. The exception was one room at the rear end which was the Science Laboratory, 'home' to Miss Drury

The Billiards Room, Armathwaite Hall

of the sarcastic tongue, spurring us on, in 1944 and later, to scientific understanding. I can remember, in my first term in middle-school (September 1943), always approaching the science lab. with apprehension! After a while though, maybe as we 'smartened up' or grew more 'thick skinned', we found she was really not so fearsome but rather an inspiring teacher! We had many happy hours there.

On the left as we entered the courtyard were the stable buildings converted into private accommodation for the teaching staff, except at the northern end, where one large high room was the gymnasium. Here we had gym benches, a 'horse' and a 'box'. A little way behind the gymnasium, in the wood, stood the squash court but this was out of bounds to the girls and used by the staff only.

On the eastern side of the courtyard was an archway leading to the path to the lake where that summer term and others, we went down to bathe. Just beyond the archway, the path skirted the front terrace lawns of the hall and here, I remember hot summer afternoons with Miss Bellamy (music teacher and Chief Guider) and her helper Miss Webster (piano teacher) encouraging us to master sundry skills to obtain 'badges' leading one to Second Class or First Class status. We learnt knots, elementary first aid, camping skills but also the mundane such as bed making and even now I mechanically make the bed with hospital corners!

A little further to the left, behind a row of tall lime trees on a high grass terrace, was a wide lawn where the outside summer play was staged. I remember being a fairy in *'A Midsummer Night's Dream'* and another year a rat in *'The Pied Piper of Hamelin'*, as parents watched from above.

Pupil access to the Hall was from the courtyard by the back door next to the kitchen on one side, third form rooms on the other, which were formerly the smoke and billiard rooms. The walls of these rooms were closely hung with glassed and framed cartoons from the late 17th and early 18th centuries, an education in themselves and very intriguing. In 1943 I was in 3A and chose the desks at the rear corner of the billiard room alongside some of these pictures and on a side platform where I could see everyone and everything! Miss Logg, I think it was, said doubtfully, 'Pat, you with your spectacles, are you sure you can see the blackboard from there?" Not my main concern! It was a lovely form room as it had a piano on which one exuberant classmate (Jean Morrison) could bash out, *'Alexander's Rag Time Band'* and other popular tunes of the time between lessons. At this time, in needlework lessons we were required to make, before anything else, one pair of navy blue woollen knickers (for refugees) entailing good practice in cutting out, running stitch, French or 'run and tell' seams, hemming etcetera (one wonders what the refugees made of the results – extraordinary!) Only secondarily could we proceed to make more interesting things such as needle cases (from linen, utilising drawn thread work and cross stitch) – one of which my mother aged 92 recently 're-gave' me! – or card cases (from flannel that was one of the few fabrics that was available in wartime for handicrafts). In art class, conducted in the same room as there was no 'proper' art room, we tried our hand at designing dress materials, painting the 'repeat patterns' in water colours, the most easily available medium, even this (in adorable little square pots) was in short supply.

Alongside these form rooms was a long 'wash-up' where we juniors repaired before the service. Here also the middle school had their weekly hair-washing supervised by Sister Marr. Poor soul, she also conducted 'bug combing' twice a term when every head was inspected by a fine tooth comb for nits! In 1944, when labour was extremely short and the school's usual laundry service curtailed, schoolgirls were asked to volunteer to do small washing and this is where they did it. I don't remember where all the washed and wet clothes were dried!

Passing on to the service, we juniors were shepherded past what was the Bar. On entry to the middle school we were to find this contained new stationery books, filling the room with the distinctive and pleasing odours of new paper – poor, grey, wartime quality though it was. It was here we joyfully obtained a pristine exercise book, unpainted wartime 'economy' pencils, Quink ink (washable blue the favourite) for use with our fountain pen. How grown up we felt with our fashionable nib and holder. Now no longer the frequent dipping of the nib into an inkwell, but continuous, hassle-free (except for the blots!) writing. However, it was fun every now and then to dismantle the fountain, to remove the nib piece and attached rubber; to squeeze it in and out repeatedly (with the nib in water) to clean it and refill it, perhaps with a different colour! No ball-points in those days! It was in this room, too, that the mail was sorted; letters into the appropriate form piles for delivery by monitors to the classroom, parcels were listed and the names read out after lunch to a hushed (for once!) dining room. The delight if one received a parcel! It had to be opened under inspection, the string untied and not cut, the brown paper to be removed carefully so it could be re-used. Any food received was stored in one's tuck box from which a small portion (very small in the case of sweets as we received a ration of 6 oz per week in toto!) could be taken each day, except in the case of the Birthday Cake when invited partakers at a special table saw its consumption! I should add that in spite of the War, we always seemed to have adequate food in the school dining room; at that time my diary for 1944 notes one occasion when we had oranges for dessert which possibly came from North Africa, another time chocolate biscuits – but these were highlights! In fact, it was worse on our return to Hunmanby in 1946 when rationing was even more stringent, as food was being directed to the starving liberated in Europe.

The Senior Dining Room, next to the Bar, stirs many memories. Most vivid is the lunchtime on D Day (6th June 1944) when Allied Forces invaded France in Normandy as the first step to liberate Europe from the Nazi Yoke. We listened to radio reports and recordings made as it happened as we ate. Some girls, whose fathers were at the Fronts, were overcome and asked to leave the room. The power of the spoken word in those days was every bit as graphic as the television screen today. We were transfixed and subdued, our prayers with the Forces.

In winter, the dark panelled majestic room would be cheerful with a huge log fire in the massive fireplace and dinnertime would seem almost like home. Preceding the meal Matron would read from the Bible in lieu of Evensong. She was renowned for her readings from the Old Testament and we revelled in Shadrach, Meshak and Abednego and the Fiery Furnace amongst other old tales. I can see her now, as she was, a tall commanding figure, her household keys hanging in a bunch at her side. Omni-present in the house, she must have had the most difficult task caring for us and to keep the household running at such a high standard. At the time I never gave it a thought, just accepted everything. Such is youth!

We sat at the long refectory tables running from the fireplace to near the window bay, across which was the teaching staff table. We girls moved two places every day around the tables so, whist having the same immediate neighbours, we had variation opposite and nearby. A steward would sit at one end of the table, often a teacher at the other. Such changing contacts were 'civilising'! Next but one position to the end on each side was that of 'waiters for the day'. We had a 'washing up' roster – one had to do a week of this every now and then as labour was short in wartime days. We also had to do half an hour's housework after breakfast – making beds, sweeping and dusting our dormitories and classrooms. For this we arranged our own rosters so that tasks fell evenly.

Moving past the Senior Dining Room one comes to the Main Hall, which was used for the occasional film show on a Saturday evening. The desks would be moved back or removed, a large screen mounted at the southern end and 35mm films such as 'Evergreen' and 'Elephant Boy' were shown. My small diary for 23rd January 1944 reads: ' saw a film, jolly, jolly nice, called "The Ghost Goes West" – it was very creepy, loved it!' I always chose to sit on the big stairs, if possible, so to be in the 'Grand Circle'.

The stairs were out of bounds except to those who undertook 'remedials' (exercises for physical problems such as flat feet) on the halfway landing every morning before assembly.

The hall was used for ballroom dancing to the gramophone (no longer wooden needles and wind-up, but steel needles and electric I think). On weekdays it was the classroom of the fourth year (13 year olds) and I can remember the tedium of reading aloud, in turn, of the 'set' book for the term – so slow! There was the occasional respite of people coming or going to the school office (first door) or the headmistress' sanctum (second door) or to the library or ballroom.

The end door (library) was the Lower 5th form room, but was also for 'extra work' on Saturdays. Girls who had been caught for certain misdemeanours and 'reported' lost appropriate marks. When these totalled a certain level per week, the culprit had to forfeit free time for 'extra work'. I can remember untying knotted string for half an hour but I think I was just lucky!

The capacious front room or ballroom, with its 1930's wicker chairs, was the Upper 5th form room but was used for large gatherings such as Sunday services, morning assembly and prayers, music recitals and competitions, presentations such as school and nativity plays, and Eurhythmics (so called 'free style' dancing). It was here we juniors from Bassenfell Manor sat, immediately inside the door, slightly apart from the older girls at the Sunday Service until we had heard our 'little sermon' before the 'proper sermon' when, on command, we withdrew quietly to return to Bassen Fell.

It was not until September 1942 when I moved into the middle school that I went upstairs in Armathwaite Hall. Thinking back in order to write this memento, I tried to map out the upstairs but fell woefully short! I could manage a few rooms, e.g. 11, 12, (no 13!), 14 and 15 on the main landing could locate only one bathroom – opposite room 12. I remember this one, not from any lavatorial point of view, but because the aspect of the deer park from its window appealed to me. As I was interested in photography, I determined to get up in the night (against the rules) at the time of the full moon and take a 'time exposure' of the moon over the park. In those days cameras were not instamatic – one had to observe, measure and set each meter e.g., distance, light intensity, lens aperture and time exposure and only then would a wonderful photograph result. Sadly on this occasion – one didn't! But I remember the bathroom. Perhaps I should add, in case you think us unclean, that we had a wash bowl per room and a roster for a bath twice a week! Wartime baths were to be only 6 inches deep or less in order to conserve energy, enough for cleaning but not for luxuriating!

As for rooms, I inherited quite a diversity in the 'never to be forgotten' winter term of 1943. My Girl Guide diary begins the term (19th January). 'I go back to school. Quite a nice journey. Am in Room 22. May change later, was reported to Miss Hargreaves'.

Miss Hargreaves had her bedroom on the south east corner of the Hall on the second floor, just around the corner from room 22 and probably heard us talking on the way to bed! However, I was not to be in there too long. On 25th January it was announced that Jean Lindley (a girl in our form) had the measles. On 26th January I went to the 'sicker' for a week with 'flu, then, presumably better, I was moved to room 29. On 7th February I relapsed and was isolated in a small room next to Miss Hargreaves (usually kept for naughty girls), developing spots later that day. It would seem that I had the measles too! We were the first of nearly half of the 120 girls in Armathwaite to go down with the disease. It was to be a terrible time for the teaching staff who were called upon to do nursing duties as well as teaching. One by one the rooms were taken over as 'sick wards'. I was up on the top landing which I think used to be the servants' quarters in the domestic wing, in room 25, the middle of three, where I have hazy memories of aching eyes and head, drawn blinds, bodily heat and discomfort, sleep and food (which I was not too sick to put down the washbowl at the earliest convenient, unobserved moment!) After a few days I was transferred to room 24 with three other girls, but not allowed to read until after the ninth day of infection and kept in bed until a full fortnight after the spots had disappeared! We whiled away the time with patience (no television!). Once up, but still upstairs bound, I remember observing the school cat down below in the forecourt tormenting a mouse! Horrid! I was not allowed downstairs until 27th

February just after we had 'tormented' room 26 after lights as ghosts, sheet-clad!

We convalesced in the junior dining room (behind the Bar) once 'downstairs' and here we played 'pick up sticks' and 'jacks' and other quiet games or read, until we repaired our strength. Eventually we were allowed out, well rugged up and in our Wellingtons for it was 'February fill dyke'. One Saturday a crowd of us went down to the lake, once there we could not resist paddling in the lake in our gum boots. Unfortunately, the girls got wet and were hauled over the coals for being 'ungrateful girls', i.e. to the long-suffering teachers who had nursed us. My diary for 6th March 1943 reads: 'Were sent to bed in disgrace straight after tea. No dancing. Foul supper. Got tuck luckily'. I do not sound particularly repentant, I'm sad to note – now I feel sorry for the staff.

The lake was the cause of another of my vivid memories. We were allowed to paddle or swim there only if we wore footwear. One day in 1944 we went down to swim and I found the button was off one of my plimsolls. Needless to say, I went into bathe without it! Shortly I felt a pain, lifted my right foot to see it streaming with blood. Putting on my loose plimsoll, I squodged up the half mile to confess to Sister, who sat my foot in Dettol (no tetanus jabs in those days!). After a little while Sister returned to find me looking white, feeling faint and the foot still bleeding. A taxi was summoned (not easy in wartime) and I was taken to Cockermouth Hospital. Not only did I see the operating theatre but, under local anaesthetic, had six stitches in my foot! Rejoicing, I wrote in my diary on 8th July 1944 'Exams. Cut my foot, had six stitches put in at Cockermouth Hospital. Jolly nice day!' A few days back at school in bed (I did my needlework examination in bed!) and I wrote in 14th July 1944 'Still in bed. Got a letter. Got a bit of toffee. Marvellous day. Had my stitches out. An ugly wound! To this day, one stitch is taped to the inside of the diary! 'In bed for a further four days' I reported sadly 'missed the excursion to Dash Falls'. Gain one, lose another!

Someone has already said: 'Another time, another place'.

After evacuation: Hunmanby Hall School returned to East Yorkshire in 1944. After Higher School Certificate I went to St Andrew's University and graduated MA in 1949 (Zoology). I was working towards a PhD (cell biology) when my father died and I went home to live with my mother in

Wilmslow. I worked for four years at the Christie Hospital and the Holt Radium Institute in Manchester.

In June 1958 I married and went to Australia with my husband and his two daughters. Archer worked as a G.P. and I worked full-time in the Zoology Department of the Adelaide University. Our son Martin was born in 1959 and I gradually returned to work in the University as a Demonstrator.

Patricia Pearson

In 1976 I was divorced and I visited the U.K. with Martin to meet up with family and old friends. Martin began work as a teller in the Savings Bank of South Australia and I continued part-time work at the University 'demonstrating', followed by teaching Biology and Botany at a private school in the Adelaide Hills. After twenty-five years I was told my services were no longer required at the University– I was pensioned-off - and took the opportunity to visit the U.K. again, this time including the Lake District.

Well, after half a lifetime in Australia I decided to become a naturalised Aussie! The ceremony was held in Brighton City Hall with family and friends present. After Martin left home on his marriage I became a "home body" - a dab hand with the paintbrush, dog walking and more time for women's lunches, film mornings, art galleries and exhibitions etcetera. Grand-daughter Elina arrived in September 1991. Another U.K. trip to see my 90 year-old mother in 1992. She died in 1994.

I had written to my parents/ mother every week since starting school at Bassen Fell but contact now is by telephone. In 1997 I became friendly with Joe Purvis (originally from Glasgow) – we shared a common interest in dog-walking. We visited West Australia (camera always to the fore!)

Joe died in 2007.

I have been tracing my family ancestry back to Littondale in Yorkshire – straight and narrow Methodist and Church of England proletariat facing hardships with good, old-fashioned Yorkshire grit - no Lords and Ladies!

In 1944 I began a love affair - with the Lake District !
AILEEN CUCKSON, COCKERMOUTH
Hunmanby School

Aileen began teaching music in 1944 at Hunmanby Hall School, which had been evacuated to Armathwaite Hall in the Lake District.

In 1944 I began a love affair – with the Lake District! Having had an interview in the dining room of Armathwaite Hall with Miss Hargreaves, the indomitable Head of Hunmanby Hall, a Methodist boarding school which had evacuated there from the East Riding of Yorkshire for the duration of hostilities, I was appointed to teach music to about twenty-seven girls, aged 7 to 9 years, who couldn't be accommodated back at the Yorkshire site when the main school returned there.

Together with other members of staff we occupied Bassen Fell (that rather eccentric building on the outskirts of Bassenthwaite village). Genista Dawson (nee Everest) and I had bed-sits at Rawlinshaw, on North Row, with the Clark family (in those days, with paraffin lamps and coal fires). Both buildings had wonderful views of Skiddaw, and down towards the central lakes, with the Langdales visible on a clear day. Emma Blockley helped with domestic work at the School and Gilbert was a 'lengthman'. Both became lifelong friends.

We stayed there for five terms, before returning to Hunmanby, and it was a very happy time. On our days off Genista and I walked, cycled and Youth Hostelled.

Was it any wonder that, later, I introduced my husband and children to the delights of fell walking, a love which has stayed with all of us?

When, in 1974, Wilf was offered a post with N.C.B. (National Coal Board) at Maryport, the wheel came full circle; we moved to Wythop Mill and renewed our acquaintance with Bassenthwaite friends and the Methodist Chapel.

In 2009, Aileen wrote: In 1945 the 'remnants' of the evacuees returned to Hunmanby. I went with them, and joined a music staff of nine.

Aileen Cuckson and Wilf

I left the School in 1949 to marry Wilf at Driffield, where my father was the Methodist Minister. Wilf was introduced to Bassenthwaite, walking, cycling and climbing the fells and eventually 'ticking off' the Wainwrights, the Coast to Coast Walk and trekking in Peru. We lived in Rotherham and Orpington, Kent and when Wilf was offered a post with the NCB at Maryport (Opencast Mines) he did not have to ask me twice!

So we came to Wythop Mill in 1947 and I became involved with musical activities at Keswick Methodist Church, played the organ at Bassenthwaite Chapel, have been a Volunteer at Theatre by the Lake and played the piano for visitors to Mirehouse, the home of the Spedding family.

We now have six grandchildren, all encouraged to walk the fells in their early days, and four great-grandchildren, all within visiting distance.

Wilf is unfortunately now disabled, but I am blessed with good health and managed to climb Helvellyn earlier this year. My fairly brief sojourn as an "evacuee" certainly got me "hooked" on the Lake District and I am constantly thankful that I live amongst the fells that I love so much.

THE LIVERPOOL ORPHANAGE

The following brief history of the Liverpool Orphanage is taken from information published on the A2A website by the Liverpool Record Office and the Local History Service and printed with their permission.

THE LIVERPOOL ORPHANAGE was an amalgamation of three institutions, the Female Orphan Asylum, the Boys' Asylum and the Infants' Orphan Asylum. Eventually the Liverpool Orphanage became Salisbury House School in 1958 but the former name was still in common use [the word 'asylum' in this case means 'a place of refuge' of course].

The rules of admittance to the asylums were strict. The children had to be full orphans, they also had to be of legitimate birth, live within seven miles of the Liverpool Exchange, be healthy, baptized in the Church of England and have no other means of support than the workhouses. Certificates had to be produced as proof of these conditions. There were, however, no restrictions placed on the number of children from any one family that could be admitted.

The specific aim of the asylums was to bring the children up according to the principles of the Church of England and to receive an education in writing, arithmetic and vocational skills. Depending on the state of their health the infants transferred to the girls' or boys' asylums at the appropriate age and the older children were set up with employment by the age of fifteen. Many of the girls were accepted for domestic service while the boys were often apprenticed to local firms. At the beginning of the Second World War I lived in the Liverpool Orphanage, a large building in Woolton Road.

We were evacuated to the Lake District, the girls and the under-seven years boys going to Wanlass How at Ambleside and the boys further north. Our first house was The Gables at Portinscale. We were not there long before we moved to the Guest House at Stair, alongside the beck and bridge in the Newlands Valley. Our next and final move was to Hause End on Derwentwater. That was the nicest place we had ever lived. Our main hobby there was climbing Catbells, Rowling End, Causey Pike and Barrow, etcetera.

We watched as an R.A.F. bomber crashed into Derwentwater
LES SCHOFIELD, LIVERPOOL

One day the boys were watching an R.A.F. Training Bomber circling the lake when it crashed into the water. We ran down to the shore and jumped into the four-oar rowing boat with Mr Hornsby, the Headmaster, Mr Smith, a House Master and a friend. We soon found the plane which was submerged nose down. We rowed around for a long time but nobody else came. So sadly we rowed back leaving the scene deserted. Four R.A.F. men had perished that day.

Needless to say, living in the Newlands Valley for so long we came to love it. My family and I head there every year for our holidays. I had two weeks in Braithwaite this year (2006).

Les Schofield died in October 2006. His daughter Helen has contributed the following account of his life after leaving the Liverpool Orphanage:

Les completed his National Service in the Irish Fusiliers and returned to civilian life to work at a number of jobs. He met his future wife Ethel Watson, also an evacuee in Keswick, at an orphanage reunion.

Les Schofield (left) with his family at Brandelhow

Les and Ethel had eight children, five girls and three boys, and they had a very happy life together. All the family holidays whilst the children were young were spent in the Lake District, in Keswick, the Newlands Valley and at the Scotgate Camp Site. They would climb Barrow or Catbells, with Les and Ethel telling the children of their past life as evacuees.

Les spent most of his life in the building trade. He was proud of his craftsmanship and went on to build house extensions for his family as they left home. He was most proud of his rebuilding and modernising a house damaged by subsidence through bombing, which remains as a family home,.

Helen added that there was so much his family could tell about their parents that it would probably fill a book on its own.

THE R.A.F. AIRCRAFT CRASH IN DERWENTWATER: On 28th December 1941 in the morning an R.A.F. De Havilland Dominie 89A aircraft, registered number X7402, was seen to crash by Les Schofield, a pupil at the evacuated Liverpool Orphanage School. According to witnesses, the aircraft flew low over the lake in good weather conditions when it crashed into the water at map reference 267215, between St Herbert's Island and the eastern shore of the lake.

None of the crew escaped before the aircraft sank. Later, salvage teams worked with a local boat company to recover the wreckage from the lake bed (the lake is quite shallow at this point) and the aircraft was removed for examination.

ROEDEAN SCHOOL IN KESWICK

Roedean School was founded by the Lawrence sisters in 1885. In 1898 the School moved to its present site at Brighton, Sussex. Roedean is an independent public boarding school for girls.

Unlike many other schools that decided to evacuate to a safer, rural location at the outbreak of war Roedean postponed the move until the autumn of 1940. The school buildings were to be used for Army purposes and, later, by the Royal Navy.

The Keswick Hotel was chosen to house the School and the necessary equipment was sent there. On 5th September 1940 Roedean School at Keswick was opened for the autumn term with two hundred and sixty girls, housemistresses, matrons and thirty-one other members of staff. Miss Tanner, the headmistress, was responsible for the planning which enabled a smooth and virtually trouble-free move from Brighton. Acknowledged as an influential educational reformer, Miss Tanner became Lady Emmeline in 1947.

The four senior Houses occupied the Keswick Hotel, with younger girls at the Millfield and Shu-le-Crow Hotels. In January 1944 a large hut was built by the side of the Millfield Hotel as classroom accommodation.

Roedean girls walking through Keswick

The staff and pupils soon adapted themselves to their new home in Keswick and the School was quickly absorbed in to the Keswick community. Help was forthcoming from Mr Howe, the Headmaster of Keswick School who allowed the sixth form to share science lessons in the School. Both St. John's and Crosthwaite Churches welcomed the girls and staff to their services. Many individual Keswick people helped by allowing their pianos to be used for practice. The girls attended lectures, plays and musical recitals in the town, and in return invited local people to their performances in the Queen of the Lakes Pavilion. A combined choir of Roedean, Keswick School and the Central Newcastle High School for Girls presented 'The Messiah' with Crosthwaite Church Choir. Several girls became members of the Crosthwaite Handbell Ringers and the Bell Ringing team in Crosthwaite Church.

It appears that examination work did not suffer from the move. In

1942 Miss Tanner wrote, *'As time goes on I became more and more convinced that in spite of obvious disadvantages the School is gaining a great deal by its evacuation. It is particularly good for the older girls to have greater freedom and more natural contact with the outer world that became possible in a small town like Keswick'.*

In 1943 she added, *'It is for us now to think out ways by which on our return to Brighton, we can combine the benefits of our new experience with the many advantages of our own home at Brighton'.*

School clubs flourished, and included the Arts Club, Music Club, History Club, Current Affairs Club and a Literary Society. One reading of *'A Midsummer Night's Dream'* on Rampsholme Island was interrupted by a violent thunderstorm. The girls were rescued by a launch and finished the play in a hotel bedroom.

The girls, sometimes in conjunction with other schools or independently, raised money for 'good causes' including the R.S.P.C.A. for the 'Russian Army's Horses' and the Keswick Cottage Hospital. The hotel garden provided opportunities for weeding, fruit picking and further afield the girls collected rose hips, sphagnum moss and herbs. The Rangers (Senior Girl Guides) managed an allotment and helped provide dinners for younger evacuees in the town. At the end of 1941 a 'Company of Service' was formed and worked, during the school holidays, in canteens and W.V.S. clothing centres, wrapping prisoner-of-war parcels for the Red Cross, selling flags and knitting socks for the armed forces.

The bonfire on Latrigg on V.E. Day (Victory in Europe Day) was celebrated with delight by the girls, who were allowed to swarm *'like white ants'* up Latrigg to join in the celebrations.

In the final school term the staff performed a play entitled *'In the Streets of London'* in the Pavilion with all the School's friends being invited – three performances were needed. Carol Sarsfield Hall, a day student from Keswick, helped her father set up the scenery. Later, there was a Farewell Concert and a dance given by the Hotel owners, Mr and Mrs Wivell.

The School could not return immediately to Brighton. The Navy had taken over the buildings from the Army. *'H.M.S Vernon'* had departed in June, but there was much work to be done to have the premises ready for occupation. Eventually, the last day in Keswick arrived – 29th November

1945. The special train was arranged for 5.15 am. All the girls were on the platform, whether or not they were travelling south, accompanied by many friends and entertained by dance music provided by Mr Wivell through loudspeakers. The girls and friends danced, farewell speeches were made, 'Old Lang Syne' sung and the train moved away, accompanied by exploding fog signals laid by the railway staff.

This account is taken, with thanks and acknowledgment, from 'A History of Roedean School, 1885 – 1985' by a former teacher of History at Roedean, Miss Dorothy Butcher.

Secret assignations in Fitz Park with the High School boys!
VIVIEN ALLEN, PLYMOUTH
Roedean School

Of all my memories of Keswick in wartime perhaps the clearest is our arrival there by special train from London, late in the evening at the beginning of September 1940. The government had closed all the schools on the south coast after Dunkirk and our position on top of the cliffs outside Brighton felt conspicuous. The Navy took over our school and we were banished.

A Roedean Special was laid on by the railways which began its journey south of London and skirted the city to the west. My mother took me to the train, at Earl's Court I think, relieved to see me off to safety as the docks had been bombed the night before and the Blitz, as it was later called, had begun. Most of us had never been further north than Oxford before and as the train trundled slowly up the country, with stops between stations for no apparent reason, we gazed out at this foreign country with interest. Eventually we were grinding up Shap and reached Penrith. After some shunting and hooting we turned west onto the late and much lamented CKP – the Cockermouth, Keswick and Penrith Railway. It was dark when we finally drew into Keswick station and, tired and grubby, tumbled out onto the platform, wondering what awaited us. The lights were dim but we soon recognised our house mistresses and the matrons, each looking for their own brood. The Junior House girls were ushered off to a coach and taken to the Millfield Hotel. The rest of us were led into the Keswick Hotel through the Conservatory that gave access to the station platform. We were astonished to see palm trees growing up through the floor and between them our familiar desks and laboratory benches from the Science Wing back in Brighton. Indeed it was in the Conservatory that we had our science lessons for most of the time.

In the main hall we were greeted by the proprietors, Mr and Mrs Wivell and the Head Porter, Dixon, in his braided uniform. Also there, we were glad to find, was Grace, the School House Maid from Brighton, who supervised the Main Entrance to the school. That first night was bewildering but we were sorted out into the rooms we were to occupy, mostly furnished with the narrow iron bedsteads from Brighton.

It was not only the Keswick Hotel that we took over, which 'for the duration' had its name covered with a sign reading 'Roedean School'. It strikes me in retrospect we took over a lot of the town! We may have lived in the hotel, and some lesssons were given there, but there were classrooms all over the place. That first term my classroom was the Ladies' Waiting Room on the station. It was very amusing when female passengers, unaware of the take-over, barged into our lessons looking for the 'Ladies'! Some classes were held in the Keswick Museum and no one seemed to mind if we had a go on the Stone Piano. I wrote my School Certificate examinations in there. A few of the staff were housed in Shu-le-Crow and the first year Domestic Science course was taught there, everything from how to clean the baths and loos to cooking three course meals for some of the staff. It was in Shu-le-Crow's kitchen that I was taught to bake bread, for which I've been grateful all my life – I still bake all our bread. One of the piano teachers had her teaching room there and that is where I had my lessons, There were pianos, also brought up from Brighton, in a number of the larger bedrooms in the Keswick Hotel where we were allotted practice time.

Every morning after breakfast we all walked through the Fitz Park from the Hotel gardens, turned right and than left into Southey Street, where the Methodist Chapel was generously made available to us for our daily Morning Assembly. Miss Tanner, our formidable Headmistress, late created Dame Emmeline, seemed completely at home in the chapel's pulpit, as she had been in our own chapel. Those of us who learnt the organ were allowed to practice there.

But lessons did not start at once. On that first morning in Southey Street Miss Tanner announced that as petrol was going to be rationed in a couple of weeks' time we were excused classes for the first week so that coaches could be hired and we could see something of this unfamiliar land. The first trip was to Ambleside to Dove Cottage and the Church. On the way back the coach made a detour along the valley below Helvellyn, the driver telling us it was an easy climb to the top and a lovely walk along the ridge! Next day we were driven over another pass to Ullswater and on the

144

way back we went to the top of Borrowdale. Boat trips were arranged to take us over Derwentwater to the Manesty Woods for a picnic.

The first Sunday were all lined up in our best Sunday uniforms – navy blue coat and skirt – and marched to St. John's. I was fed up to be stuck in the congregation as at Brighton I had been proud to be in the chapel choir. It was not long, however, before were told that any members of the school choir who cared to join would be welcomed in the choir of Crosthwaite Church. I couldn't wait to volunteer and was delighted to be accepted in the altos there, under the guidance and tuition of Mr Brown, the organist. I soon stared organ lessons with him and he was so good a teacher that in 1943 I was able to win the Henry Smart Organ Scholarship to the Royal Academy of Music. In the choir I was placed next to a Keswick High School girl, Anne Hodgson. We quickly became friends and remain so today.

That first Christmas a number of us, whose homes were in or near London, were not able to go home for the holidays and stayed in Keswick. The summer of 1940 had been warm and sunny but it turned into a cold winter with snow on the fells. As the Keswick Hotel was only a summer - only hotel there was no heating in the bedrooms and conditions were arctic. We used to take our underwear into bed with us at night and dress under the blankets before venturing out of bed. Our breath froze into ice on the blankets pulled up to our chins and two girls ended up in the Cottage Hospital with pneumonia. There were compensations, however. The lake froze and we all went skating and sliding on the ice. Two girls who were better and braver skaters than me skated all the way across to Derwent Island and back, to the consternation of the teacher in charge of us.

Another place that we saw regularly was the small theatre, The Pavilion, which was on Station Road by the river. It was sad to see on a post-war visit that it had been pulled down and replaced by a block of flats. Sad, because it housed some epic performances which we were privileged to see. ENSA, the wartime organisation which not only provided entertainment for the troops at home and overseas also sent tours round the provinces to keep up the morale of the population. We were not all sated with TV in those days – there was none. Among epic productions we saw was one in which Sonia Dresdel starred as Portia in *The Mercant of Venice*. Her performance in the trial scene was so memorable, not least

145

the famous 'Quality of mercy' speech, that it is with me still, thanks to the Pavilion. It was there that we were able to put on our school play. One year it was *Quality Street* in which the leading part was played by Jill Balcon.

There was music, too. A professional performance of '*The Marriage of Figaro*' made me an opera lover for life. However, the Pavilion saw one song recital that was close to history - making. Those of us taking Music for our School Certificate were escorted to the recital by Miss Monk, the head of the history department. Walking back to the Keswick Hotel afterwards she said, 'You girls have heard one of the great voices of the 20th Century. She is an unknown bank clerk from Carlisle now but remember the name Kathleen Ferrier'. As indeed I do. That evening in the old Pavilion remains clear in memory though I heard her on many later occasions, including her London debut while I was still a student at the Royal Academy of Music.

One more part of Keswick we were involved with was the Keswick High School. We went to concerts and recitals given in their school hall, one or two by our own music staff. We did our science exams in the High School laboratories. And there was a certain amount of fraternising, sometimes amounting to secret assignations in Fitz Park with High School boys, but that is another story.

Vivien Allen wrote in 2009: After leaving Roedean in April 1943 I volunteered for the WRENS – Women's Royal Naval Service. However, I failed the medical due to an old back injury so instead went to the Royal Academy of Music on an organ scholarship. Later, I switched to the Drama Department and emerged with an LRAM (Speech and Drama). Adding a diploma in Phonetics, I took up teaching EFL – English as a Foreign Language. In 1949 I married Michael Allen and we had a daughter and two sons. In 1966 we went to live in South Africa where we both had relatives. Not being qualified in Afrikaans I could not teach so went into journalism, writing first as a freelance then as a 'staffer' in the Pretoria Bureau of the Johannesburg 'Star': having been divorced I needed a job. I married my boss, Archie Atkinson and we moved back to the UK when he retired in 1976. When he died in 2008 we had been married for thirty-two years. My first book was published in Pretoria. I went on to write five more for UK publishers and am still at it!

146

The dismal diary of Adrienne Mole

NANCY BANKS-SMITH
Roedean School

Honour the worthy
And honour the keen
Honour her daughters
And honneur aulx dignes

Roedean School song

Fifty years on it strikes me that it may all have been a dreadful misunderstanding. My parents ran a boozer in Blackburn which everyone called t' new pub. Except my mother who called it The Mill Hill Hotel, taking pains with the unaccustomed aitches.

The name may have confused the Roedean bursar into believing that, like many colonial administrators dislodged then from their rubber plantations by the Japanese, they were sitting out the war in some country hotel. Then there was the Banks-Smith. I believe the double-barrelling comes from some fisherman none too sure about his father, but I do realise that Nancy Banks-Smith sounds like someone falling off a horse at Hickstead.

In the hell of total war these little mistakes are easily made.

I was an only child and my parents were great believers in bettering yourself. In the quiet afternoons, when the last customer ("Na then, lads and lasses!") had hit the cobbles, my father would read my Arthur Mee's Children's Encyclopaedia over and over again and regale the boys in the back room with the bits he thought they would enjoy, like:

I often wonder what the vintners buy,
One half so precious as the goods they sell.

Education, my dear Omar, that is what the vintners can buy.

Which is how, much to our mutual surprise, I found myself at Roedean thanks to the boys in the back room whose hoarse, sweet, homesick, Irish tenors rose like smoke every evening singing that they would take you home again, Kathleen, to where your heart would feel no

147

pain. Though, in a way, I never did go home again.

Roedean rallied, like a good hostess, without a flicker of surprise. The first thing they did was get rid of the Lancashire accent I didn't know I had. Rather Pygmalion, really. I had to recite poems like

It was eight bells ringing
And the gunners' lads were singing
And the ship she lay a-swinging
As they polished every gun.

until I stopped hitting my ings like dinner gongs. The way I speak is an interesting social curiosity. I'd change it if I could be bothered because it sounds ridiculous now. Bloody cut glass as the boys in the back room would say. Of course, the way my parents spoke didn't change. The moment I noticed that we sounded different a little fissure grew between us, the earth shrugged and shifted. I don't think I'm imagining it. I don't believe we ever really talked to each other again.

To lose one parent may be regarded as a misfortune. To lose two looks like a first class education.

Roedean was evacuated to the Keswick Hotel, the kind the bursar had in mind. Dame Emmeline Tanner, the headmistress, was reputed to have moved the whole school overnight from Brighton to the Lake District with a Bradshaw in one hand and a bible in the other. She had one of those undivided bosoms popularised by Queen Mary on which her pince-nez, leaping from their perch under the stress of strong emotion, would flutter to rest.

If she was quite a nice old bird really, I don't wish to know that. She once delivered such a powerful oration on the subject of Gels Seen Buying Chips in Keswick that several blameless children had to be escorted out in floods.

The deputy head, Topsy, so called because she just growed, asked us to calculate the percentage who left sobbing. Topsy was a senior wrangler who saw everything in terms of mathematical purity. She had such a clear mind that now and then, like the disappearing rear light of a train you had just missed, I almost thought I got the hang of maths.

We were permanently, achingly hungry. The hotel was run by a couple called Ma and Pa Wivell who were, to my mind, quite suspiciously fat. The cheers we were ordered to give for them at Christmas stuck in my

148

throat like a pauper's pudding.

On half holidays we were detailed off to climb a mountain. There was a depressingly large choice. As Dame Emmeline wrote in the school magazine: "On a perfect October day, 43 girls climbed Great Gable, 16 climbed Scafell Pike, 79 climbed Helvellyn, 16 bicycled to the Langdales (46 miles) and seven walked all round Derwentwater. I was obliged to go to London."

I groaned up Helvellyn which, as Wordsworth remarked, is remote from human road or dwellin' and damn well deserves to be. On the saw-toothed ridge my packed lunch, a pork pie, fell from my frozen fingers and leaped exuberantly down the mountainside, each bound more exhilarated than the last. Topsy said that given Helvellyn was 3113 feet high, could we calculate the time of arrival of a pork pie at the bottom. I still feel quite violently that all mountains are a great mistake and that all pies should be made square by law.

While travelling somewhere east of Suez where the best is like the worst, the maiden ladies who founded the school had come across the djibbah. They adopted this as the ideal school uniform as it disguised the growing gel at all salient points. We wore blue serge djibbahs by day and, dressing for dinner, velvet djibbahs at night. My best friend, Ros, was so tall and willowy and I was so short and fat that, when we walked up the aisle to be confirmed, the same suggestible small girls had to be escorted out sniggering. In djibbahs we looked much of a muchness.

The Outlaw was showing around this time and we heard that Howard Hughes had designed Jane Russell's bust-bodice (as the school called it) on the soundest aeronautical principles. Ros and I, who felt strange stirrings under the djibbah, cut a couple of bust bodices out of the school blackout which was the occasion for another Dame Emmeline special on Gels Who Have Taken Leave of Their Senses. Though, strictly speaking, this applied more to Howard Hughes who later went completely off his head.

Gels were expected to be clever, alert, athletic, loyal and most seemed to be. I never seemed to get the hang of it at all. Not for a minute. Any of it. A damp diary reveals me as Adrienne Mole aged 13 and three quarters.

Mon: Unpacked. Can't find fountain pen. Very unhappy about it. Prunes and junket.

Tues: Bike not arrived. Lost? Snowing.

Wed: Found bike. Lost laundry book. Felt bitter against God.

Thurs: Found laundry book. Lost brolly. Thunderstorm.

Fri: Amy shared her fish paste and everyone got diarrho. Minnie (a teacher called Minnie Ha Ha because of her resounding laugh) said she nearly polished us orl orf.

Sat: Broke my watch that had just been mended for 10s 6d. Wrote bitter poem. Rattle windows! Blow O Wind! Flail your branches broken tree! Though the world be washed away, What concerns it me?

Sun: Rained, snowed and hailed all the way to church. Terrible man from the United Society for Christian Literature shouted at us. Rice pudding. Lost 'crosse stick.

Lacross is a Red Indian game. I believe they played it with the heads of their enemies. That is how Roedean played it. I was usually put in goal on the grounds that they might go easier on someone in glasses. This was entirely fallacious. They came in like Sioux, hair streaming, supporters screaming "G squared D No. 3!" (Grit, Guts and Determination No. 3 House). I found that if I closed my eyes, I didn't scream. "Played No. 3," says my diary. "Lost 15 – 1."

Where did they all go, those clever, alert, athletic, loyal gels? I never came across any of them again but I did meet one or two misfits who were doing rather well. It was as though kicking violently against the regime sent you into some kind of eccentric orbit.

The great thing about public school is that life comes as quite a nice surprise.

Nancy Banks-Smith is a television critic for The Guardian. This article was printed in the newspaper on 4ᵗʰ February 1994, and is reproduced with the permission of the author.

Bitter winters – we muffled ourselves in long woollen cloaks

DAPHNE HOARE, WEST SUSSEX
Roedean School

In September 1943 I travelled by the school special train from Victoria to Keswick to begin my first term at Roedean which had been evacuated to the Keswick Hotel. Until then I had attended a day school so on the journey I had mixed emotions about leaving home and family for the first time. The school special train left at 1.30 pm and the journey seemed endless. We arrived at Keswick at 7.30 pm and at the end of term we departed at 5.30 am to arrive back at Victoria by 1.30 pm where we were met by our parents.

My first term was spent sharing a room with three other girls on the top floor of the hotel. Your room and room-mates changed each term. It was a tough life with no central heating. In the bitter winters we muffled ourselves in our long woollen cloaks and wore mittens in class but still suffered from chilblains.

Although we complained of not having enough to eat, our parents thought we looked remarkably well on the diet which was no doubt due to the healthy outdoor life we led. We would queue up weekly to receive our sweet ration, either so many sweets counted out by our Deputy Housemistress or a 2oz bar of Cadburys Milk chocolate. I used to make that last the week by sucking a square each day and two on Sunday.

Some lessons took place in the station waiting rooms. I can well remember attending a scripture class there when an elderly couple came in and sat down to wait for their train. The class continued with the visitors sitting silently until their train arrived which was an amusing diversion for us. Other lessons, including dancing, music and gym took place at various locations around the town. Chemistry was always in the Palm Court conservatory leading from the hotel down onto the station platform.

Each day began with prayers in the Wesleyan Chapel. The Junior House was in Millfield Hotel on the other side of the River Greta where some of our lessons were held. All games and matches, lacrosse, cricket and tennis, were played in Fitz Park.

151

Our art studio was in the garage at the back of the hotel which was scrubbed out and decorated by our art mistress Miss D.B. Martin. Many of the plant drawings she made there are now housed in the Lindley Library at the Royal Horticultural Society.

At weekends we often had matches. For those not involved there would be walks. On other occasions, staff would accompany us on an all day outing to a particular beauty spot. If it was a long outing we would have a packed lunch provided. I was introduced to fell climbing when we went up Latrigg during the first weekend in Keswick. On another weekend as part of our war effort, the whole school had to collect rose hips which were put into sacks on our return to the hotel and sent off to be made into syrup. This became an annual event while we were there. We were also encouraged to knit socks and scarves in oiled wood for the Navy. Thereafter I happily joined in with friends on any long walks or fell climbing. Our housemistresses were very keen on the outdoors so they maximised the opportunities provided for us to see as much of the Lake District as possible.

We were privileged to have stayed in Keswick in those days when it was so peaceful. I have happy memories of the walks to Friars Crag and around Derwentwater, learning to swim in the lake and of seeing it completely frozen over in 1945. On that occasion, we were permitted to go down to see the skaters and watch the curling on the completely frozen lake which was quite something to enjoy. When the thaw came, huge icebergs came down the Greta and crashed against the bridge in Keswick.

At weekends, we either attended St John's Church or Crosthwaite Church, neither being large enough to accommodate the whole school as well as all the other parishioners. While at school, I was confirmed at St John's. We attended two services on Sundays and always enjoyed going to Crosthwaite for the walk along the river, particularly when the salmon were tossing.

My lasting memories are of the sheer beauty of the Lake District, the lushness of the grass everywhere, the beautifully manicured bowling greens on the right walking up to the station, the Keswick Museum where we held some of our exams, the Alhambra where we held our plays, the Cedar Wood Shop with the lovely smells, Derwentwater, Friar's Crag, Ashness Bridge, Borrowdale, and of climbing Helvellyn as well as many other fells. On our return to Brighton in January 1946 we very much missed the relaxed atmosphere of Keswick and found we had far less contact with the staff from then on.

In 2009 Daphne wrote: I was a PA (Personal Assistant) in my working life. In my retirement I assisted my husband who was the first Secretary General of the International Association of Research Institutes for the Graphics Arts Industry until his retirement. This appointment allowed me to travel with him when he attended conferences and courses he set up in the U.S.A., Germany, Russia, Japan, Hungary, Austria, Switzerland, Italy, France and Spain. We both loved to travel. My husband died last year after forty-seven happy years together.

I have two delightful cats, I still love gardening and growing plants by the sea we could not grow in our home in Surrey. I have two sisters and step-daughters nearby, grand-children and great-grandchildren. I am looking forward to Christmas!

Always misty, raining and damp.
We were always hungry.
PAMELA JENNINGS, WORTHING
Roedean School

I joined the School in January 1944 aged twelve and began in the Junior House (No 4 House), which had taken over the Millfield Hotel by the side of the River Greta. Later, I joined my sister in the Upper School in the Keswick Hotel, just a few yards from the Keswick Station.

The School was large and lessons were held in various places such as the Station waiting rooms, a small hotel called Shu-le-Crow, the Art Gallery and the hotel conservatory as the Science Laboratory. The huge hotel garage was used for art lessons. Sometimes we had to practise our piano lessons in private houses near the hotels.

The hotel bedrooms were very cold in winter and mice were everywhere. Most rooms had washbasins but toilets and bathrooms were far away down the long corridors.

Each day we had morning prayers in the Wesleyan Chapel. In the afternoon we played games in Fitz Park, lacrosse, netball, rounders and tennis, weather permitting, or else on endless walks.

It seemed to me to be always raining, misty and damp. Wartime food was dreadful and we were always hungry.

On Sundays we attended St. John's or Crosthwaite Churches.

Getting up really early at the end of a term for the holidays was an adventure we all enjoyed. We were each handed a packed lunch and then boarded the special train in the dark to travel south. The steam trains were quite smelly and our sandwiches usually ended out of the windows for the birds.

Pamela wrote in 2009: After school I trained as a General Nurse, then as a midwife and, for experience, worked in several hospitals and also as a District Nurse. Then I worked in hospitals in Australia, including Victoria, New South Wales and Alice Springs. Before returning home I visited Tasmania and New Zealand. Nurse

154

Pamela Jennings

Administration positions followed. In retirement I did a City & Guilds Embroidery course.

I keep busy with my hobbies – needlework, gardening, flower arranging and enjoyable walks on the beach on most days.

I have returned to Keswick several times and appreciate the beautiful scenery more than in my school days, and I intend to go again next year.

MEMORIES OF ROEDEAN
AT KESWICK

The following extract from "Memories of Roedean, The First 100 Years" (1998) compiled by Judy Moore with Ann Voigt as Consultant Editor is reproduced with the kind permission of Roedean School.

The first term at Keswick lasted fourteen weeks, to make up for the short summer term, and by Christmas 'everyone was very cross and tired', Susan Gatti (Booth) said. But after the rigid restrictions of Brighton, the girls revelled in a new freedom. 'It was fun, and crazy – not really like school,' Ruth Misa, (Spielman) said.

Vivien Allen wrote: 'I loved the relative freedom and the beauty of the fells, but one friend said she couldn't stand all those mountains breathing down her neck, and left early. We had been so penned in at Brighton that walks and bicycle rides were a great joy. I remember one beautiful Saturday in May bicycling all round Bassenthwaite and meeting no other traffic. The only person we saw was a man ploughing with a team of horses, and seagulls following him. It reminded me of Masefield's *Everlasting Mercy* – "With holy white birds flying after".'

'Living in a large hotel and having lessons in the station waiting room was a novelty.' Ruth Maclean (Gimson) said. 'Skating on the lake and walking and cycling in the fells made it the happiest year of my schooldays.'

'All its shortcomings were more than compensated for by my being allowed to go anywhere with my sketch book, a quite extraordinary change from the Brighton rules,' Isobel Bernstein (Forsell) said.

The shortcomings included mice (and sometimes a practice piano) in the bedrooms, crowded accommodation (squashed luxury, one OR called it), bitter cold when jugs of water froze in the bedrooms and flannels became 'hard and crisp', frozen pipes (but the plumber was dishy and the subject of scandalous rumours) and chilblains.

In the hard winter of 1944/45 there were twenty-seven degrees of frost, and eighteen inch long icicles hung at the windows. Bedroom ceilings collapsed at the Keswick Hotel and the bedrooms were so cold, Ann Portnoy (Levy) remembered, 'that we rolled ourselves in blankets and then got into bed.' In class the girls wore mittens to keep their fingers from turning blue.

'We walked each morning to the Methodist Chapel for Prayers and Fitz Park became our sports field. We had bicycles and made use of them to see the Lake District. The situation at Keswick was more informal and we enjoyed a different school life there,' Audrey Kenyon (Hinchcliffe) said.

'School at Keswick was more flexible because an hotel and a railway station are built differently from a school,' Rosamund Huebener (Bensen) wrote. 'We were usually four to a bedroom instead of the two or three at Brighton. The house identity was blurred and the whole school (except Junior) ate together. Staff were somehow less distant, because they were also scattered about the building. We walked daily through the town and were not cut off as in Brighton.'

Diana Poole (Wilson) remembered long dining tables of ten or twelve with a member of staff at the head of each. 'We sat in houses, and there was a complete change of seating plan about two or three times a term. The hotel owners, the very portly Mr and Mrs Wivell, always stood and surveyed us all rather sternly.'

There was little heating in the Keswick Hotel – until then just a summer resort hotel – and at bath time girls were allowed only three inches of water and ten minutes to wash. Incredibly, cold showers were introduced, Pamela Thalben-Ball recalled. 'After the first one I was excused as I remained blue for half a day!' Pamela also remembered snow in the Lake District in June. It was so cold in Miss Martin's art class, Margaret Bashford (Kay) said, that to keep warm girls would all get up and dance the Sir Roger de Coverley.

Jillian Gordon (Albury) was one of the girls who returned from Canada in October 1944. She loathed Keswick – 'the food, the Wivells, the isolation – it was one of the worst years of my life. I was teased mercilessly for my Canadian accent and I had free elocution lessons to get rid of it.' [In June 1940 Roedean had received an invitation from The National Council of Education of Canada to have fifty Roedean girls attend Edgehill School in Nova Scotia..]

The classrooms in the station waiting room had 'frequent strange visitors – a marvellous distraction from a tedious lesson,' Jean Peacey (Thirlby) thought. Ann Portnoy explained that there was nowhere for the public to wait for the noon train to Carlisle 'so they sat at the back of our class while we were being taught German (in World War Two!)'.

The conservatory science lab was more of a glass-roofed corridor linking the station to the hotel. 'I can hear now the indignant, high-pitched Scottish voice of Miss Will squeaking, "Well, really and truly" as her botany lesson was interrupted yet again by a dripping wooden crate of kippers being carried through to the hotel kitchen,' Margaret Williamson (Blench) wrote. Margaret Bashford remembered the biology class's frogs escaping into the large potted palms, and Miss Lloyd Williams trying to explain the mysteries of chemistry while snow dripped through the glass roof.

Susan Tolfree (Kelly) took her School Certificate in 1940 in the station master's office and the waiting room; Margaret took hers in the local museum 'among locks of Wordworth's hair, strange maps and old prints'.

Six Roedean girls were taught physics with six boys from Keswick School. Jean Marwood, one of the girls, said the boys did the practical experiments, leaving the girls to make the analytical deductions and write up the results. 'Very sexist, but it didn't bother us in those days,' she said.

The sick bay was presided over by Mrs Wilson – The Willy – formerly matron of Number Four. Dilys Jordan (Dunn) and another girl spent one Easter there with mumps. 'The Willy was so kind and the Wivells served us special food – but we couldn't eat the pigeon (supposed to be a delicacy) and it wouldn't go down the loo!'

If life was sometimes difficult in the cramped accommodation for girls and staff, it must have been equally fraught for the hoteliers, but the Wivells, who owned both the hotels, made great efforts to house and feed their guests as well as circumstances allowed. For the duration of the war they were honorary staff and entered into the spirit of school activities. In her 1941 diary, Eve Bysouth (Dowson) wrote: 'To-night it was Hallowe'en, and at supper, after we had just sat down, the lights were turned out and through the dining room door came Mrs Wivell and three maids all draped in white sheets and long pointed hats with another sheet over the hat and face. They came dancing in shaking rattles and holding a large bowl with minced potato in it. They doled out the potato to everyone and told them to eat it carefully. They then danced round the room again and went out. Some people found charms and others found silver three-penny bits wrapped up in paper, in the potato. When the "witches" had come in everyone shrieked and hooted with laughter and stamped on the ground. I found two threepenny bits but Roysia found nothing.'

Dilys remembered 'a wonderful little man called William who spent his entire time stoking the foul-smelling anthracite stoves in the Keswick classrooms'; and she recalled the younger girls' loo roll rolling contests on the long, linoleum-covered red top floor corridor at the hotel. 'War time loo paper was shiny, and scarce,' she said, and inevitably there was trouble when contestants were caught.

'Keswick seemed to be perpetually shrouded in mist,' Dilys said. 'The rain seemed to isolate us from the rest of the country. I found it unutterably depressing to be so hemmed in by mist-shrouded mountains. So rare was good weather that we were usually given a day's holiday when it came.'

She remembered playing games amongst the sheep in the park, the Sunday trek to Church and seeing the salmon leap in the river. There were rehearsals for the colour play in the museum and piano practice in houses in the town.

'There were hilarious comments from soldiers arriving at the station on their way to the commando training on seeing schoolgirls hard at work in the waiting rooms, and even more astonishing, the sight of nubile young women drilling as Rangers outside the station – one or two never did learn to co-ordinate legs and arms when marching!' Dilys added.

Jeanne Reeves (Stranack) said: 'In the Rangers we had a man to teach us mechanics, which I enjoyed and it was very useful in later life. He showed us how to strip a car engine and put it back, and explained what the parts did.'

Roedean was welcomed into the community, not least for the prosperity it brought to the town, and many enduring friendships were made, but there were inevitable small rivalries and animosities, and Janet

Bailey (Ross) recalled Keswick children's taunts of 'Rodie rat poison!' as columns of girls walked to lessons or to chapel.

Junior House in The Millfield Hotel was about ten minutes' walk from the Keswick Hotel. After the 8am breakfast girls had to walk to the Methodist Chapel for Prayers, and lessons were held in prefabricated huts in the garden and at Shu-le-Crow. Some of the girls slept in the guesthouse and others were lodged in private houses in the town. Ann Hulme (Prall) slept out at 51 Blencathra Street for one term. 'The hand bell was rung out of the window at Millfield, and woe betide you if you were late for breakfast,' she said.

The dormitories in Millfield were named after the local mountains, and the classrooms after current war leaders – Churchill, Roosevelt, De Gaulle and Stalin. Belinda McKinnel (Bleckly) remembered passing time outside in the garden, playing ball against the wall, hopscotch, skipping and keeping caterpillars and snails as 'pets'.

Diana Kay (Johnson) was desperately homesick and hated Junior House life at Keswick. 'We had a matron called Wallie who could make life hell. One poor girl ran away and her punishment was to be kept in a dark sick room for over a week, with no books or anything. She ran away again and stayed away in the end.'

Because of the difficulty of travelling in wartime, few parents visited their daughters at Keswick. Jeanne Reeves remembered the time when she had chicken-pox and her parents splurged their saved petrol coupons and travelled all the way from Malvern, in an Austin 7. 'My father was six feet six inches, and how he got behind the wheel and squashed in his legs I don't know, it was a labour of love,' Jeanne said. 'Great excitement seeing them, and then The Muck said I couldn't go out with them as I still had one scab on my back. Naturally, I was very disappointed, but she was called out and my father got his penknife and removed the scab, and when The Muck returned he said, "I think Jeanne's scab seems to have gone now", and The Muck looked, and was amazed. A friend and I were allowed out for a meal – a great treat.'

In the winter of 1944/45 Derwentwater froze over and girls sent for their skates. Janet Bailey (Ross) recalled that the girls back from Canada were very much envied for their *white* boots.

For the war effort, girls collected rosehips for syrup, and sphagnum

Salmon leaping in the River Greta (lino cut by Roedean girl)

moss, to be made into bandages. They knitted sea boot socks and balaclavas in oiled wool for sailors and organised sales of work to raise money for good causes – the Russian Army's horses, the Red Cross and Keswick Cottage Hospital.

The traditional Saturday evening dances continued, pupils performed in plays and concerts for local people, and occasionally they went to the cinema.

Some of the girls joined Crosthwaite's depleted team of bell ringers, others sang in the choir, and memories remain of fellow choristers – Tom Wilson, who drew caricatures during lessons, prayers and sermons, Billy Thompson, the joking policeman, Percy McKane, the printer, with his terrific nasal bass and Mr Fleming, the decorator, with his one flat lock of hair plastered round the front of his bald head, and his large ruby ring.

On VE Day in May 1945 the girls celebrated victory on top of Latrigg, behind the hotel. 'We climbed to the top of the mountain and lit a huge bonfire in the evening. There was singing and dancing, and we ran home in the dark, very late,' Gillian Pemberton (Cameron) said.

Mary Driver, who spent most of her Roedean schooldays in Keswick, said: ' I cannot speak highly enough of what was done to help us in difficult circumstances by the all the staff.'

The return to Brighton was accomplished amazingly smoothly, Mathilde Edward remembered. But it was to a Roedean very different from that of 1939. In the bleak post-war years shortages and rationing continued and no longer were there some fifteen men working on the estate and seventy-five resident domestics.

FIFTY YEARS ON –
THE REUNION

.In September 1990 women who had been at Keswick as schoolgirls held a two day reunion in the Keswick Hotel on the fiftieth anniversary of Roedean's evacuation. It was organised by Pamela Allen (Day-Winter) who said, of her schooldays: 'For those of us who had been in Brighton it was a wonderful feeling of release to be surrounded by the ever-changing views of the fells, and to enjoy the freedom of movement between classrooms, the town, our outings and our expeditions'.

Old Roedeanians attended from all over the world. 'Some of us were trendy in culottes, some sensible in tweeds, but we were all agreed that at our age our clothes should not actually hurt,' ran an account in the *OR Magazine*. 'Had anyone fallen ill we need not have worried – six of us were doctors. We also mustered two diplomats, a musician or two, a deacon, a lawyer, a journalist, a recently retired headmistress, a ditto Head of BBC Children's Radio, a number of businesswomen and plenty of straight up and down housewives. But for two days all that was of no consequence; we were a happy group of old friends and a high old giggly time we had of it.'

Pamela devised a programme that included walks and talks, a dinner and a service in Crosthwaite Church. Ann Longley, the then headmistress, arrived from Brighton for the dinner and another guest was Brigadier Anne Field, who before her retirement was head of the WRAC, and ADC to the Queen. To the ORs she was Anne Hodgson of Keswick School and a member of the Crosthwaite Church choir. Also present was Carol Sarsfield Hall, who had the distinction of being Roedean's only day girl at Keswick.

Excerpts from memories of Keswick written by some of the ORs during the reunion.

'Fifty years on the truth can be told. It was a remarkably hot day, incredible in the heart of the fells and velvet green hills that usually held mist and rolling clouds like a fur collar around Keswick. Our close group of four friends were all preparing mock exams and were on a fairly loose rein between revising. We were also sub-prefects so we could go off on cycle rides. Jane Goldsmith, Joyce Pinney, Maureen Miller and I headed towards the lake and without much ado we hired a boat, a skiff, to row out to a further island.

'By the time we had manoeuvred oars and rudder almost to the middle of the lake we were falling about with laughter and a sense of freedom that a year at Keswick had blessed us with after the isolation of the old gaunt school high up on the flats of Brighton.

'We grounded the boat on a pebbly strand and decided to sunbathe in the remarkable heat. In those days there was no teenage culture, no Ambre Solaire, no search for the ideal shade of brown tan. It was war time and life was honed down to the bare essentials. We decided to do the same with ourselves in the blazing sun. So off came all the clothes and in we went into rippling clear unpolluted water. There were no tourists in those days, no coach tours, wind surfers, sail boats or launches. Derwentwater was in its pristine, innocent, original essence, a lake of clean water.

'Consider then our consternation when another skiff glided silently and swiftly round the curve of the island. It was Miss Godfray – Minnie Hal Ha of the waters! And we were skinny-dipping with nowhere to hide.

'Taken in tow we were, dripping hair, hastily dragged on shorts clinging to our wet bodies. We were rushed up to the hotel by this irate staff member, straight in to see Miss Middleton. All I can remember was her hawklike, speechless stare, and a rapid transfer to Dame Emmeline Tanner's study where her august frame, in its ruched and pleated bodice with many tiny buttons, seemed to tower over us.

'I can't really remember the admonitions we must surely have received, but I do remember all four of us were un-sub-prefected in front of the school next day, like so many hens being de-beaked.' Anon

'Dressed in my very ill-fitting uniform – nearly all secondhand, or made rather badly from ex-naval blankets, and bought to allow for lots of growth – I say goodbye to my parents, and we set off on the long journey north ... Finally we arrived at Keswick Station. It had been raining heavily, but the rain had stopped and the sun had come out. Every leaf sparkles, the air has a sharp freshness and the view of the mountains which surround us is intoxicatingly beautiful. It is one of the most magical moments of my life.

'Memories of Millfield .... the hard yellow field peas, the almost uneatable pies that we used to hide in the napkin bags, the bread dipped in tepid bacon fat, the lumpy porridge.' Susan Crosfield (Martin).

'Grey skies, grey stone houses, the smell of smoke from the trains, Grace walking up and down the platform ringing the bell between forties. Trying to get chocolate out of the machines on the platform – they soon ran out. Being hungry – kedgeree and rabbit and damson jam on semolina. A bun and an orange to sustain one on long Saturday walks up hills. Seeing Dean Inge, which meant nothing at the time, but whose prayers and sayings I rather like now.' Anon

'There was a letter box outside the station with a stamp machine above it. Every time we passed on the way to lessons in the station rooms we lifted the flap of the stamp machine – once a girl had found a stamp there. There was a continuous "click click" as we all dashed past, lifting the flap.' Anon

'My abiding memory is our total obsession with food. The basic fare was quite disgusting – oceans of yellow custard and loaves of grey National Bread on which one spread a nauseating mixture of chocolate spread (made at one's scrum table from cocoa, sugar and milk) ... The fear of being tongue-tied when sitting up to Minnie Ha Ha, who in any event did not wish to listen to chatter whilst she tackled her kipper; the complicated procedure of selecting tables; the difficult art of staring at the girl opposite until she remembered to ask if you would like some water, bread or whatever. I recall how I cajoled dear Dr Mills into prescribing yummy Radio Malt for me (not that horrid Cod Liver Oil and Malt) and persuaded him that Marmite was essential for my well-being.' Anon

'It was amazing how we all adapted to the new way of life, and I remember vividly that first autumn we were here, the freedom of movement, the beautiful surroundings and the discovery that hill walking was the most exhilarating activity ever.

'Derwentwater froze over that first winter and we skated on the lake and the snow was thick enough to make an igloo on the front lawn of the hotel.

'Our education continued, as before – there was no drop in standards, only a change in conditions. I shall always appreciate the way Miss Monk and Miss Lucchesi came up from Brighton by rail to give us our music lessons; their description of their wartime journeys was quite horrific, but they never missed, and the orchestra continued as before.

'We made our contribution to the war effort, gardening and knitting (sweaters for the Argyll and Sutherland Highlanders, thick mittens with trigger fingers for the Russian front soldiers). Anon

'The windswept Downs of Sussex gave way to beautiful, wooded, welcoming mountains. At the same time the rigid discipline of the Brighton days was replaced by a far less formal way of life. .... The freedom must have gone to my head. On the way to the Chapel one morning I discarded my hat – unthinkable. My punishment was that I had to play games in my hat – a fate worse than death at that self-conscious age. Anyway, at the last minute the heavens opened and it poured with rain. No games! Maureen Eastwood (Miller).

'My recollections of Keswick school days include being taught bridge by dear Lloydy Bill at the house prefects' weekly get-togethers; going down the long corridor to quell the noise of some exuberant youngsters in their bedroom, to hear the lookout say, when I reached the door, "It's all right, it's only Squance"; a picnic on one of the islands in the lake with Miss Fyleman and spitting cherry stones into a bottle. Anon

'I was one of the few members of the Francis Holland School to go with Roedean to Keswick. I remember particularly the great friendliness and feeling of togetherness I met on every side. Never for a moment did I feel out of things or lonely, and being an outdoor girl the wonderful challenge of climbing with Miss Spearing thrilled me and provided me with an interest that I've never lost. Patty Maxwell (Scott).

'I think my first memory of Roedean at Keswick was of Miss Tanner – large and impressive, but not at all formidable. I had arrived from a boarding school on the south coast which had closed because of the war,

166

my mother had just died, and I must have been immersed in grief and lack of confidence. However I felt reassured and supported by her kindness and understanding, as well as amazed by her prodigious memory of the names and circumstances of every girl in the school. Jane Spicer (Mackinnon)

'My memories include lines of pixie hoods bobbing through Fitz Park; the occasion of Pastor Niemuller's visit when we in the congregation were singing *A Safe Stronghold Our God Is Still* while he sang the hymn in German – a great moment; the queue for hair washing by the team from a Keswick salon, followed by a session by the fire, or using the drier in the maid's room; the Music Club singing Gilbert and Sullivan to a "pressed" audience of the local servicemen – we hope they enjoyed it; how the garage was transformed into a studio with murals, printed curtains, but cold, very cold in the winter. We sat muffled in scarves, cloaks, extra socks and mittens while, I swear, the paint froze on our tin palettes. Anon

'Aircraft used to fly low over the lake; later we learned that they were practising for the Dam Busters' Raid. Watching them from my bedroom window one day, I saw a plane coming low out of the Jaws of Borrowdale. It disappeared from sight over the lake, there was a bang and it did not reappear. For three days we were not allowed near the lake while the wreckage was located and lifted, and the bodies recovered.

'I remember taking all my clothes, apart from tunic and shoes, into bed with me on winter nights and dressing under the blankets next morning. I remember being hungry and buying rum butter in the town to be eaten after lights out with the handle of my toothbrush. Vivien Allen (Hallet)

'I faked a tummy pain to avoid a maths lesson, was put into sick bay and from there, in spite of protestations, was taken to the cottage hospital. There I had my appendix removed – the first Roedean girl to be operated upon. I had two lovely weeks of recuperation at a guest house on the other side of Fitz Park.

'An abiding memory of envy of Hilary Garstin, who fell over the handlebars of her bike descending a mountain path. She suffered temporary concussion, as a result of which she was excused from taking any exams that term, and sat, wreathed in happy smiles, reading books of her choice from the fiction library, while her unfortunate friends continued on the unremitting path of sweat and swot. Pamela Gilbast (Seager)

'At the end of term we would bag our seats on the train the night before we left. The carriages had all been shunted on to a sideline at the station and we were up at 4am for breakfast before being shooed on the train for home.

'I remember Hilary Garstin falling off her bike half-way up a mountain. She was concussed and I stayed with her, stripping off as much as I dared to keep her warm (it was sleeting). The others cycled off to alert a doctor, who had to reverse his car up the track as there was no turning point.

'Hilary, Daphne Dawkes and I got lost on an expedition above Rydal Water. We were meant to aim for Grasmere. Eventually we were picked up in the dark in pouring rain by a couple driving home to Ambleside, who telephoned the school. Mrs Wivell, The Tanner and Lloydy drove over to collect us. The sixteen or so miles back to Keswick were passed in stony silence. I don't remember any punishment, but I do remember Lloydy suggesting that we should be chained to responsible girls, also that no one should go on an expedition again without twopence to telephone if we got lost.

'I remember picking soft fruit in the vicar's garden and picking hips and haws; the salmon leaping in the Greta as we walked through Fitz Park; the cedar wood shop in town and its lovely smell; the cockatoo in the aviary in the hotel gardens. I remember Daphne stuffing books and a pencil box up her knickers coming from the station classroom to the school bedroom to swot (illegal). A train had just unloaded hundreds of commandos, who had come to train in the hills. Daph's elastic gave way on the platform, showering pencils and papers everywhere, much to her embarrassment and confusion. But the soldiers loved it. Margaret Hill (Davies)

'I remember trying to persuade the hotel cat to stay just a little longer on my knees, to keep out the cold; laying pennies along the pavement in Station Road for the Wings for Victory Week mile of pennies; sitting hunched against the driving rain and eating a sodden picnic lunch; bathing in Derwentwater with the novelty of fresh water waves; the odd and unpredictable movement of the suspension bridge over the Greta.

'Best of all I remember standing in the space between the carriages on the 5am train for home, and watching the sparks fly and the undertinge of reddish gold on the steam cloud as the engine raced down Shap to Oxenholme. Rachel Nugee (Makaver).

'At one House Fancy Dress Elizabeth Hall, Susan Lloyd Williams and I dressed up effectively as Hitler Youth. Late that Saturday evening we went on to the station platform to fetch something from the form, and passengers were alarmed to see a line of goose-stepping, saluting brown shirts advancing on them. Gillian Cotgrove. (Grindley)

'I remember the awful head colds we had. We never had enough handkerchiefs so we had to wash them out ourselves and flatten them on the bedroom walls to dry. My blazer sleeves often had to catch the drips. I also remember darning and re-darning stockings and navy blue knickers until they were covered in darns.

'I loved the surroundings – seeing the hills and mountains on waking up and going to sleep. We learned Wordsworth's poems my first year for School Certificate and living in the Lake District made it so relevant. Sheila Oberdieck (Miller)

'It seemed a real adventure – coming to Keswick in September 1940. I had never seen mountains before, and found them at first quite frightening.

'I remember the warmth of Mr and Mrs Wivell, the cockatoos and other birds in the garden aviary, the fun of having lessons in a station waiting room and a hotel conservatory. I remember the countryside around the hotel – the beauty of Derwentwater and Friar's Crag, the pigs rooting wild in the woods and the excellent bacon they provided for breakfast. Nancy Pirie (Crow).

S. Katharine's College

Liverpool Institute of Higher Education

In Thy Light

1844-1994

S. KATHARINE'S COLLEGE - THE LIVERPOOL INSTITUTE OF HIGHER EDUCATION AT LIVERPOOL HOPE UNIVERSITY

'In your light we shall see the light'

College motto translated from the Latin

The College was founded in 1844 as a Church of England College for the training of women teachers at Warrington. The College transferred to Battersea in London in 1923 after a fire at Warrington and the College moved again in 1930 to new premises in Childwall, Liverpool – but still called 'Warrington Training College'. In 1938 the College was re-named S. Katharine's.

In 1939 with the outbreak of hostilities it was realised that the

College needed to relocate to a safer part of the country – and in any event the premises were requisitioned by the Ministry of Health to be converted into a hospital. Little notice was given of the take-over. A telephone call at 9.30 am on Saturday 3rd September announced that the Northern Hospital was coming 'into residence' at 10.30 am the following morning!

Arriving in Keswick, the Principal, Miss Allen, erected a notice board outside the Queen's Hotel on which was written *'S. Katharine's College, Liverpool, War Headquarters'*.

During their exile in Keswick the students were at first billeted with Keswick families, and eventually distributed over some seventeen different houses, rented by the College for use as hostels. The top floor of the Queen's Hotel became available for the use of the College in September 1939 and there the Principal gathered her staff to prepare for the arrival of furniture, goods and, of course, students. Blackout curtains were made for the Hotel windows and an inventory made of hotel property. Local craftsmen made alterations to the electrical wiring and the gas supply. In early October the first delivery of College possessions were made and stored in the large hotel garage. As new pieces of furniture arrived, that which had already been delivered had to be taken by staff, maids and volunteers to their new locations. The hotel bar became the temporary store for the College Library, the dining room was reserved for personal possessions with the main hallway and steps used to stack items ready for a handcart delivery to the various 'billets' negotiated by the Principal.

During October two of the large bedrooms were carpeted for use as lecture rooms, the dining room adapted for use as a lecture room and a library with selected books (there was not room for them all) catalogued and shelved ready for the arrival of the first students on Monday 30th October.

In the first year of the war twenty-one second year students (the College course was for the duration of two years) lived in the Hotel – they shared bedrooms with the luxury of washbasins and baths. Other rooms were used as a sick-bay and Chapel, with the Vicar of St John's Church acting as College Chaplain. For the second academic year the number of students in the hotel was reduced to eight, with the then available space being used for staff sitting rooms, additional sick rooms and a student common room. But, it appears that the resident students had to endure the sound of seemingly endless feet ascending and descending the 67 stairs for lectures. The students appreciated the common room facilities where they were able to toast bread on homemade toasting forks and hold parties. Although the hot-water system was said to be 'noisy' it was much appreciated, especially in winter when students from other 'billets' where water pipes were frozen had to go to the Hotel for bathroom facilities.

The Waverley Hotel (now the Edinburgh Woollen Mill shop) was acquired in September 1939. The kitchens and dining room at The Waverley (the building had also served as a cafe) enabled the accommodation at the Queen's Hotel to be altered for its new functions. Originally, twenty-five students were accommodated at The Waverley with shared bedrooms but no common room. Compline, the final church service of the day, had to be held by the students around the fire in the café downstairs. More hostels were found, enabling the largest bedroom to be furnished as a common room. Soon the three staff and twenty-two students were able to organise social activities – including the formation of an amateur pipe band.

Students from other hostels enjoyed meeting most of the College members at dinner in The Waverley. But, The Waverley was also used for other purposes. 'Granny' Gradidge taught needlework there. One recollection by a student was of someone singeing a garment being ironed and Miss Gradidge's comment, 'Isn't the smell of baking lovely in The Waverley'.

Burleigh Mead on The Headlands was the nearest hostel to Derwentwater. This was the residence of the Principal, the Deputy Principal and 'the senior student'. Apart from the senior student the other thirteen second year students who arrived in October 1939 shared rooms, normally three or four to a room. They felt themselves privileged because Annie, Miss Allen's own maid, looked after them also.

Like Burleigh Mead, Parkfield was built of local stone and afforded beautiful views of the lake and the mountains. This three-storied semi-detached guesthouse became the home for twelve students in September 1940, together with two wardens, a refugee Austrian housekeeper – and two kittens. The house was not fully furnished, but additional furniture and a piano arrived to help Parkfield become 'a musical hostel'. By

172

S. Katharine's College in Keswick

September in the following year Parkfield had combined with the adjoining West View to accommodate 28 students and three staff.

Millfield, a hotel on the Penrith road, was acquired. The students shared bedrooms and two common rooms, allowing a relaxed atmosphere. But, the house was not convenient for the Queen's Hotel or The Waverley, and in the summer of 1940 the College surrendered its lease to Roedean School. A young evacuee from the north-east of England remembers Millfield House being used by Roedean girls for dining, with crisp white tablecloths and sparkling table cutlery seen through the windows. Millfield is now a retirement home.

The Blencathra Hotel on Southey Street, now renamed The Easedale Hotel, housed another twenty students. The Advanced Music students at the Blencathra Hotel provided music for the Compline Service and organised a percussion band. The Common Room was also used as a lecture room. In September 1943 the Blencathra Hotel closed as a hostel and the students transferred to Northbridge House and Laburnum House, guesthouses that have since been renamed. Hostels were opened at Lynwood House and Sunnyside (Southey Street) to accommodate students who were able to use The Waverley's restaurant for meals.

173

The Terrace (Derwentwater Terrace) consisted of large boarding houses, with numbers 1, 2, 3 and 8 being used by the College. Number 1 has been renamed The Cumbria Hotel, 2 and 3 became the Chaucer House Hotel (now apartments) and Number 8 is still named Greystones. In the autumn of 1939 these four houses became home for 24 first-year students and three academic staff. The church clock chiming every quarter hour was not altogether appreciated! In the first Spring the water pipes froze, with several bursts. The students ingeniously used the contents of their hot-water bottles for their morning wash.

Frequent changes in accommodation appeared to be the rule rather than the exception, possibly driven by the varying numbers of students, and by the start of the 1940 - 1941 academic years only Number 8 The Terrace was used for six students who came late to the College. The Hollies, off High Street and The Seams, was used for housing nineteen students and two staff members from September 1940. It was described as a beautiful and convenient hostel, with flower beds, views of Skiddaw above the house tops, a large common room, kitchen, craft room and piano. In later years The Hollies became the Headquarters of the Royal Air Force Association, and eventually was converted into separate apartments with additional houses built in the grounds.

Fawe Park, surrounded by woodland and rhododendrons, was situated on the western side of the lake. It was the home of Commander and Mrs Fox. Commander Fox was a serving Naval Officer. In 1939 twenty-eight second-year students and four staff lived there. The students shared seven bedrooms, three of which contained curtained four-poster beds – the latter to be admired, not used for sleeping! On three days in the week the students travelled by bus to Keswick for lectures, using the Fawe Park drawing room for lectures on the other two days and evenings. Fawe Park had its own chapel, with candlesticks and a cross from S. Katharine's in Liverpool.

The first winter at Fawe Park was a severe one and several students took up ice-skating. One group posed for a photograph on the ice, which cracked, leaving one of the students in the water. On another occasion the water mains burst and the students had to walk into Keswick to use the Queen's Hotel facilities. The electricity supply failed on another occasion, causing some hardship to the needlework students in particular. The second winter in Keswick was so severe that buses were unable to operate and all supplies to Fawe Park had to be transported by toboggan.

Another large house, Lairthwaite (later becoming a Secondary Modern School and eventually the site of the present comprehensive school in Keswick, Keswick School) became another College hostel in September 1940. The extensive grounds, tennis court, orchard and profusion of shrubberies were most appreciated by the students. Indoors, there was a large common room and all the bedrooms had views of the lake or the mountains. The lecture room could be converted into a dance hall. Items from a 'treasure trove' in the cellars consisting of chairs, mirrors and dressing tables were taken by the students to 'beautify their rooms'.

The students at Lairthwaite were able to eat in the hostel – and the hot water system survived the worst that the cold Keswick winters could throw at it! But, one Keswick downpour lasted six weeks and six days non-stop. With the students having to walk for lectures at sites more than a mile apart, some had to change from soaking clothes to dry outfits four times in one day.

The Vicar of St John's, the Reverend Mr Mathews, Chaplain to the College, offered his Parsonage to the College. He and his housekeeper welcomed fourteen students and one staff member in September 1940. Crosthwaite Vicarage also offered accommodation to students from time to time.

In May 1944 the Church of England Central Board of Finance paid £12000 for the large mansion known as Derwent Hill at Portinscale with the expectation that S. Katharine's would lease the building, contents and grounds. It was their intention that Derwent Hill would be a permanent annexe to the Liverpool College after the war was over. This would, it was hoped, secure the now-established links with Keswick and the County of Cumberland and facilitate a special course for the training of rural teachers in addition to accommodating the increased number of students.

Derwent Hill is a stone built house, originally 18th Century but added to considerably in the 20th Century. It is situated about a mile from Keswick, with a field path leading students directly to Greta Bridge, across 'The Howrahs'.

The first group of thirty-six students moved into Derwent Hill in September 1944. They found a very comfortable house, and used the large entrance hall as a dining room, another luxurious room as a Common Room and a dark panelled room as a Chapel – formerly the billiard room. With its large gardens and ample bedrooms and lecture accommodation Derwent Hill was probably the best situated and most convenient of all the Keswick hostels. In later years, after the end of the Second World War, Derwent Hill was used by final year students and for Liverpool-based students as 'lodgings' for teaching practice in the area. The students were sad to leave Derwent Hill, and the College fought long and hard to keep it, which they did until 1962, when it was bought by the City of Sunderland for use as an Outdoor Pursuits Centre. Several students who attended S. Katharine's College in the post-war period married local men and are still living in Keswick and district.

Apart from the buildings used for hostel purposes, many other Keswick premises were used for the varied needs of the College. Art Lectures were held in the Keswick Art Gallery (part of the Museum building). The Drill Hall on Southey Street (now the home of 'The Keswick Reminder') was used appropriately enough for physical education and Fitz Park was used for games. The Keswick School of Industrial Arts showroom was used for needlework classes, weaving and other crafts. The Co-operative Hall (in St John's Street, now converted into several shops and offices) was hired for social events, including dances, musical and dramatic competitions. The Pavilion on Station Road was hired for lunches, dances and Christmas parties. From 1943, members of the armed forces stationed in the district were invited to these occasions. The Royal Oak was hired for special dinners and the Rawnsley Hall was the setting for a joint concert with pupils from Keswick and Roedean Schools for the 'Aid to Russia Week'. And, the Church of St John's was the venue for the traditional Nativity Play as well as being the major College Chapel.

During the war years the Principal tried to maintain as much of the traditions of the Liverpool College as was possible under, at times, very trying conditions. The actual task of maintaining a teacher training college in Keswick, with the number of hostels and problems of delivering the curriculum called for a high degree of organisational skill and she was to

Queen's Hotel in 1939, with Miss Tanner's Notice Board

be congratulated in achieving the success she did, along with a devoted staff. Miss Allen tried to maintain the ethos of the Liverpool campus. In theory, the students would rise at 6am, attend chapel and then have breakfast. Lectures were from 9 am to 1 pm, with a mid-morning break. Generally, the afternoons were free, apart from school visits once a week, but with more lectures from 5pm to 7 pm following afternoon tea. Then students were given half-an-hour to change before a formal dinner at 7pm. After dinner the students attended a Compline Service followed by a study period from 9 pm to 10 pm. In Keswick, Saturday morning lectures in speech training were abandoned to enable the students to 'explore the beauties of Lakeland'. Sunday was a day of worship and rest.

The subjects remained as they had been at Liverpool, but the organisation of lectures gave problems in that students often had to walk over a mile from one lecture to the next, whatever the weather. Exceptional weather, especially in winter, created havoc with organisation, but both the staff and students appeared to overcome the

Student Teacher Lucretia Odensi pond-dipping
with St. John's School girls including evacuees

sometimes severe difficulties.

From the moment hostilities ceased the College contemplated their return to Liverpool and their solicitors were instructed to terminate the various leases, but in 1946 the tenancies had to be extended and even more premises obtained for temporary occupation. In addition, The Towers and The Gables at Portinscale, near to Derwent Hill, were leased for longer-term occupation from September 1946. It appears that the second year students living in Keswick were pursuing advanced courses in geography and biology, subjects appropriate to their surroundings. Later, the Derwentwater Hotel in Portinscale was used during the winter, when it was closed for visitors, for extra accommodation. The Keswick 'Annexe' was under the control of the 'Keswick Vice-Principal', a Miss Trueman.

The College re-assembled in Liverpool for the first time after the war on 28th January 1947, the beginning of the Easter Term, but still maintaining a definite 'Keswick connection' at Derwent Hill.

During the war years teaching practice was held in schools ranging from Whitehaven in the west to Carlisle in the north, Penrith in the east and Ambleside in the south, in addition to Keswick. The then railway line, the Cockermouth, Keswick & Penrith Railway, was much used for transport for school practice. Many older Keswick residents will remember the teaching practice sessions by the purple-clad students, armed with the visual aids and other equipment they had prepared in the hostels ready for the week or more spent in Keswick Schools. And, of course, many of the children they were teaching were evacuees themselves.

Dr Hollinshead's account ends with these words:

'Evacuees, both staff and students, entertain very warm memories of the Lake District, its people, and the war years. They wax eloquent on the spectacular beauty of Lakeland, and the kindness, tolerance and hospitality of the people of Keswick and their fellow refugees, and of the new closeness and camaraderie of the hostel groups and of staff and students in relation to one another. The 'students' were first so called in the Executive Council Minutes in May 1945; until then they were referred to as 'pupils'! All felt that the War pulled down barriers and created a unique sense of unity among people who were equally frightened, equally homesick, and equally determined to win through to the end'.

This summary of the activities of S. Katharine's College in wartime Keswick has been largely adapted, with thanks, from 'In Thy Light: S. Katharine's College 1844 – 1994' by Dr Janet E. Hollinshead, 1994.

The exhilaration of skating across the lake to Fawe Park

JOAN BERRY, MANCHESTER
S. Katharine's College

I read in 'The Reminder' that the Keswick Museum had assembled a file of evacuees' experiences in Keswick and so in October this year, while staying in the town, I headed in that direction. When I mentioned my mission to the Curator, he asked which years I was in College and on hearing the dates he indicated where the file could be found and added, "I think you will be surprised." The 'surprise' was a contemporary of mine with the file open on her lap: Joan Kirkham. We had not known each other in College but our shared experiences led to a stirring of memories with an hour-long flow of chat. When Joan and her daughter left, the latter told the Curator it was a pity a tape-recorder had not been available.

When I read the articles in the file, I marvelled at the details of names and times. My memories are mainly a series of anecdotes, but in contrast to the student who spent a miserable first year, rarely a day passed in my two year College-cum-Keswick life without my feeling a sense of wonder at my luck.

Several weeks into the term, I arrived in Keswick in October 1941, because, having applied for the following year, I received a telegram asking if I could go at once. After a serious illness when I was in the Sixth Form at school, I had spent a "gap year" in the Public Complaints Office of the L.M.S. Railway Company in Manchester, working with six men, where I sharpened my wits in their company and learnt useful skills in dealing with a critical public, but as I sat in the train I wondered whether I would cope with academic work again and if I would feel friendless in view of many relationships having been established already. Even so, the prospect of living in Keswick through the changing seasons when, previously a week's holiday had been my lot, was uppermost in my mind.

In the event, I felt that those of us who went to College not directly from school – unless it had been a boarding school – settled more easily into our new life. For the boarders used to communal living, it was more of the same, whereas some of those recently at day schools and eagerly anticipating independence, found it surprisingly pitted with difficulties: homesickness, the give and take of shared living, trivial regulations and the self-discipline of organising personal work schedules. The Senior Student, Edna Dowling, in her late twenties and having worked in a Lancashire mill, said that she could laugh at or shrug off, the nannying and petty rules in view of the many benefits offered by College and Keswick. I felt the same – though it did not stop us from trying to amend a directive now and again.

Any new term started with handing in a Health Certificate and having one's weight recorded by a very small but intimidating Sister. Once I forgot my Health Certificate – I rang my parents from Preston Station to send it as soon as possible – and had to report to the Principal Miss Allen regarding its non-appearance. This was not a formality: I entered her room nervously and stood to receive a severe reprimand for irresponsibility. When I mentioned that both my maternal grandparents had died during the holiday, the tenor of the interview changed and concluded with warm expressions of sympathy that were almost sentimental. This contrasted with her response to Benita Hyam's request to observe a Jewish festival: she was reminded that she was at a Church of England College. While appreciating Miss Allen's brilliant mind and her accomplishments in organising the transfer of St. Katharine's from Liverpool to Keswick, neither my friends nor I felt we knew her as a person.

Apart from the Health Certificate incident, I spoke to her three times: Once when summoned for a misdemeanour, again to ask for 'Late Leave' and finally to be handed a reference when I was leaving.

First, the misdemeanour. My roommate and friend at Parkfield West View, in my first year, was Joyce Green from Blackpool. One Friday evening she suggested that we should skip Late Prep. from 5.00 pm. to 7.00 pm. It was the one-day of the week that we did not have lectures at that time; instead we dispersed to hostels for two hours study in the Common Rooms. The day had been wintry, the week humdrum and we needed a boost. It would never have entered our heads to nip into The George, but the temptation of ham and chips, with bread, butter and tea at Friar's Café was irresistible. The food and the café appealed equally:

181

Friar's had the charm of an old-fashioned teashop, whereas The Waverley, at the foot of Main Street where we ate with College, was necessarily basic. (Other ham and chips places that we patronised were Swinside Lodge and one of the farms at Watendlath.)

As we started to eat, feeling more cheerful already, the door of the café opened to admit Miss Gill, our hostel warden and Pam Bell, a clever second year, who had that day taken scholarship papers for a place at one of the London University Colleges. My instinct was to run for it but Joyce, with a steadier nerve than mine, protested that we could not leave good food, and, in any event, Miss Gill must have seen us. It would be interesting, she added, to observe whether Pam's post-exam treat matched our end-of-week one. We took some satisfaction from noting scones and jam at the other table.

The next we heard of the matter was at the following Monday's Assembly, held in the former dining room at Queen's Hotel, when the two students who had been in Friar's Café on Friday evening were asked to report to Miss Allen, which we did. We resented the fact that Miss Gill had not mentioned to us, as a matter of courtesy, that she had reported us to the Principal. After all, we lived under the same roof.

When my boyfriend, John Berry, serving in the Royal Artillery and stationed in North Yorkshire, stayed at the George Hotel for part of his leave, I asked Miss Allen for 'Late Leave' – 9.30 p.m. on Saturday and Sunday, the only days for which it could be granted. Her questions were: 1) did my mother know John? 2) did she know of this visit? 3) would I be alone with him?

Having come from Catterick Camp, where he was sleeping in sub-zero temperatures on a training exercise and bumping over the North Yorkshire moors, tapping out Morse in the back of a truck, with rifle-shooting and bayonet practice in between, he found it astonishing that we were so cocooned. The line of questioning and the 9.30 p.m. deadline led to an outburst of Army language.

Others have referred to officers at a nearby training camp being invited to dances but in my two years, there was no such contact. (Was it perhaps an arrangement for the group at Fawe Park?) The only eligible male we saw as we walked up and down Main Street was known as the Pot Shop Boy because he stood outside his family's china shop. It was not long before his eye fell on Gwyneth Rowlands, an auburn-haired, pale-skinned beauty: they had a brief romance.

As for the lecturers, only Mrs Berrie was married. She was Deputy Warden at Lairthwaite, where I spent my second year and when her husband came on leave, she told us in a sort of excited whisper, "Remember, girls, there's a man in the house", reminding us, I suppose, not to wander to the bathroom scantily clad.

Our single-sex social activities flourished. College arranged a memorable St. Katharine's Day dinner at the Royal Oak in alternate years. We dressed in our best, defying the introduction of clothing coupons. Few of us visited hairdressers in term-time; instead, we cut the tops off our stockings, stretched the bands round our heads and tucked our hair into a roll over them. We went as a body to special showings of 'Bambi' and 'Fantasia' at the Pavilion and to a Denis Matthews piano recital at Rawnsley Hall. Great rivalry between hostels in the Music and Drama Competitions led to frenzied yet hilarious rehearsals. Lairthwaite won the 1943 Drama contest, with a production of Frank Sladen-Smith's 'The Invisible Duke' but our celebrations were short-lived because Mock Finals started two days later.

At Lairthwaite, the large lecture room, probably the previous owner's ballroom, served as a less glamorous substitute for us. Mary Blackhall, my close friend, was the only pianist in the group; so she was called on to provide the music while we danced. She responded cheerfully but remarked ruefully once or twice that she wished she had never mentioned that she played the piano. In December 1942, the Vicar of Crosthwaite invited Lairthwaite residents to a party at the Vicarage. A jolly affair with old-fashioned games.

Roedean, evacuated to the Keswick Hotel, asked any Lacrosse players to join them in the afternoons on Fitz Park but although I had been considered a reasonable performer at school, I was completely out-played by those boarding school girls and consequently only turned up twice. We were a match for them at tennis, however. We played on the shale courts in the park, which were remarkably well kept, notwithstanding the war.

We did not need to be games players to keep fit. Fresh air and exercise figured in our daily routine, as hostels, lecture venues and churches were scattered across town. Queen's Hotel, with numerous lecture rooms and College H.Q., was the centre of our activities. Everyone, except those living at Fawe Park and Lairthwaite, assembled at Waverley four times a day to be fed; we hiked up the hill to St. John's for compline and sometimes in the mornings too; dispersed to the Museum for Art, to the Industrial Arts Centre near Greta Bridge for Needlework and Handwork; to the Drill Hall in Southey Street for P.E. and to Lairthwaite for one lecture a week.

We filled our leisure time with outdoor activities. At least, most of us did: there were a few people who seemed oblivious to the appeal of our surroundings. Free afternoons between lunchtime and resumption of lectures at 5.00 p.m., were there to be filled. Before we were allowed to take out a boat on Derwentwater, we had to be able to swim and to pass a rowing test, the first element of which was to manoeuvre the Fawe Park boat out of the boathouse, watched by Miss Caughey, the P.E Lecturer. As we covered a short stretch of water, she noted how we handled the oars and turned the boat around, after which the freedom of the lake was ours. The islands fascinated us and we circled them many times, trying to imagine life in the grand house on Derwent Isle and delighted by the primroses and wild daffodils on Lord's Island.

In January to February 1942, the lake froze and we spent hours by the boat landings, day after day. I wrote home for my skates, which I had only worn previously at Manchester Ice Palace, never out of doors. The exhilaration of skating across the lake to Fawe Park, with the sun shining from blue skies and the mountains snow-capped, could be one of those definitions of happiness we often seek. Friends clamoured to borrow my skates, which I lent not quite readily because my feet are size eights and I feared for the ankles of those wobbling on the ice in ill-fitting boots. Most of them resumed sliding after a brief attempt at skating.

We cycled, too; round Derwentwater and Bassenthwaite, along Newlands Valley, into Borrowdale and once to Caldbeck to see John Peel's grave. On one ride round Bassenthwaite we spotted a large patch of snowdrops on the grass by the road and we dismounted to marvel at our first sight of these flowers in the wild.

Those of us who had walked and climbed in the Lake District on holiday got out our maps – those nice pre-war linen ones – and found newcomers to the area keen to join us on our Saturday expeditions. So we tackled Walla Crag, Grange Fell to Watendlath, Catbells, Grisedale, Skiddaw and Causey in my first year and some of them again in Year Two, when our enthusiasm brushed off on our juniors at Lairthwaite. Being a 'feisty lot' they were soon urging us to try something more challenging, so, one day in late autumn, we climbed Great Gable via Sty Head. As we descended on the Green Gable route, a mist swirled round us – it had been clear at the summit – and we lost the path; our compass reassured us that we were heading in the right direction but we covered the ground slowly. By the time we had reached the valley, walking briskly now towards Seatoller, dusk was falling and our watches told us that we had missed the bus that would have got us back to Keswick in time for supper. From a phone box near Seatoller, I rang Miss Holford, informing her that we were all right but faced a two-hour wait for the next bus. "Indeed you don't," was her reply. "You start walking immediately." For once, the Borrowdale Valley held no appeal. As we approached Rosthwaite, two cars came up behind us. We stuck out our thumbs. They stopped and the seven of us piled in for a speedy drive to Keswick. Miss Holford registered surprise and relief: she had kept our food warm and arranged for hot water bottles to be put in our beds. No wonder she ran a happy house.

Joyce and I had our sights set on Saddleback – a first for both of us – and we chose a bleak but clear early spring Saturday for the venture. We took a bus to Threlkeld, and then started to climb towards one of the ridges that led to the summit. Picking our way along the steep and stony path meant that we moved at snail's speed with frequent rests, so by the time we reached the fearsome stretch of ridge, we were tired and cold. A strong wind had sprung up, which caused us to advance almost on all fours to keep our balance in the buffeting. I don't know which of us said it but the words had been running through my head for some time: "This is crazy. Let's turn back". We retreated to a pub in Threlkeld, frustrated and cross with ourselves, yet relieved to be eating our sandwiches by a log fire and warming our hands on mugs of tea.

College food kept us healthy; we grumbled of course. I liked prunes; a regular dessert with watery custard but many did not and heaped them on to my plate. Rice pudding topped with a blob of flavourless red jam or a thin slice of jam tart made a change. We ate a lot of mince and spam. Miss Yeoman, housekeeper at Lairthwaite, where we thought the food was better than in the main College dining room, made an excellent vegetable pie and did wonders with our cheese ration. Our one egg per week was boiled. Parcels from home brought plain cakes, which we ate for Sunday tea (we were responsible for providing our own) and at bedtime, the only two occasions when we were allowed to use hostel kitchens. Some of us packed a jar of dripping at the start of each term, to eat with toast for Sunday tea. On teaching practice in Carlisle we ate in a British Restaurant - our vouchers provided by College. These wartime institutions were basic in structure, furnishings and food.

Minor irritations could become matters for indignation. We did not like to be addressed as 'Miss' by staff, or to be told that First Years must call Second Years 'Miss' when speaking directly to them and when referring to them in conversations with staff. The seniors we knew well told us to dispense with the title when with them but in all other circumstances the rules applied. In my second year at Lairthwaite, with thirty girls from both years living, sleeping and eating under one roof, it seemed a nonsense to observe such formalities, so we used Christian names from early in the term.

The bath rota came as something of a shock: once a week in water at the wartime level of five inches and not always hot at that.

Those of us brought up as Methodists, accustomed to attending Chapel hatless, wondered at the insistence of hats in Church. If we forgot our hats we were not allowed into Compline and often Miss Allen stood near the door to enforce this rule. I had a woolly cap that stayed folded in my pocket until I reached the Church porch. We were slow to adjust to 'the always once and sometimes twice a day' services at St. John's. At home, we had been Sunday Churchgoers and questioned the time spent coming, going and attending so frequently but came to accept it, grudgingly, as probably customary at Church of England Colleges.

Stockings were another aggravation. Before coming to College, girls of our age often went around in daytime with bare legs, keeping our stockings for best wear. Clothing coupons were precious. We accepted that stockings should be worn with skirts, blouses and ties on Teaching Practice but as we watched bare-legged holiday makers and local girls passing 'Queen's' there was resentment that we had to wear them at all times, even with summer dresses.

Miss Butcher, Warden at Blencathra in Southey Street, called my year to a meeting in the summer term when we were about to vote for the next Senior Student. It had come to her notice that some of us – she would not mention names – had been electioneering, a practice that was deplored at St. Katharine's. Indeed, it would not be tolerated and must not happen again. We were flabbergasted.

At the same time, we were asked to submit our choice of Second Year hostels, along with the names of friends with whom we should like to share a room. The Parsonage, a spacious house in a convenient situation with no lecturers in residence, attracted many of us but was open only to those who had been confirmed.

During my first term an incident at my hostel introduced me to a new word. Brought up in a small Lancashire town by Methodist parents, I had never heard of 'lesbians'. I was nineteen and not alone in the house in this lack of knowledge. As I walked to Queen's with a student living in the room above ours, she told me that her room-mate had moved out, except for leaving some of her belongings in drawers and a wardrobe and joined a Second Year, who had single accommodation on the ground floor. She stayed there for the rest of the year and the pair were very open in their displays of affection.

I have barely touched on the Course. We took two academic subjects. Mine were English at Advanced Level and History at Ordinary Level. An A level in History was necessary for the advanced group. Everyone took Art or Music and Needlework. The professional subjects comprised Principles and Practice of Teaching, including Psychology, Hygiene and Physical Training.

Standards were high. We worked hard but had time always for personal leisure pursuits. In addition to the Course, College arranged outside speakers of note to broaden our areas of knowledge. Dr Viola, a Child Art Specialist and refugee from Austria, held our attention from his first sentence as he looked out over a sea of purple blazers: "I must start by admitting that purple is my least favourite colour." Someone involved in the production of the Beveridge Report told us of the plans for social legislation in the future; it could have been Beveridge himself. Dr

Elizabeth Clark, a writer of storybooks for young children, gave us a lesson in the art of storytelling, relating a tale from one of her books, and then asked if anyone could repeat it. Kathleen Windle stood up and retold it almost word for word.

The most stressful period of each year was the month of Teaching Practice. Finding places for 80+ girls to teach must have been a mammoth task, considering the isolated situation and the size of Keswick. In the first year, a double-decker bus took many of us to Carlisle, some of whom stood on the open deck at the back, trying to keep down their early breakfasts. I wondered why we were not asked if we had a serious travel-sickness problem but perhaps students economical with the truth would have seized the opportunity to teach locally. Schools in Keswick and nearby villages were used; I can't remember whether anyone went to Penrith. Although we taught a limited number of lessons, those of us who travelled found the days exhausting. We had not a minute to ourselves. Back at the hostel, after a hasty supper, we wrote an assessment of that day's teaching before preparing the next day's lessons with their accompanying materials for models and drawings and paintings as illustrations. The most laborious task involved worksheets. In a sort of Swiss roll tin containing jelly, we put, face down, a sheet written out in special ink, peeled it off, then made the necessary number of copies, often smudgy. Mary and I bought a jar of Robeline, a sort of sticky malt, to sustain us. Ashley Street Girl's School, in a deprived part of Carlisle, where I taught a class of 13 to 14 year olds, gave me an easy introduction to teaching. The Head Mistress started the Lord's Prayer at Morning Assembly with a brisk 1-2-3, which indicated that she ran a tight ship.

Second year Teaching Practice was timed for the last month of the spring term. Those of us travelling to Cockermouth, Workington and Whitehaven caught the coach to Keswick Station, when it was barely light. The train took us to Cockermouth, where we changed trains for Workington, where buses were waiting to drop off students at Workington schools and to take the rest of us some miles further to Whitehaven. As we assembled on Keswick station, we peered through the half-light to see which lecturers were travelling with us to observe our lessons: only students with a dramatic flair enjoyed this audience of one. Each of us had a personal supervisor but Art, Music and P.T. had to be assessed as

188

well. I had a lively class of 8 – 9 year-olds at Bransty School on the edge of a Council Estate, which had become run-down with the collapse of the mining industry before the war. The unemployed became soldiers; the Estate was taking a pride in itself once more and the children were delightful.

On Saturdays, we met lecturers to discuss the week's ups and downs and to prepare for the week ahead. People often returned to the hostel depressed. At Lairthwaite, in addition to Compline, we had First Years who gave their time most generously to help with our evening preparations and some got up early to stand on the railings that separated Lairthwaite from the railway line to wave to us as the train passed. Sounds quaint now, but we liked it.

We seemed to take exams in our stride. When the sweet-scented yellow azaleas flower in my garden, I think of those days in June 1943 when I sat on the lawn by the bank of azaleas in Lairthwaite gardens, a pile of books by my side, awaiting revision.

Residents of Keswick must have felt overwhelmed by the arrival of wartime evacuees. We were made welcome and I hope that we gave something back. I think we did. Some students ran a playgroup for young evacuees on Saturday mornings and the College choir performed at local functions. Schools benefited when our lecturers took stimulating demonstration lessons; those same schools received Students for Teaching Practice, when established staff helping the trainees would perhaps pick up one or two new ideas. Members of the Student Christian Movement volunteered to help in any way they could at St. John's; that meant cleaning the Church sometimes. We spent money on books from Chaplin's, cakes from Birkett's, art materials from Mayson's and so on. The boatmen were glad of our custom and so, I presume, was the laundry (wherever it was) where we sent sheets, pillowcases and towels once a fortnight. The Post Office despatched personal items of clothing for washing to our homes: the hostels had no facilities for us to deal with them, so we brought brown paper and string at the beginning of term. College hired buses to ferry Fawe Park girls in and out of Keswick and for Teaching Practice. Visiting parents, siblings and boyfriends booked in at hotels and guest houses and we ate ham and chips whenever we could get them.

An earlier contributor mentioned not remembering names of lecturers, so I will list those I remember to jog the memory of any future reader.

I have referred to Miss Allen (Tilly), a Divinity Specialist. She lived at Burleigh Mead on The Heads, where a few students were resident. It was not a popular venue - who wants to live with The Boss? Her companion, Miss Evetts (Little E), played little part in College life - she and I never met.

Miss Williams (Big Bill), Maths and Fawe Park, large and jolly, told us of her mother going to Cambridge before women were awarded full degrees, then facing criticism because she did not take a paid job but she had thirteen – I think that is right – children, each of whom went to University. With her at Fawe Park was Miss Clarkson (Clarkie) – slight and unworldly, responsible for Principles and Practice of Teaching, including Psychology. They were great friends. Miss Caughey, the P.T. Lecturer, lived with them. She had the foresight to realise that some of us would be taking jobs in schools where male teachers were serving in the Forces, so she taught us the rules of football, which we put into practice in Fitz Park.

Miss Gill (Little Gill) – small, round and grey haired, with a must-have-been-pretty-when-young face, looked after us at Parkfield/West View in my first year. I say 'looked after' but she kept a low profile in the house. After our encounter in Friar's, I think that she had reservations about Joyce and me. Out of the blue, she called me a rebel when I was sitting next to her at supper one evening. History – her subject – was also mine. Subjects taken at Ordinary Level merited a Credit for a mark above 70%, whereas the same mark earned a Distinction at Advanced Level. I hope that she was pleased when I got the only Credit in the group: she wrote to congratulate me, mentioning in passing that I had only achieved it by a margin of one mark. Her lectures were always interesting and meticulously prepared and her comments on essays a reward for one's work. Her Deputy Warden, Miss Charlesworth (Charlie), a strongly built, no-nonsense Scientist, had a Lancashire accent, similar to many of ours.

In the upstairs room at the Keswick Industrial Arts, near Greta Bridge, Miss Gradidge (Granny Grad) taught needlework. Her job was made difficult by wartime constraints. I parted with precious clothing coupons for a length of peach-coloured rayon, a difficult material to convert into cami-knickers and slip.

At the same venue, Miss Taylor (Birdie Tweet), homespun from head to foot, took us from plaiting to weaving, ultimately on a large loom at which we worked in pairs. My partner, Kathleen Davis, and I wove diligently at our weekly lessons but never felt drawn to the building in our spare time, which caused Miss Taylor to accuse us of living in Arcadia, if we imagined that we could produce a piece of cloth with so little effort. Another exercise involved collecting fleece from the hedgerows, carding, combing, spinning and dyeing it, then knitting a rather knobbly glove. Miss T was Warden at No. 8, The Terrace.

Miss Butcher's Art Classes were held in the Museum, where we learnt and practised skills that were to be useful in the classroom. Joining the Art Group was Hobson's Choice for some of us: we were not talented artists but had even less aptitude for Music, so we appreciated Miss Butcher's practical approach; we did stick and potato printing, making patterns, both geometric and from leaves, flowers etc., and calligraphy. Nevertheless, we were expected to produce pieces of work to show what talent we had. I painted the staircase at Lairthwaite and a heron with a fish in his beak – at that time an exhibit in the Museum but I could not find him on my recent visit. Blencathra, in Southey Street, was a large hostel in Miss Butcher's care (Butch her nickname).

Miss Dobson (Dolly Dobbs), whose subject was Divinity, prepared every student for the Archbishop's Certificate. Her hostel, The Hollies, was very popular.

Miss Brookes, Advanced English – angular, stooping and scholarly, with a grating voice – told us more than once that music, to her, was just a pleasant kind of noise. The Course ranged widely from Bacon's Essays to Galsworthy's Social Problem plays. I cannot remember if she had a hostel. Loopy Loo was her nickname.

Although she never taught me, (she was a Geographer) Miss Warren (Bunny), Warden at Lynwood on Ambleside Road, steered me through Final Teaching Practice with morale-boosting humour. We got on famously. Eton-cropped, slim, smartly–suited, she seemed an appropriate, no, an essential friend for Miss Johnson (Johnny) – her co-warden and music lecturer, who was both disorganised and dishevelled.

Mrs Berrie (Winnie), recently married and younger than most of the staff, looked girlish in pretty blouses and trim skirts. Her subject was English (Cambridge Degree) with some Speech Training but my only contact with her was at Laithwate, where she was Deputy Warden. Her love of Keswick kept her there for life. When Boyd was demobbed, they bought a house in Rogerfield. He worked in a local bank initially and their two children were reared in the town.

Miss Holford (Lizzie) of the big-toothed smile, Education and Psychology lecturer for those training to teach infants, ran Lairthwaite in a mature and independent way, never intrusive, always observant. Her attitude to the men in our lives differed from Miss Allen's, although the 9.30 p.m. deadline applied, instead of hollow questions, she invited me to bring John for a cup of tea in her elegant sitting room. Some first-years were thrown together in a bedroom for six and found sharing one of several difficult elements in a world of new experiences. Finally, we were all called into the sitting room where Miss Holford, during an understanding talk, said; "I really don't know how you expect us to win the war when you are fighting among yourselves here". We laughed, she laughed and they lived happily ever after.

She told us that the view over Lairthwaite grounds to the mountains more than compensated for having to share the house with thirty noisy students. Twenty years after I left College, she wrote that, notwithstanding having travelled widely, Keswick was still her favourite place. When she retired early, she joined Dr Bullen, a former St. Katharine's lecturer, who had opened a small boarding school for delinquent children in East Grinstead.

Earlier writers have mentioned their lasting love of Keswick; we came as evacuees and we have returned again and again. Two years after leaving College, I married my 'Late Leave' boyfriend and as soon as our daughters (born 1949 and 1950) were on their feet, they were directed towards the fells. We wanted a base in the area and so we bought a caravan, which the Huttons at Springs Farm let us site on their land. One daughter married a clergyman. As they would never have a home of their own on the job, they had no hesitation in choosing Keswick as the place to start buying their 'real home' in Brundholme Gardens in 1978. They head north from Essex whenever they can and they, with their two mid-twenties offspring, climb the same fells that my St. Katharine's friends and I did in 1941 – 1943. It was from their house that I walked to the Museum to read what my fellow evacuees had to say.

Joan Berry wrote in 2009: In a five-year teaching career I taught in a primary school in a desperately poor area of Manchester, English in a Secondary Modern Boys' School in Worsley, followed by "special needs" children and then the "Scholarship Class' at the local Methodist Primary School.

Although I never returned to teaching after my daughters were born, I served as Governor at the above Secondary Modern for twenty years and at the Methodist Primary School for twenty-five years. As a volunteer, I taught illiterate adults and did a long stint on the Bench, including much juvenile work.

The link with education continued when one daughter became a headmistress and the other Editor of the Times Educational Supplement. The Keswick connection continues; the latter, with her clergyman husband, bought a house in the town in 1978, which they regard as 'home'.

Lectures, work, fun and companionship!
MARJORIE FAULKNER, MANSFIELD
S. Katharine's College

It was inevitable that I should choose S. Katharine's College which was still evacuated to Keswick for a while after the war ended. I had been born in Cockermouth and spent my early Primary School life in Cumbria until our family moved into Nottinghamshire.

My first hostel was the Queen's Hotel. I met Anne Singleton who became my room-mate and great friend until she died in 2002. Her elder daughter Joanna is my dear God-daughter.

After a year at Queen's our group were transferred to Fawe Park where we were welcomed by Commander and Mrs Fox. With three colleagues I enjoyed the wonderful views of Derwentwater from the "Long Room".

My memories of Keswick are many and very varied. Mealtimes at "Waverley", lectures at Lairthwaite, games in Fitz Park, P.E. in the Drill Hall, services at St. John's Church, lesson observations at Crosthwaite and St. John's Schools and teaching practice at Cockermouth. A very vivid memory is a sermon preached by the Bishop of Liverpool on the text, "I can do all things through Christ who strengthens me" (Philippians Chapter 4, Verse 13). It has been an inspiration and strength to me throughout my long and happy career. In December 1946 we bid a sad farewell to Keswick and in January 1947 the College returned to Liverpool where we settled into a life of lectures, work and lots of fun and companionship with all students living on one campus. Then came the ultimate final exams and teaching practice.

In September 1947 I began my teaching career in Nottinghamshire, first of all in two primary schools. Then I was very fortunate to become Headteacher of the school at the famous Harlow Wood Orthopaedic Hospital which was situated in the wooded countryside north of Nottingham. It was a very interesting and absorbing life helping to continue the education of long-stay specialist orthopaedic cases from many parts of England and also being able to contact or visit other

194

Hospital Schools in the country.

Now in retirement I am a Governor at my Church Primary School and also a volunteer at the local Hospice. I am a Past-President of our local Ladies' Probus Group, keep in touch with other "old girls" of S. Kath's College – and receive "The Keswick Reminder" by post each week!

So, my memories of S. Katharine's are happy days in Keswick and Liverpool and a fulfilling teaching career.

The Liverpool students missed the ships' sirens on the Mersey

MOIRA HEWITT, WIGAN
S. Katharine's College

Moira's reminiscences have been edited. The complete transcript may be seen at the Keswick Museum. Moira's elder sister preceded her at S. Katharine's College in Keswick, attending from 1939 to 1941.

I don't remember my first journey to Keswick; but on subsequent ones several girls from the Wigan area met at Wigan North-West station and were joined by others from St. Helen's. As we made friends with girls from other areas, we would look out for them at Preston and Penrith.

Most of our luggage, which had to include a Concise Oxford Dictionary, a complete Shakespeare and a Bible, had gone in advance. We had to send a painted orange box, with a curtain in front, which was used as a bedside cabinet in which to store our books.

As well as a list of books that were needed, we were sent a list of clothes. These included P.E. kit, but because of clothes rationing the college uniform could not be enforced. Most students used their old school uniforms. I was lucky because my sister's purple tunic and purple and white striped blouses had been saved for me. I had a college blazer.

I seem to remember that amongst the list of necessities was a dress for S. Katharine's Day dinner, a travelling rug and a warm dressing gown. The last two proved to be a great comfort in the cold January of 1945.

On arrival at Keswick Station we were met by 2nd year students from our hostels. One took me to 'Lingmell', now 'The Crow Park Hotel', on The Heads.

On the day after our arrival all 1st year students assembled while Miss Allen read out the groups that we had been put into, and the subjects we were taking.

I considered myself lucky to be at 'Lingmell', as our meals were provided there. The owners of the house, Mr and Mrs Aston, must have lived in back rooms. Only occasionally did we see them going out. They had a gift and fancy goods shop in the arcade off Station Street – not used by students – too expensive.

Very few students could afford to go to hairdressers. At 'Lingmell' we were supposed to wash our hair on Saturday afternoons at an old brown sink in one of the basement rooms, so as not to clog up the wash bowls in our rooms. With thirty-four students, two lecturers and a housekeeper, there was never much hot water for washing and bathing.

The view from our back bedroom was of Skiddaw, and that first term it was almost always completely shrouded in mist. Some days the mist would rise a little, and reveal a scattering of snow, and then descend again. There were also gales and driving rain, and we got very wet going to and from 'Lingmell' to various lecture venues in Keswick, and to S. John's Church for Morning Prayer and Compline.

I had three raincoats of different types – one was a waterproof cape – and some days all three would get wet, and would be hung in a basement room to drip. Someone said that we had five fine days that term.

My two room-mates became very homesick. A lot of the Liverpool students were affected. They missed the ships' sirens on the Mersey. Some felt claustrophobic amongst the mountains. A walk to the Stone Circle to look towards Penrith and see the way out cheered them.

January 1945 was very cold. There was snow and the lake froze round the boat landings and in Calf Close Bay. Attempts to keep open a passage for the boat to the island failed. It was possible to walk across.

One night several of us walked to Friar's Crag in the snow, and I shall never forget it. The sky looked like dark blue velvet and the stars seemed to be hanging in it – no light pollution!

Our room, with that big bay window, was terribly cold. I tried to fill my fountain pen from my bottle of ink. It wouldn't fill so, thinking there wasn't enough ink left, I bought another bottle. When the thaw came, I filled my pen successfully from the first bottle. It must have been frozen! That's when the dressing gown and travelling rug were such a comfort.

A notice board in the common room was filled with lists – rotas for baths (one per week), those going out for study hour, and those responsible for rousing the household at 7.00 am. When it was the turn of one girl on the 2nd floor, she did this very successfully by accidentally kicking her stone hot water bottle out of bed in her anxiety to get up promptly.

197

Our first teaching practice was in the summer term. Mine was at Lowther Street School – a junior school in Carlisle. The last time I was there the school building was used for some other educational purpose.

While on school practice, students from 'Lingmell' had to go to The Waverley Hotel for breakfast. We set off by special bus from the Moot Hall about 8.0 am. I think the children were third year junior. The only reading books were ancient, some of the desks were long ones without backs to the seats, and the teachers announced with pride that they had not used the P.E. equipment since the last students were there. Balls, hoops, skipping ropes, etc, used for the 1933 P.T. syllabus were in excellent condition, but the children had to be taught what to do with them. A question often asked of the P.T. teacher was – Is any benefit to be gained from doing rhythmic jumps in clogs on a dirt playground?

We were picked up by coach about 4.30 pm. Dinner at 'Lingmell' was at 7.00 pm. Every other evening the bus returned via Wigton to fill up with petrol at the bus depot, where the smell of petrol was terrible. This added several miles to our journey. During the whole month of teaching practice I felt travel sick, in spite of having got pills from a chemist.

While we were on teaching practice the war in Europe ended, and we had a two-day holiday – V.E. days. The evening before the holidays, we threatened to kill the bus driver if he went via Wigton. He didn't! On the way back to Keswick I remember seeing the flag flying at Crosthwaite Church, and being so thankful that the war was over. We had no access to a radio to hear the news, and very few could afford to buy a newspaper. One girl at 'Lingmell' used to buy 'The News of the World' on Sundays and distribute pages round the common room.

We used to stand outside cottages with doors and windows onto the streets and listen to the news. It must have been between 9.30 pm and 10.00 pm, after study hour.

On V.E. Day Miss Stott provided a radio for the common room – just to hear a speech in the afternoon. I can't remember whether it was the King or Winston Churchill. We started to dance to some music which followed the speech, and Miss Stott immediately removed the radio.

A bonfire had been prepared on top of Latrigg. S. Katharine's students were not allowed to go, but I believe Roedean students went.

There was a Victory Dance in the Pavilion. Students could go but had to be back in hostels by midnight. Very few could afford the five shillings to attend.

One girl went up Latrigg, failed to return by midnight and was threatened with being "sent down". Miss Allen's threatening remark was always, "You may pack your bags and go!"

Each year there was a college dance at the Pavilion. It finished at midnight, but Miss Stott the Warden insisted that those from her hostel had to be in at 12 midnight. So students from Lingmell had to leave the ball early before the clock struck 12 – like Cinderella.

Most of us got only 5 or 10 shillings per week pocket money. File paper and essay paper bought from Chaplin's cost 9d for twenty-five sheets which could soon be used up if any essay took 4 – 5 sheets.

Each month we bought our sweet ration, which was quite generous. Perhaps because our food was short of sugar, I felt I needed chocolate, and think I ate more than at any other time in my life. Occasionally oranges that we could buy arrived unexpectedly. I was too old for bananas! Each month we were given our soap coupons. Some girls sent soap and washing powder home. There was postage to pay for letters, and some girls sent their personal washing home. I used the Keswick Laundry, and my washing had to be taken to the Queen's Hotel, and collected from there. Laundering of our clothes, bedding and towels was the students' responsibility. Fortunately bread and cakes were not rationed while I was at college, so we were able to buy buns and cakes when finances allowed.

We all had little jars for our butter, sugar, jam and margarine rations. Some was kept for cooking of course. Rations were put out each week. When my sister was at Fawe Park, naughty Squirrel Nutkin got into the dining room, and helped himself to someone's butter.

By the end of term, most of us were broke and sometimes a library levy of 3d for lost books was the last straw! Some girls would try to sell stamps for the bus fare from their nearest railway station to their homes.

We were expected to go to church on Sunday. I was one of those who went to Crosthwaite for Matins. Roedean School girls went to Crosthwaite Church two by two in a supervised crocodile. Some of their uniforms looked quite shabby. Keswick School boarders went in small groups, unsupervised and in their grey uniforms looked much smarter than the Roedean girls.

In my first year I had a needlework class at Keswick School of Industrial Arts at Greta Bridge. The syllabus had been altered from my sister's year because of clothes rationing, and included some "make do and mend". On Saturday lunch was at 1.0 pm as usual, and we had high tea at 6.0 pm – often pilchards. This allowed time to go to the pictures!

Occasionally we were in trouble for not having the right coupons in our ration books. One day I was summoned to Miss Allen's presence before lunch at 1.00 pm because my tea coupons were missing. They were certainly in the book when I handed it in. Miss Allen blamed students for everything that went wrong – never domestic staff, or in the case of missing coupons – Keswick Food Office.

In my first year I made friends with two girls from my group who lived at 'Lairthwaite', and we used to meet and go walking for the day – starting on a bus – if we could afford it – we would go to Grasmere or Seatoller. We had to be back at the bus terminus to queue for the return journey in good time, because the buses were always full. The buses from Seatoller were overbooked. Each passenger took another on her knee, and the centre aisle was packed with standing passengers. Most were instructed to get off at St John's Church to avoid the police in Keswick!

The only food I can remember being supplied in the packed lunches was bacon and egg pie – now called quiche. I expect it was made with dried egg. On one occasion this was so awful we left it on the top of Honister Pass. I should think it fossilised there. It must have been awful because we were always hungry. On another occasion I remember eating at the top of Newlands Pass. My mother had sent a tin of sardines. We bought buns in Keswick, and put the sardines in them, and the buns were sweet! As we were there an eerie silence was only broken by the sound of ravens. After a short while the three of us felt we had to move on.

When my two friends from 'Lairthwaite' and I met for games in Fitz Park on Friday afternoons we would plan walks for Saturday and Sunday.

All 1st year students had games on Friday afternoons. Each group played a different game each week so that we were able to teach them – handball, netball, hockey, rugby touch, rounders etc. My group seemed more academic than athletic. Before we could start we had to chase away the sheep, and the local Keswick dogs liked to join in the fun. We used to encourage the dogs to run off with the balls, even loosening the laces of the old-style footballs to give them something to get hold of. There was only one P.E. tutor to supervise us all, and when she saw us standing around, we would say that the dog had run off with the ball. It was during these interludes that our week-end escapes were planned, but standing around when the snow was on the tops was a bit chilly!

On free afternoons, usually Tuesday and Wednesday, I used to walk, when the weather permitted, to Calf Close Bay, Castle Head, the Stone Circle or Walla Crag. The last time I climbed Walla Crag it took all day, but I came down the new path to Ashness Bridge, and I had one of Sir John Charnley's hips! [Sir John Charnley was a surgeon at Wrightington Hospital who performed the first hip replacements].

One night each week at St. John's Church there was a service or Intercession for St. John's congregation instead of Compline for the college. One night there was a collection. In a panic the girl next to me said she had no money. I had two halfpennies, so I gave her one. On another occasion, the hymn *"Lead, Kindly Light"* made some very homesick – *"Lead kindly light, amid the encircling gloom – the night is dark and I am far from home"*.

Shortage of money made us thrifty. Most of us came from "working class" families. My father was a clerk who sometimes worked long hours with no overtime pay. My mother didn't work, but stayed at home making cheap, nourishing meals, and was good at dressmaking and make-do-and-mend.

We had no grants. I think ours was the last year that didn't get grants. We hadn't to make any contribution to the education fees, but had to pay for accommodation and food, our own books, cardboard etcetera to make apparatus for teaching practice, and file and essay paper.

The fees for St. Katharine's were among the most expensive at £52 per year – similar I think to Whitelands, Putney and Homerton College, Cambridge. These included medical care if needed – pre N.H.S.

There were no concessions for students – cheaper rail fares, admission to concerts etcetera.

I remember the choral competition the first year. 'Lingmell' choir sang some Scottish songs. I think the themes were chosen by Miss Johnson, the music tutor who coached us.

In the second year we had a drama competition judged by Joan Littlewood. I think Fawe Park did part of *'Richard of Bordeaux'*, but I remember very little of it. We must have rehearsed after study hour at 9.00 pm. It was produced by a student from London.

These events must have taken place in the Pavilion, which was the only building in Keswick, apart from St. John's Church, big enough to accommodate all the college.

Every Monday morning at 9.00 am the college met in the Pavilion for what Miss Allen called "The Business Meeting". It began when she walked in, and we stood in absolute silence.

After the chapel notices, the results of matches were announced. I wasn't very interested. I know the college had a hockey team. They sometimes played the D and M (Army Driving and Maintenance) School at Portinscale and "Tilly" gloated when the girls beat the men.

On one occasion she dismissed all the tutors and said it had come to her knowledge that students were saying that the staff had better food. She pointed out that they ate with students. They joined the students for breakfast and dinner, but served themselves for lunch when they had a choice from a side table and we never saw what they got for tea.

I remember attending a parish tea at the Pavilion at the invitation of S. John's congregation – a real treat.

The Pavilion was used as a cinema. I remember one visit there to a Saturday matinee. No one under 14 was admitted without an adult. Two boys approached us and asked if they could go in with us. When we booked the tickets we were asked sternly if we were over 18. The film – *'The Wizard of Oz'!*

The only luggage in advance that I sent between 1st and 2nd years was my orange box containing books. During the war a lot of luggage was stolen from railway stations. People wanted clothes when they were rationed.

Sending parcels by post was much safer. The cost of a 15 lb parcel, the maximum weight allowed, was 1 shilling, and 3d to register it. Estimating the weight of a parcel was rather difficult, and sometimes when put on the post office scales they were overweight! The scales at Keswick Post Office were near the customers' side of the counter, and it was possible to surreptitiously put one's thumb under the scale with an apparent reduction in weight. One girl, sending home a doll's house she had made, was rejoicing it weighed less then 15 lbs when the P.O. assistant whipped out a tape measure and said it was too big!

I remember going to Fawe Park from Keswick at the beginning of my 2nd year. When we arrived Miss Clarkson allocated our rooms. My two friends from Lairthwaite and I fancied West Room which accommodated three students, and where my sister had spent her year at Fawe Park. Somehow we were left till last and put in Yellow Room with two other girls.

My memories of the Yellow Room at Fawe Park are very different from those of Doreen Taylor who had occupied the room the previous year.

There was nothing yellow about it! The walls were "off-white" – very "off", and there was a patch of plaster missing from the outside wall on the exposed lakeside. The curtains were black-out of course – very dark and dusty. The hangings of the four-poster bed were dirty, dark orange and droopy. The pattern of the carpet was unrecognisable, and it was threadbare near the door. We used to pull out loose warp threads to tie up our essays. We were expected to keep our rooms clean and tidy. Occasionally we used to a get a carpet sweeper of the Ewbank type, and that would send clouds of dust flying. It was rumoured that the elderly maid employed by the Fox family had said the carpet hadn't been up for 50 years!

One bitterly cold night we pushed our four divans together and draped the dusty curtains over for extra warmth. Our heads were in a draught from the door, and one of my friends went to bed wearing a headscarf. There was some heating in the corridor, but none in our rooms.

On one occasion Miss Clarkson let us know very tactfully that she could hear our conversations through the open window. She repeated a conversation she had overheard when Joan told us that if we could save some of our margarine and sugar rations, she would send them home for her mother to make a cake for us.

I think when my sister was at Fawe Park Mrs Fox used to have dinner with the staff on "high table". While I was there Commander Fox came home.

One of my sister's friends got caught licking the trifle spoon when clearing the table after Hugh Walpole had been to dinner.

Sometimes Miss Williams would sit at a students' table while students went on "high table" with Miss Clarkson for dinner. We used to invite Miss Williams to our table for a laugh. We would ask her to serve the pudding, which was brought to the table. She always began by dividing it into eight, saying I'll divide it mathematically; (she was Maths. tutor), but she always finished with the biggest helping. We had a lot of semolina. On one occasion the bowl of semolina for eight contained just one sultana. The girl who got it put it on the side of her plate to save till last, and her neighbour pinched it.

On Sunday afternoons two friends and I liked to escape. We were allowed to miss Sunday tea and be absent from lunch until supper. If funds allowed, we went to the Borrowdale Hotel, or The Swan at Thornthwaite for afternoon tea – luxury for two shillings! We were shown into the lounge while tea was prepared – sandwiches, scones and fine crockery – sometimes toast at the Swan.

Towards the end of our final term, "we three" walked from Fawe Park to the King's Head at Thirlspot on a Saturday afternoon for tea. Having ordered our tea we went and sat about six feet up Helvellyn and waited for tea-time. We asked for afternoon tea and one egg, which cost 2/3d. We all felt tired after the walk and blamed our weariness on poor college food. At tea-time we descended Helvellyn and went for tea. There were two eggs each, cost 2/6d. After paying for this we hadn't enough money to return to Keswick by bus as planned. We set off to walk with the hope of getting back to Fawe Park for the next meal when along came a car driven by a man who worked for the Forestry Commission, and he gave us a lift back to Keswick. We had shared a table with two Dutch airmen.

"Matron", the nursing sister, was a character. She was an Irish Catholic who said she attended S. John's Church as it was "as near the RC church as made no difference". She named all the students who didn't wear vests, and ended with, "…. and Miss T. wears one you could shoot peas through".

On the Whit weekend of the last term, a friend of one room-mate came to Keswick for the weekend. The weather had been lovely, and a group of us decide to go to Watendlath. Most said they weren't taking rainwear, but I looked across the lake from 'yellow room' window and saw a cloud like Elijah's – the size of a man's hand – over Watendlath and put my mac cape in my rucksack. The day was fine till we got to Watendlath when the heavens opened! Most had not raincoats and some one said that in the rain, the less on the better – less likelihood of getting a cold. Several went to the ancient toilet, and took off as many clothes as they dared and we set off back to Keswick. One girl had a hand-knitted blouse in some sort of yarn which stretched when wet. By the time we got back to Keswick it was very revealing and she had to find her way through all the back streets to avoid the holiday makers (we knew all the back streets and short cuts which led from one lecture hall to another).

In contrast to the first year, the autumn of 1945 was glorious except for a bad storm with wind and rain at half term. One student said the water in Fawe Park boathouse rose six feet in 24 hours.

Tuesday and Thursday afternoons were free, and whenever the weather permitted, my friends and I would walk along the west shore of Derwentwater as far as possible between lunch and tea. Usually we got to Brandlehow. If we stayed in, it was possible to get an extra bath. We were allocated one each week after study hour at 9.00 pm.

On Friday evenings an old - fashioned cane clothes basket full of bread had to be collected and taken on the bus to Fawe Park. I don't know where it was collected from as two students who didn't have music had to collect it, but I had to take my turn with a friend to get it up the two or three steep steps on to the bus. We had then to lift it off the bus and carry it up Fawe Park drive - in the dark in winter – and down to the basement kitchen. The bus driver would park at the bottom of the drive so that the headlights shone, and helped us up to the first bend. We were then in total darkness. Keeping to the right to avoid the drop on our left, we walked into spiders' webs and wet greenery, and stumbled in potholes and puddles. I don't remember the bread being covered.

One night, when the carriers got to the basement they found a loaf was missing. It had fallen off the top of the heap; but they didn't worry very unduly because it was a brown loaf, and only the staff had brown bread! There was not time to go back for it then, before dinner, so they sneaked out again later, and found the loaf in a puddle, cleaned it and dried it, and took it to the kitchen.

Mrs McKay had a cat which started to come into Yellow Room, and we suspected it was looking for a mouse. It got stuck behind the wash stand. We daren't report this to the staff, or we would have been accused of keeping food in our room, which was true and forbidden (it should have been kept in a cupboard in the basement somewhere). We all contributed and bought a mouse-trap – 5d, 1d each. I was made responsible for this, baited the trap with chocolate, caught a mouse, put it in a paper bag with a stone, and dropped it in the lake.

The view from Fawe Park chapel across the lake was wonderful, and the cross and candlesticks from the college chapel were on the altar in front of the window. The chapel was at the end of a corridor occupied by Mrs Fox, and we had to walk along in silence.

The lecture room was above the chapel, with the same view. Sometimes the small launch coming to Nicol End would have a rough crossing in winter.

The common room had an open fire. It would be laid ready for the evening. One maid, 'Thistle', used to put a large lump of coal with a piece of cardboard on top. There must have been some good Girl Guides because the fire always seemed to get lit somehow (smoking was allowed in common rooms, but no-where else).

At the beginning and end of every term we were all weighed by Matron. In the first term my weight increased from 7 stone 7lb to 8stone 4lb. At the end of the first teaching practice my weight was back to 7 stone 7lb and never gained again. Matron thought I had no "insides". At the end of the second year we were all examined by the local G.P.'s young assistant. One of the ladies who worked in the Waverley Hotel was heard to remark that she didn't think that young man should see so much of those young girls!

The arrival of the R.A.F. Mountain Rescue team and their vehicles outside the Moot Hall used to cause a stir in the library at Queen's - "MEN"! I think the serious implications didn't enter our heads then. I have since seen the wrecked aircraft remains on the fells.

When my sister was at Fawe Park, they invited R.A.F. officers from Silloth to a college dance. Occasionally students had boyfriends visit them in Keswick (I think they were usually "cousins"). It was well known that Miss Allen did not approve of going for walks. When students asked permission to meet men friends, and 'Tilly' asked what they were going to do, they always said they were going to the Royal Oak. She approved of this, though I can't think why, as when we went to S. Katharine's Day dinners, it seemed to be full of Commonwealth R.A.F. officers.

Students were allowed to go home for a week when brothers were on embarkation leave.

On Saturday evenings, three of us from Fawe Park used to go regularly to the Alhambra Cinema. We would book on Monday at the back row of the 9d seats – there were three rows at 9d and those on the row behind paid one shilling. On the way back we called at Postlethwaite's chip shop, almost opposite the Post Office, before walking back to Fawe Park. There was another chip shop in Bank Street, known as M's. My god-daughter says her mother, who was at Lairthwaite, used to have chip butties round the bus station.

Miss Allen disapproved. She said we were, "taking the food off the people of Keswick".

After their sheltered life in the college in Liverpool, the move to Keswick must have been very difficult for the tutors. Those who lived at hostels in Keswick had to go to the Waverley for meals, and walk from one lecture hall to another. As I walked to Lairthwaite on a Friday morning, I used to meet a tutor from there walking into Keswick. From Lingmell I could see Miss Allen and Miss Evett walking from Burleigh Mead to the Waverley Hotel.

College ended on Midsummer's Day and some from Fawe Park walked to the Stone Circle to see the sun rise. We had to change rooms so that those going out did not disturb those who were staying in. A visitor to yellow room slept on the four-poster bed and frightened the rest of us by smoking. We must have set out soon after mid-night because it was double summer time. The circle was well populated with college girls and we saw the sunrise as predicted.

CONNECTIONS WITH KESWICK

In an accompanying letter. Moira refers to her family connections with Keswick, which began many years before she arrived there to begin her teacher training.

My connections with Keswick began long before College. My

maternal grandmother worked at the Queen's Hotel (chosen by the Principal in 1939 to be the 'headquarters' of the college in the war years). Her job was described as 'book-keeper'. I think she must have been the receptionist. She worked for her uncle, Edwin Edward Poole, described as 'farmer and hotelier' in the documents that came into my possession when my sister and brother-in-law's house was cleared. I think that E. E. Poole died in 1879, leaving no will, and the documents dealt with disputes that arose from this – and a suspect solicitor in Birmingham.

According to my mother, my grandmother travelled from her home in Shropshire to Liverpool by coach, from there to Maryport by sea and from Maryport to Keswick by coach. Mother talked of Uncle Poole and the Lodore Hotel and the Derwentwater at Portinscale. She also mentioned an 'Eskin Field'. There is an Eskin Street off Ambleside Road near S. John's Church. I think she may have inherited a bit of money from this! She used some of it for myself and my sister at College, but was rather secretive about it.

The squirrels used to come at mealtimes and eat our bread

MARY LIVER, KENDAL

S. Katharine's College

I was a pupil at Lancaster Girls' Grammar School before going to S. Katharine's College in 1938. When World War Two broke out in 1939 the college was taken over by the David Lewis Northern Hospital and so S. Katharine's had to find new premises. To my great delight our new home was to be Keswick. Several hotels and private houses were taken on lease for student accommodation - mainly in Keswick itself. The Queen's Hotel in the Main Street became the college headquarters and the Waverley Hotel became the "Diner" where most students had their meals.

Twenty-eight of us were based at Fawe Park - a lovely house on the shores of the lake at Portinscale - about two miles from Keswick. We made one room into the chapel with the cross and candlesticks from the Liverpool chapel. We said morning prayers and evening Compline here. For Sunday Eucharist we went to either St. John's Keswick or St. Kentigern's, Crosthwaite.

The winter of 1939-40 was very severe. Derwentwater was completely frozen over, and although we didn't have skates we made the most of walking, sliding and dancing on the ice. We had a wonderful time - many tumbles and falls - but exciting and enjoyable days. We had to go into Keswick for some of our lectures and while this severe weather lasted we had to walk because the snow blocked the road and no vehicles could use it. In some parts of the route the snow was so deep that we were actually walking on the top of the hedges, but being young and ready for a challenge it didn't deter us, and the bonus was that the countryside looked like fairyland.

We had our own cook at Fawe Park and except for the days when we had lectures in Keswick we had our meals in the spacious dining room - plenty of room for the twenty - eight of us.

Looking back to my time at Keswick has made me recall many incidents and memories that I thought I had forgotten - such as when the squirrels (red) used to come in through the open windows at meal times and help themselves to our bread. They loved the butter too and we ended up putting a dish of butter on the window sill for them.

They still came onto the tables to see what they could find. They were not at all shy and would eat out of our hands.

Another memory that comes to mind is that the children from an orphanage were evacuees living in Lingholm, the house next to Fawe Park, and six of us used to go there on Sunday afternoon and have Sunday School with them - practice for our teaching careers! The lady of the house regaled us with tea and cake.

My real "school practice" was done at a Comprehensive school in Workington. I confess that I cannot remember much about this except that the staff were very helpful and supportive - coming to my rescue when ever I got a bit lost during a lesson, and that I enjoyed tremendously the bus journey from Keswick to Workington each day, travelling along the western shore of Bassenthwaite. There was a different aspect to the lake, hills, trees and wildlife every day which made that journey very special, and every time I have travelled along that road since then the memories still come to my mind.

My special interests were Botany and Biology, and if we had been in Liverpool I intended for my thesis to study a stretch of shoreline on Morecambe Bay, but when the war came that area became a government factory and a fuel store, so it would have been a non -starter for me. Finding myself near Derwentwater it seemed logical to study the region where I was living. The area proved to be a very good one indeed and worthy of much more detailed and searching study than I was able to give it in the short time I had - only having Spring and Summer my observations were unfortunately limited, but nevertheless it gave me great pleasure, and the fact that it was different from what I had planned made it exciting and unpredictable, so I called my thesis "The Biology of Fawe Park."

After reviewing the area I found that there is evidence of a direct succession from water plants to deciduous and evergreen woodland. I divided my findings into six chapters plus an introduction and conclusion:

a. Reed swamp; b. Marsh; c. Shale Region; d. The Alder Willow Region; e. The Woodland; f. Birds.

Here is an extract from e. The Woodland: This chapter describes the flora found on the woodland floor under the Horse Chestnut trees, and this paragraph tells us about the Wood Sorrel (*Oxalis acetosella*).

"This very dainty fragile plant appears in clusters and can easily be overlooked by a casual observer. It is a very small plant usually growing amongst the moss, and its drooping flowers make it inconspicuous when it is not in large numbers. The leaves of the Wood Sorrel are a very delicate pale green and are very sensitive, they fold over if you touch them or if there is a sudden change in the weather. It is probably the original Shamrock which St. Patrick used to demonstrate the truth of the Trinity."

Having said goodbye to the snow and ice, the summer of 1940 was sunshine all the way and we were allowed to use the rowing boat belonging to the house. It came in very useful when one day I had to go to the dentist in Keswick to have a tooth removed, and my friend rowed me across the lake and back again when the ordeal was over. On June 8th 1940 our P.E. Lecturer Miss Coy was married in the local church and became Mrs. Barrie. We of course went to the wedding and afterwards enjoyed tea and cakes - a lovely day to remember.

Another incident which I would rather forget is when several of us went to the local cinema. As we came out and walked down the outside steps into the street, my skirt which must have come unfastened during the film, fell round my ankles. The person behind me quickly pulled it up and I was decent again, but not before I had been seen and subjected to pointing fingers, quiet giggles and astonished sideways glances. I shall not forget that afternoon.

In July we held our Sports Day in Fitz Park and crowds of local people came to watch us, running races and playing netball with and against students from other educational groups who like ourselves were war-time evacuees. Many friendships were made on this day.

Saturday was usually a free day and we could pursue our own interests, and many of us chose to go for walks and take advantage of seeing the beauty of the scenery. One day a group of us walked up the Borrowdale valley and climbed the ladder on the Bowder Stone.

I first saw it when I was about 11 years old and said to myself, "I wish I could climb that ladder". I didn't know then that only seven years later I would do just that and my wish would be granted. Another place we visited was Castlerigg Stone Circle - and pondered on what those standing stones meant and who were the people who put them there and what / who were they worshipping. One Saturday we set off very early and climbed Helvellyn to watch the sunrise. It was a spectacular sight and well worth the effort. We had breakfast at the inn at the foot of Helvellyn - ham and eggs (yes, two eggs if you could manage to eat them). They had their own hens and rationing had not yet reached them. My favourite place was Catbells. I did a lot of my "swotting" sitting or lying on a rug which my great aunt gave me and which I still have, and hopefully getting inspiration from the gently rounded slopes and the breathtaking views of the lake and the mountains.

Back to Fawe Park. As I was Deputy Head Student I was allowed to sleep in one of the "posh" beds. The room was called Oriel as there was an oriel window near to my bed and I took the photograph of the moon shining on the water from this window. It was a serene and uplifting sight which made me and other students realize how fortunate we were to be in this tranquil place whilst in other parts of our country - even the places from which we had come - were going through the trauma of war. Many of us, after our time at Keswick did go back to see and experience this. My first job was in Manchester where night after night we were in the air raid shelters and I myself supervised the evacuation of children from Manchester to "safer" places in the country, but I am sure that the time in Keswick gave us strength to "do our bit".

If I had known that I was to write my memories of S.K.C. at Keswick 67 years on I would have taken more meaningful photographs and written down more names and places. There was of course much more to my year and a half at Keswick as an evacuee than I have been able to remember, but I hope you have enjoyed hearing about a few of the things I have remembered. When at church I hear the Priest say "Lift up your hearts" and we reply "We lift them up unto the Lord" I am reminded of S. Kath's and how much the time at Keswick meant and still means to me. The college hymn is of course "Lift up your hearts" and the last verse is:

"And when the trumpet call in after years
Lift up your hearts rings pealing in our ears
Still shall those hearts respond with full accord

We lift them up-we lift them to the Lord"
In conclusion I would like to say that to organize the move from Liverpool to Keswick must have been a tremendous task. I don't think we students realized at the time how much thought, planning, and sheer hard work went into this operation and our thanks are due to all those who made it seem such a smooth transition.

A bottle of Nut Brown Ale – thrown in the lake!

MABS NICHOLSON, BARNARD CASTLE
S. Katharine's College

This is a light-hearted account of two years spent in Keswick during the Second World War. My single name was Mabs Bainbridge and I lived in Keswick during the years 1942 to 1944.

September 17th 1942 was the date of my arrival in Keswick to train as a teacher. It was wartime, and the S. Katharine's Training College population was evacuated from Liverpool to Keswick.

I left my Egglestone home and travelled the two and a half miles to Romaldkirk railway station by taxi. From there, I travelled to Barnard Castle where I changed to a train going by Kirkby Stephen to Penrith. At Penrith, I caught another train to Keswick. It is sad to relate that these railway lines are no longer in existence. It has been said that it is easier to cross the Rockies than it is to find transport from east of the Pennines to what is now known as Cumbria. Previously, we knew the counties as Cumberland and Westmorland.

Recently, a private company stopped running a bus from Lofthouse, Yorkshire, via Darlington and Barnard Caste to Penrith, Keswick, Grasmere and Kendal. This had functioned at weekends and provided a return service, enabling walkers and other visitors to have a long day at their destination or to stay for a longer period. Now it is possible to travel by minibus from Barnard Castle to Brough, to change there to a Stagecoach bus going as far as Penrith where four hours may be spent in the town before returning, or to take a taxi from Penrith if Keswick is in mind. If a day trip only is possible, this gives a short stay in Keswick. Enthusiasts are attempting to open up parts of the railway lines but it will be a long time, if ever, before the whole route will be available. I had always enjoyed travelling by train but I never had encountered any route as attractive as that between Penrith and Keswick.

I was enthralled by the scenery between Penrith and my destination. I remember diving from one side of the carriage to the other, repeatedly,

Mabs Nicholson on Derwentwater

to drink it in. This was the beginning of a long-lasting, still-continuing love affair with the Lake District.

Leaving the train at Keswick Station, I walked along Station Road and near the War Memorial stopped to ask for directions to the Blencathra Hotel, which, given time, was always referred to as 'Blen'. It was but a short distance. At 11am, I was the first student to arrive at that hostel, and I introduced myself to Mrs Evans, the proprietress, who showed me to the bedroom I was to share with two other girls on the top storey.

Today I pause at the entrance to Southey Street and look up towards the little window, on the left, facing me. It seems a long time ago, but I remember the room clearly, the three beds, a table, a chair and a wardrobe but no very necessary bookshelves. This lack was remedied by begging orange boxes from the local fruiterer and making them as attractive as possible.

Mr Evans was a railway signalman, and he and Mrs Evans had an adult family of three. Edwin and Archie were away in the armed forces but came home occasionally on leave. Mary, aged 22 I think, and in the W.R.A.F., contracted meningitis and died. Her name is to be seen on the War Memorial.

Mrs Evans must have found the presence of so many girls in her home something of a trial, I fear. She said she couldn't understand why on earth visitors wanted to climb mountains. She hadn't gone climbing, and she didn't think that many locals had.

Fitz Park was within easy reach of the Blencathra Hotel. The area bordering Penrith Road was a lovely place for relaxation and study and offered flowers and bushes, subjects for the "artists" amongst us. On the lower part beyond the Museum we played hockey and tennis and I remember, at one time, we used to run round the perimeter in an effort to shake off the surplus pounds gained through eating too many helpings of

Waverley steamed puddings. Walking and climbing resulted in very healthy appetites.

We stayed at the Blencathra from September 1942 until July 1943 when we moved to other hostels. I was fortunate in being able to reside at Fawe Park, Portinscale, and the home of Commander and Mrs Fox, from 1943 to 1944.

Some Keswick buildings remain in mind because they were used regularly by the College. Chaplin's Bookshop was situated in Station Street. It was necessary to buy certain books there, but it was expensive, and we became frequent visitors to Mr Brown's second-hand bookshop in Southey Street, where prices were within our means. The Drill Hall, also in Southey Street, was used for P.E. Just round the corner from Southey Street was a small shop, near where McKane's is now. It was owned by a cockney gentleman with a noticeable accent, who was a cobbler. When we went into the shop to ask if we could have something or other done he never failed to reply with, "There ain't no law to preventcha!" This survived through many years as part of our repertoire. We were amused by it, and liked it.

Further along the street, on the same side, was a shoe shop, Ritson's. I had arrived in Keswick without suitable hill-climbing footwear. In this shop I bought a pair of shoes which I thought would be suitable for ordinary wear in bad weather as well as for climbing. They were golf shoes and were tough. I should have broken them in gradually, but stupidly I wore them for the first time to walk around the lake. In some discomfort, I managed to get as far as the Lingholm area where I could stand the agony no longer, and walked, shoeless, back to the Blencathra. I remember resting on a wall in Portinscale and tears, mixed with laughter, were not far away.

Birkett's had a cake shop and an upstairs café in Station Street. It happened that, although I did not know the family, my uncles had gone to school with the Birkett boys who started the firm in the South Tyne area. I developed a kind of loyalty towards Birkett's and until Greggs took over from them recently, I used their shops whenever I came across them. Even now, a grocery van, originally owned by Birkett's calls at my home on a weekly basis. The driver now owns it as his travelling shop.

In my Keswick days we occasionally used to pop into the café for teas and a bun. In a corner of the room was a lift, which worked on ropes and was used to transport food up from the downstairs kitchen and used dishes downstairs. Orders were shouted down through the lift way and there was one waitress with a loud voice who used to shout down, "Egg and cheeps! Egg and cheeps!" I was reminded of this, years later, when a friend married into a Welsh family and said that her in-laws referred to "fish and churps".

The food at Birkett's was of good quality but partly, because we had to be thrifty, we didn't have main meals there. Sometimes on a Saturday two of us would meet up with Mr Fred Tee (Manager of the Pencil Factory), have a walk in Fitz Park then he would treat us to tea at Birkett's. We appreciated this and enjoyed his company and conversation. At the time, he would be in "digs" in Keswick. I remember once his taking us to see the salmon leap up the weir in the park.

Storms café, which I think was where Woolworth's is now, was the café where we went for a change of scene and for conversation with local people we knew. Again, funds limited us to coffee and a scone. The chairs were of bentwood and of course there were tablecloths, very different from the plastic and formica of today but involving more work. Mr Temple had a drapery shop across the square from Storms' and the name, Temple, is in evidence today.

Purple blazers and silver badges: Queen's Hotel was the College H.Q. The room to the right of the front door became the Library. Much work must have gone into preparing the many rooms in Keswick for us. At the back of the Hotel were washrooms where we did minor laundry and, in the same area, were two bathrooms. It was a case of a bath per week and we had a rota. There was a gap above the dividing wall between the rooms and we looked forward to this weekly luxury when we soaked, at the same time eating apples and carrying on a conversation, calling through the space above. Bed linen was taken to be washed at the Lakeland Laundry, where the collecting point was next to the rear of the Queen's.

We were daring enough to do a bit of hitch-hiking (again, finances and a certain lack of public transport dictated). Once, aiming at Carlisle, we were given a lift in his van by the Lakeland Laundry van-driver who had to make a delivery to Armathwaite Hall where one of the church dignitaries, an archdeacon connected with the College lived. The driver volunteered to take us a little further along the route. So afraid of repercussions, should the archdeacon happen to see us, we had to hide among the baskets in the back of the van whilst, parked in the drive, the driver made his delivery.

The Waverley Hotel, owned by Mr Wilson (Tom), provided bedrooms and a large dining room. From the Blencathra Hotel, at just before 8 am, girls wearing their purple blazers with silver badges could be seen tearing down Standish Street, through Queen's from back to front, then down Main Street to Waverley for breakfast. Butter, sugar etc. were, as for everybody, rationed, but we never seemed to go short of food and Mr Wilson's hot breakfast rolls were excellent. What a pity it is no longer a hotel.

The Royal Oak, owned by Sir Percy Hope, was where official College celebrations were held. They and the place were impressive. A small room, now part of another small hotel, with the entrance from Main Street, was where the International Society held its meetings. Lady Rochdale, a small lady dressed in black, was the President. Keswick did seem to be cosmopolitan at the time, there being French sailors, Poles (two students married Poles), Czechs and others. The Czechs were very emotional about wartime circumstances and would read poems, aloud, tears streaming down their faces. French and English were my main subjects so I joined this Society.

The Rawnsley Hall was the scene of concerts and other performances. At a time when friendship with Russia was being encouraged Russian music and ballet were performed by Russian companies. Canadian soldiers were involved in a different way. They were involved in a noisy brawl outside the Golden Lion. That sort of behaviour was unheard of at that time and was all the talk of the town.

Lairthwaite was another lovely house where students lived and lectures took place. Many years later, when it became a school, a conversation with a boarder revealed that he was very bored; there was "nowt" to do. The grounds offered scope for outdoor drama. On one occasion I, perforce, had to act the part of a nymph hiding behind a rhododendron bush, feeling a complete idiot. Training to teach occasionally involved pretending to be a child and entering the mind of a child.

The Derwentwater Hotel was where the D & M officers were billeted. They were invited to be escorts at our dances, rare occasions held in the Pavilion. We were not allowed to dance with any soldier more than twice. The Principal and Vice-Principal sat at the side of the room to ensure this rule was obeyed. Why they forgot to foresee that the soldiers could walk back to Fawe Park with the students will never be known. The Pavilion and the Alhambra both functioned as cinemas at the time, but outdoor activities, whatever the weather, were too attractive an alternative for us to visit them.

Jennings Nut Brown Ale: two of us once entered the portals of the Farmer's Arms at Portinscale. It was not the thing for women to go into pubs in those days so we were quite daring. I am not sure who it was who praised the virtues of Jenning's Nut Brown Ale to us but we decided we had better try it and went into the Farmer's and bought a bottle. Back at Fawe Park, we hadn't the courage to drink it so we put it unopened behind some books in the corner cupboard in the bedroom. It stayed there until we were packing to leave College when we had to get rid of it. Somewhere, in the depths of Derwentwater, in the middle of the lake, lies one bottle of Nut Brown Ale. What a waste!

The only other inn we visited was the Swinside Inn. We knew Mr Simpson (Syd) through his bus connections, and were invited to play a board game, 'Tip It', with a group of elderly farmers. The inn now has completely changed and I shouldn't think that 'Tip It' is ever played.

S. Katharine's was a High Church establishment and Mr Matthews, Vicar of St John's, was our chaplain. He struck us as being a saintly man in appearance and character. His churchwarden could not have been more different in appearance. The bluff and hearty Sir Percy Hope would make his way after morning service to the Royal Oak where, we used to joke, he was off for a pint but, probably, he had Sunday lunch there. Probably, both.

I was confirmed at St John's by the Bishop of Penrith. We had to wear veils, and were instructed by our very religious and intolerant Principal that the edge of the veil must come down to our eyebrows and must not rise above that level. A great deal of importance was attached to this. I tried it, privately, and was not at all pleased with the effect. I had no intention of looking like a nun, and managed to ease the veil upwards as I made my way from the pew to the Bishop.

Once, going to Evensong, and knowing that the church would be very cold, maybe because of wartime conditions, we collected hot baked potatoes from the Waverley and went with these in our pockets. St John's seemed, at this time, to be a beautiful church and the services were peaceful and reverent. Mr Matthew's home, The Parsonage (The Snidge) was another hostel.

The Museum in Station Road was where art lectures were held. It is a small Museum with strong local associations, occupying a site with an attractive view over Fitz Park.

Shortage of swimsuits: from Fawe Park we were regular callers on Mr Gill (Richard) and spent hours with him, listening to his stories, helping him by rowing some of his customers across to the Keswick side of the lake and enjoying the use of his boats when they were not in use. A pal and I used to sit in his cabin, listening to his reminiscences. He had a wealth of stories. One that he used to chortle over was about the fact that he had to take parties of Americans and a few titled people who where guests at Lingholm out on to the lake for midnight swimming parties. On occasions, there appeared to be a shortage of swimsuits and he had to make great pretence of not looking. I remember that when we left Fawe Park we gave him a pipe and baccy pouch as a 'thank you' for his kindness to us.

Dennis Marshall and Teddy Hall were "characters" who kept a yacht at Nichol End. We were invited to go for a sail on one occasion. It was an experience, but we realised that we had been asked so that we could be employed to "swing the boom". However, there was a picnic lunch (chicken) at Hawse End, so we were rewarded.

Once, Teddy Hall, who was not averse to a spot of over-imbibing, took the yacht on his own to the southern end of the lake and went ashore. Possibly, through more imbibing, he had forgotten that he had sailed down and walked back to Keswick where he lived at or near Greta Hall. Two of us went with Mr Gill to retrieve the yacht and we showed our skills with the boom.

Nichol End almost deserves a chapter on its own. Several characters, visitors to Keswick, gathered there. Amongst them was a Czech called

Benny. I'm not sure how he came to be resident at Portinscale at the time. His English was not very fluent but he had mastered some expressions which he used with gusto. "Plutty hell! Plutty hell!" he would say when things went wrong. "Py colly" was another of his expressions. I remember Dick turning away to laugh. What an enviable life he had at Nichol End!

A lost pair of pyjamas: the police station was in Bank Street next to the Post Office. I once went into the station as support for a friend who had managed to lose her needlework, a pair of pyjamas, en route from Keswick to Fawe Park. The police were highly amused by her request. Amazingly, the parcel was handed in.

Paddy, the policeman, was not on duty at the time, but we used to come across him in the town and we got to know him very well.

Needlework and lectures took place near Greta Bridge, at the School of Industrial Arts. Needlework was not one of my strong interests but the course was compulsory. The only time I taught it was when I did a month's teaching practice at Kells, Whitehaven. Because of the shortage of time allotted to needlework, I was instructed to do the preparatory work myself, i.e. cutting out the parts for twenty padded tea-cosies, then the girls would do the sewing. At 2am, at Fawe Park, I was still cutting out sixty cover parts, sixty pieces of padding and sixty linings before going to bed. At 7am it was a case of racing down the drive to catch a "utility" bus, driven my Mr Steele (Basil) who was an Inspector at Keswick Bus Station, to be taken to Whitehaven. The so-called 'utility' buses had no upholstery. The seats were made of wooden slats and were far from comfortable. We felt corrugated.

Whitehaven was part of a depressed area at the time. This was evident in the town and in the people. When the Headmaster handed me the maths syllabus, I found that I was to instruct the boys about writing a cheque. They and I knew that they were unlikely to need to do this. Perhaps, in older age and better times, they might remember.

Multi-coloured, herring-boned skin: during the two year stay in Keswick we climbed most of the surrounding hills and mountains though we didn't reach the Langdales. Skiddaw was to be remembered because in November we didn't really have adequate clothing. Despite warm sunshine at the start, it was icy at the summit. Rationing and clothing coupons would influence our choice of clothing but very few people in those days had climbing gear. Years later, as a founder member of a local fell-rescue team, I felt I knew what I was talking about.

On Helvellyn we met the sheepdogs, Moss, Lou and Ken. One of them had appeared in a Lassie-type film. Gable was reached in fine weather but at the summit the heavens opened. I was wearing a multi-coloured tweed skirt with a herring-bone pattern. When I dried out, back in Keswick, the wartime dyes had soaked through to my skin. I was multi-coloured and herring-boned.

On Scafell we ran into thick mist and remained sitting until it cleared when, to make up for lost time, we descended by way of a scree. We were very wary about this yet today it seems that scree-running and ice-climbing are accepted sports.

All these walks and climbs and others were enjoyed and repeated but I shall never forget the sheer beauty, one perfect September day, when, on the shortest climb of all, my first, I looked down on Derwentwater from Catbells.

Keswick was an oasis in wartime Britain. I do not remember any war incidents there at all. The nearest we got to them was a fire-drill at Fawe Park with Mr Blamire (Percy) in charge. Rationing was the same as elsewhere. The population was interestingly mixed. Some were refugees. The soldiers with their vehicles were active on the lake and in the hills. Keswick was lively and full of voices. Now, even when it is crowded, I find it quiet!

We must have been intrusive as far as the local population was concerned but we were welcomed and gained so much. I hope that we contributed in some ways to the life of the town.

S. Katherine's College students at Fawe Park

Fawe Park

Caught in the mist climbing Causey Pike
DOROTHY ROBERTS, LIVERPOOL
S. Katharine's College

Before I attended S. Katharine's College I was at St Edmunds' Grammar School in Liverpool. The Principal of S. Katharine's (known to the students as 'Tilly') came down from Keswick to Liverpool and the interviews were held in the old Church House which was bombed soon after! All that I can remember from the interview was facing a dim figure across a table and being asked if I had passed my School Certificate first time. After I had answered in the affirmative a rather gruff voice said, "Good. I like people who succeed first time." I was accepted. That must have been about November 1940 and the College term began at Keswick in September 1941.

So, I was a student at S. Katharine's College, then based in Keswick, from 1941 to 1943.

My close friend and I travelled by train to Keswick to be met at the Station by a former St. Edmund's scholar who was just beginning her second year. She took us to the Queen's Hotel with our two suitcases balanced on the saddle of her bicycle. Coming from a much-bombed Liverpool it was so good to arrive in Keswick. It seemed a haven of peace and tranquillity.

During my first year my friend was billeted at Lairthwaite House and I was billeted in the Burleigh Mead Hotel on the Headlands with seven other young ladies, three of whom had already spent a year in Keswick, so were 'seniors' – the rest of us were 'juniors'. I shared a room with another student who came from Widnes. One disadvantage of living at Burleigh Mead was that our very strict Principal was also billeted there, so we had to be very good!

One particular memory I have was of a miniature Niagara Falls. The hotel was a rather tall building. We only had jugs and basins to perform our ablutions in and the water was put in buckets on each landing. One morning the girl from the top floor slipped as she was coming down and the whole bucketful came dashing down to the ground floor. The Head was not amused.

In my first year we travelled to Carlisle by bus for school practice and in my second year to Workington, travelling by train. The train was always delayed on the way home and we arrived late, had our evening meal and then went to the Compline Service at St John's Church – not leaving us much time for preparation for the next day!

In my first year school practice I had an accident with Indian ink when preparing a visual aid for the practice. We were working on the floor – always short of space – and I tipped a bottle of ink over the precious carpet belonging to the owner of the Burleigh Mead Hotel. Two of my second year friends came to the rescue and poured cold water on the stain until, it disappeared. We were left with a wet stain. We put a chair over it and hoped that the Principal wouldn't move the chair when she inspected the Common Room as she did every evening. My roommate and I waited with bated breath in our own room, next to the Common Room. But, there was no sound of movement and the stain had dried out by the morning.

Another little adventure we had was when six of us decided to climb Causey Pike. I had already done this climb so I was appointed leader. However, we only got about halfway up when the mist came down and we turned back. On the way up we had passed some workmen and a lorry. As we came down the men were packing up and kindly offered us a lift into Keswick. The Principal would have gone mad had she seen her students alighting from a lorry! Fortunately we were not seen by anyone in authority.

Two more incidents have stayed in my mind. There used to be a café where Woolworth's is now which was patronised by us students. At the time I enjoyed the odd cigarette and the people I was with at the time likewise. One of them had a celluloid cigarette case which she put in the middle of the table to use as an ashtray. We had finished our cigarettes and were just talking when suddenly there was a flare up in the middle of the table from the cigarette case – someone had not put out their cigarette properly and the case had caught fire. I was the culprit. One of the waitresses rushed in with large shovel and carried the burning case outside. I don't think there was much damage done, fortunately.

Another little incident stays in my mind. It concerns the lovely coffee shop which was next to the Waverley Hotel. Sometimes, if someone had a postal order from home, we would have a little party on a Saturday afternoon. We used to have to queue at the cake shop on a Saturday morning as the cakes went very quickly. One particular Saturday morning my friend and I were first in the queue and were standing close to the door when suddenly the door opened and a rather irate lady begged us to stop leaning on the bell! I think she kept us waiting a bit longer.

I visited Keswick in July this year (2006) and there was still a cake shop in the same position and we had lunch in the restaurant above it. I don't remember there being a restaurant there in 1941 – 1943, but there could have been.

I shall always remember one winter when Derwentwater was frozen over and we were able to walk on it.

In my second year I was billeted in the Queen's Hotel. We had beds in the attic. We also had a few lectures in the Queen's. We had our meals in the Waverley, which, last time I was in Keswick, housed the Edinburgh Woollen Mill. The food was not good, but it was wartime. We had nicknames for some of the dishes – one I remember was a sort of milky pudding with jam which was called 'Death on Skiddaw'. Another time we were given a horrible sort of stew, which tasted as though the remains of the week's meals had been put into it and we walked out. We had a lecture from the Principal the following Monday telling us how students in Greece were living on a few raisins.

Living in Keswick was a big bonus and I fell in love with the little town and all its surrounding area and have been to visit several times since.

One of my friends and I both enjoyed climbing – we went up Causey Pike, Catbells and of course Great Gable. Funnily enough we never climbed Skiddaw.

We went on lots of lovely walks on S. Katharine's Day, but on one occasion there was to be an evening meal at the Royal Oak and everyone was to attend! Six of us went for a walk down the Borrowdale valley to Seatoller. On the way back we began to realise that we were going to be late for the evening meal and were all getting a bit worried. A taxi passed us going towards Seatoller and then returned (owing to petrol rationing taxis could not go any further than Rosthwaite). So, the taxi, having dropped its passengers off at Rosthwaite was on the way back to Keswick and the driver very kindly offered us a lift – we were saved from trouble and we were very grateful.

It has amazed me how much I can remember of my time in Keswick. I have enjoyed writing of my memories as a trainee teacher in the Lake District.

In 2009 Dorothy wrote: I returned to war-torn Liverpool in 1943 to begin teaching – fifty 5 year-olds. Supply-teaching followed, and then a permanent appointment in Woolton, and a post as Deputy Head of a north Liverpool school. I married a Welshman and moved to Wales. I was unemployed - because I was married! My husband worked for Trinity House as Buoy-Keeper on the River Dee. Eventually I did obtain a teaching position in Flint for fifteen years.

During my spell in Liverpool I was a "Court Missionary" for the Magistrates' Court – giving comfort where it was needed. I was once asked if I was an undercover cop! I joined the Needlework Guild in Liverpool and eventually became its Secretary. I had the pleasure of meeting the late Queen Mother when I accompanied the Guild President to London. I worked for the Red Cross on the wards in Sefton General Hospital. When I was widowed I returned to Liverpool in 1979, to be near my family, and worked 'behind the counter' for Oxfam for twenty years.

I spent many happy holidays in the Lake District, Derwentwater being my favourite lake.

Do not sleep in the four-poster bed!
DOREEN TAYLOR, BARNSLEY
S. Katharine's College

September 1944, Fawe Park, Keswick. Mrs McKay, the Housekeeper, greeted us and ushered us into the Common Room and rooms were allocated. The second year students sought us out and took us to our rooms. Ann Raby (F2, Fawe Park 2nd year students) was my 'College mother'.

The Yellow Room. It contained five divan beds along one wall from the door of the room to the window. Blue covers, fitted, made a contrast to the yellow walls and curtains, which matched those on the four-poster bed. We were warned not to sleep on it. Bedroom furniture consisted of wardrobes and drawers, to share, and at least one large dressing table.

The students who joined me and Anne Raby were Margaret Prest, Margaret Hemingway, Marjorie Bonser and Sheila McLaren. Margaret Prest and I were friends. We came from Barnsley Girls' High School. Margaret Hemingway came from Burnley, Marjorie from Altringham, Cheshire and Sheila from Stoke-on-Trent.

We became firm friends from that first meeting. In fact, the twenty-eight students were all friends. F2 helped us very much, especially when we were on our first School Practice. What a shock it was to travel to Maryport, Cockermouth and, in my case, Whitehaven, and to have to prepare lessons during the evenings after dinner. Our seniors helped us to set out notes and evaluate the day's lessons.

Our 'Baptism' at Fawe Park came on the Saturday, after our arrival, still suffering from shock when we realised our home was the beautiful Fawe Park and the view from our bedroom window across the lake was lovely. We thought we were in heaven!

High Tea. Saturday. This was something new. A buffet meal at 5pm would be normal on Saturday, to give kitchen staff time off until Sunday morning. Students took turns to clear away and do the dishes in the kitchen.

On that first Saturday, Amy Clowes summoned us to the Common

Room and took charge. We introduced ourselves. After that, in alphabetical order, we were called to the piano and told to perform from sheet music. I was asked to sing *'My Hero'* from *'The Chocolate Soldier'*. I knew the tune and a few of the lyrics and I screwed up my courage and sang!

I cannot remember what my friends did however, the evening was well spent and we began the term on the right foot. Our seniors wanted to see what we were made of and often we gathered round the piano to sing some of the popular songs of the day.

We eventually formed a choir to compete in the Inter-Hostel Competition in the later part of term. We sang *'Brother James' Air'*, *'I Waited for the Lord, He inclined Unto Me'*, *'Sanctuary of the Heart'* and *'O, Lovely Peace, with Plenty Crowned'*.

The adjudicator was the composer, Armstrong Gibbs, who awarded the first prize to the girls who sang a selection from Edward German's *'Merrie England'*. He decided that although we made a heavenly sound our choice was sombre.

Lectures at Fawe Park on certain days were welcome. Our tutors came to us and enjoyed lunch there. Miss Boardley was the History tutor, Miss Evett took us for English. Miss Williams took us for Maths and Methods of Teaching. On other days we were taken to Queen's Hotel and had our other lectures in certain halls in town.

Friday afternoons were devoted to games for the First Year Students in Fitz Park.

We had lessons in voice production from Mrs Berry, a wonderfully patient lady who tried to help students from Bolton and Bury (and Liverpool) but whose success was marginal.

Days and evenings were structured. Dinner at 7 pm was formal and we took it in turn to sit 'On High' and enjoy the company of Miss Clarkson (the Vice-Principal) and Miss Williams. After dinner we had private study in the Lecture Room. At 9 pm we gathered in the Chapel for Compline. We were 'free' thereafter to spend time with our friends.

I had to check F1 (the First Year Students) by 10.30 pm and report to Miss Clarkson that we were all safe and sound. I don't think we went out very much in the evenings except when we were allowed to report to Mr Kitching, a teacher at the local secondary school, for choir practice at

St. John's Church.

We lived life to the full for thirteen weeks. We walked for miles and made some attempts to climb. We had no climbing gear and stuck to Catbells and the lower slopes of Skiddaw. We ventured up Saddleback but the mists descended suddenly and we escaped.

In Keswick we had lunch at Bryson's. I have met certain elderly ladies at the 'Drop in Club, Keswick who used to work to feed the students (I met them November 2001). We bought meat pies from the bakery and our skirts grew tighter. We gave them up (the pies) for Lent in 1945 but the weight dropped when we did our first school practice.

We learned to row. There were two boats in the Boat House. We loved to row to Derwent Island, thought we'd done well and felt no fear. We swam in the water near the Boat House but not for long. It was too cold to persevere with it and none of us was a strong swimmer.

There was a cottage in Fawe Park woods and we were allowed to use it on Sunday afternoons to entertain friends to tea. I do not know what has happened to the building. We have visited Keswick several times in the last few years and have walked past Fawe Park to the Lakeside. I have searched the woods – as much as I could, up to Lingholm's fence, but have not seen the cottage. Fawe Park belonged to Commander Fox, R.N., who was on active duty. Mrs Fox lived in her private apartments and was often seen in the garden and the greenhouses. I remember the grape vine in one of them.

Fawe Park gardens are in Beatrix Potter's story of 'Benjamin Bunny'. The buttresses and pear tree are there too and still exist. I have a photo of them taken last November.

My year at Fawe Park is unforgettable. We had perfect living conditions and were well looked after, perhaps too well. We had very little freedom but there was no ill-feeling – except – Saturday mornings. F1 had to go to Keswick to have lectures and practical work in Handwork, Needlework and Art. There was one month when this did not happen. In January, 1945, our senior students went to Liverpool to do their Final School Practice and certain members of staff went with them. Saturday mornings were ours. We loved it. We also changed hostels, went to Lairthwaite House for four weeks and met Miss Pack, one of the younger tutors, who was in charge of us.

Miss Pack was friendly. She treated us as young women, not schoolgirls. She joined us in the Common Room and took an interest in our days. I liked her. She invited us in twos and threes to her sitting room to have cocoa and biscuits. That does appear to be girlish but we appreciated it.

In May we were busy revising and our F2 group were rather grumpy about 'Finals'.

Amy Clowes, F2's group leader, was a wonderful young woman. She was never too busy to help anyone! After her last examination she went home to enter hospital to strengthen and correct a leg which was shorter than the other. In September 1945 Miss Allen (College Principal) told College that the operation had been successful. The Head girl 1944 – 1945 was Margaret Eden.

November 25th 1944. The Bishop of Liverpool came to Fawe Park to meet us. We had to wait in our rooms until he arrived, accompanied by Miss Clarkson. He shook hands with us, moved over to the window to admire the view, then said "Goodbye".

We had dinner at the Royal Oak, Keswick, to celebrate S. Katharine's Day. I have no souvenirs of that event, just memories of students 'dressed to the nines', lots of noise, laughter and speeches. Can't remember the menu. The Head Girl opened the speeches. The Bishop complimented her, told her that her surname, Eden, fitted the Vale of Eden and of Keswick. We agreed, it was a heavenly place.

The Vicar of St John's and Miss Allen gave their speeches too. I've never been in the Royal Oak since 1944, have gazed in the windows at times. It has a new name now so perhaps I shall never step inside.

May 1945. Finals for F2, into June and then the excitement of packing trunks and preparing to leave us. There were tears shed. Our groups had melded and I don't recall there being any bad feeling – ever. We were left behind to do our first year exams. The dining room minus F2 was eerie! I feel sure that Miss Clarkson and Miss Williams also felt sad to lose F2.

June 1945. When F1 completed exams we prepared to leave Fawe Park.

We had celebrated VE Day on May 8th by cycling to Honister Pass, to Borrowdale, to Keswick calling at Queen's, to talk to other students and to celebrate. Back to Fawe Park to have a bath, to change into dresses, to have dinner and then to be taken by bus to The Pavilion in Keswick to dance until midnight. Most of the College attended and so did the O.C.T.U. (Officer Cadet Training Unit). It was an exciting evening.

We walked back to Fawe Park. So much energy and youthfulness in those days made life wonderful. There were some tired muscles next day, but it was worth it.

Doreen Taylor (nee Gooder), who was a student of S. Katharine's College in Keswick from 1944 to 1946, gave photographs and her story to the S. Katharine's College Archive in October 2002. They are now kept in the Sheppard-Worlock Library, Liverpool Hope University at Childwall, Liverpool L16 9JD.

Mrs Taylor died in 2002. Her daughter, Mrs Christine Landon, has given permission for her reminiscences to be placed in the 'evacuees folders' in the Keswick Museum and Art Galley Project on evacuees in Keswick and to be included in this publication.

The Keswick Museum and Art Gallery is grateful to Christine Landon for this help with the project.

My mother was often greeted by a grinning postman handing her my washing with my underwear dropping out.

ISABELLA THOMASSON, BOLTON
S. Katharine's College

My story will be different. It is a tale of how I came to love Keswick after a very inauspicious beginning and how I hated College, particularly my first year.

The College friends I have now are very surprised by this, as they never realised how unhappy I was. Their memories were not the same.

Even now my heart goes out to those children who were evacuees. It was hard enough for an older teenager but for a child .... however, I am sure there were many kind motherly ladies in Keswick to put their arms round these children when they cried.

I came from a happy and loving family and was horrified to find that there would be no weekends when I could travel home. All travelling was banned – except by foot and bicycle. When I finished my exams at the convent school I attended I was too young to go to College or University, so I had worked in a bank for a short time before I started at S. Katharine's college. This taste of freedom made matters even worse.

My "hostel" was "Lynwood", which was a little further out than many of the hostels around Keswick. I seem to remember that a Mrs Richardson, whom I always thought of as being kind, owned it but, of course, she only provided the accommodation. I duly reported there on arrival and was shown to my room. Later, when it was time for dinner, I walked to the Waverley Hotel where we had all our meals, only to be called out along with other unfortunate girls to appear before our Principal, Miss Allen, to whom apparently we should have reported. How were we to know? We were ushered into a room at the Queen's Hotel to be soundly ticked off by this formidable lady. Nothing like this had ever happened to me since the Infant School!

This was nothing like College life as I had anticipated. There was no proper base. Starting off the day trudging from the hostel to The Waverley for breakfast, we continued the pattern all day – from The Waverley to lecture room, from lecture room back to the Waverley, to a further afield lecture room back to The Waverley, from The Waverly to church, from church to hostel and so on. I did not mind walking. What I did mind was getting wet and often I stayed wet all day. Much later I read that these years, 1942 – 1944 had been the wettest in Keswick on record. So it didn't just feel like it!

As far as I can remember we had no facilities for washing our clothes in our first year. Well, if there were any in my hostel I never found them. I parcelled up my clothes regularly and sent them home to be washed! My mother told me that she was often greeted by a grinning postman who handed her a badly wrapped parcel with my underwear dropping out.

I got by reasonably well. I rang my parents every weekend, reversing the charges and used to chat to the telephone operator. I wrote constant letters to them saying that I might as well come home now as I could never pass the needlework and handcraft exams and they just as constantly reassured me. The girl who became my closest college friend, and with whom I attended French lectures, taken by the charming Miss Wileman, was made of bolder stuff. She sent a telegram home, "The greatest mistake of my life. Coming home." And that is what she did, only to be brought back later by an aunt.

My parents also came to see me, staying in a guest house, which I believe is situated on "The Heads" and I was allowed to stay with them for the weekend. There I also met the esteemed cricketer Herbert Sutcliffe whose daughter was a fellow student and a man employed as a locum in Keswick who it later turned out appeared to have no medical qualifications whatever!

About this time I was summoned on a second occasion to Miss Allen's room. I had accepted an offer to go for a walk on a Sunday afternoon with one of the young soldiers stationed in Keswick and was no doubt just as home-sick as I was. Unfortunately I came face to face with Miss Allen who was also having a Sunday afternoon walk. "What would your mother say?" she asked. Well, as I came from a home where friends from either sex were welcomed and I had taken another girl with me I could only answer that she would not have minded. After that I learned to keep my head down. There were obviously some double standards here as one of our students managed to get herself engaged to an army captain based nearby.

I was however beginning to see the funny side of all this. When I developed a corn on my toe - because of all that walking in wet shoes – I asked the nurse if I could go to a chiropodist. "Oh, no!" she said. "It might be a man and Miss Allen would not like it!" Then there was the time when Miss Allen was approached to ask if we could attend a dance held by the soldiers based nearby. She refused, but the head of Roedean School, made of more liberal stuff, allowed her girls to go.

My second year was quite a different experience. A large number of us were based at Fawe Park, that beautiful house on the edge of Derwentwater. I shared a room with four friends. It was called "Night Nursery" and the bars are still at the windows. Now this was more like it. We studied, had most of our meals and lectures and slept under one roof. The Misses Clarkson, Williams and Dobson made it a happy place for us. Commander and Mrs Fox owned it and when the Commander was home he would sometimes ask one of our girls to row him out while he did a spot of fishing; for this we had to pass a rowing test.

We went by bus to Workington, Whitehaven and Carlisle to do our teaching practice. Some of us felt sick before we even arrived! Even at Fawe Park we did not escape the shadow of Keswick. One day a brave soul complained about the food – not at Fawe Park, where it was excellent – and we were all promptly punished. We were put in a rota for washing dishes.

Although the food at Fawe Park was excellent it was never-the-less rationed and, as teenagers, we were always hungry. Two of us in our room were often sent food by our mothers and I can still remember one of my mother's fruitcakes being promptly cut into four when it arrived.

Just before we took our final exams some of us went down with flu and were confined to bed. On the morning of the exams we were told that we had to take them in a separate room. We were seated round a large table not really feeling able to cope when, like a guardian angel, the doctor arrived and packed us off to bed again.

Soon after we left College, and to be fair, we were very well qualified in spite of the conditions. I was off to start my teaching career, and with no regrets at leaving College and hoping never to see Keswick again.

Two months after I started teaching my dear father died at the age of

Isobel Thomasson with her family

48. I was so glad he had seen me settled in my new job. About a year later I met the boy who was to become my husband. Although it could have easily ended then when I found out what he had missed most when he was in the Royal Navy was cycling in the Lake District and, more, his brother lived in Kendal.

He re-introduced me to the Lake District and to Keswick. It was our favourite weekend haunt for fell walking, rowing and picnicking. We spent at least one week's holiday in the Lakes every year and our two daughters had climbed the Langdale Pikes when the younger was only three and Helvellyn when the elder was only eight – the younger one and I not quite making it to the top.

Disaster struck again when our children were still in their teens. My husband died at the age of 44. Our lives were thrown into turmoil and once again I thought I should never see Keswick again. Then fifteen or so years ago some College friends got in touch saying that we should meet in Manchester. From that first meeting developed luncheons in Manchester and a yearly holiday at the Borrowdale Hotel, continuing up to the present day. I think that one could say that from that beginning in 1942 Keswick has now become part of the fabric of my life.

Isabella wrote in 2009: After College, I taught in both Senior and Junior Schools before leaving to raise my family. When both daughters had started school I returned to teach children who were unable to attend school in their own homes – and some 'supply' work. In the late sixties I changed direction to join a small group of pioneers at a Language Centre, operated by the Bolton Education Authority, in anticipation of the numbers of Asian children, unable to speak English, whose families would settle in the town. When our teachers moved into the schools I became a co-ordinator for the primary service, liaising with the schools, supervising our teachers and teaching myself where numbers did not warrant even a part-time teacher. I found this work very rewarding and continued until I retired. Even then I was a volunteer for many years, helping with reading etcetera. A glutton for punishment!

Our elder daughter won a scholarship to St. Hilda's College, Oxford and our younger daughter went to Mather College of Education and, following in my footsteps, became a teacher. I could not dissuade her!

Meanwhile, I studied for a degree with the Open University. My interests now include the theatre and bridge, but the most important thing in my life has always been my family.

CAN YOU HELP?

Were you evacuated to Keswick, had evacuees at your home or have talked with elderly relatves and friends about their evacuation there?

Your contribution to this project would be very welcome, whether it is a short account or something more substantial.

Your response, with your permission, will be placed in the Keswick Museum Evacuee Folders for others to read.

If you can help in this way, please contact Brian Wilkinson at the Keswick Museum, Station Road, Keswick, CA12 4NF.